A Parent's Guide to Autism Diagnosis

by the same author

It's Raining and I'm Okay
A Calming Story to Help Children Relax When They Go Out and About
Adele Devine
Illustrated by Quentin Devine
ISBN 978 1 78592 319 7
eISBN 978 1 78450 631 5

Flying Starts for Unique Children
Top Tips for Supporting Children with SEN or Autism When They Start School
Adele Devine
ISBN 978 1 78592 001 1
eISBN 978 1 78450 241 6

Literacy for Visual Learners
Teaching Children with Learning Differences to Read, Write, Communicate and Create
Adele Devine
Illustrated by Quentin Devine
ISBN 978 1 84905 598 7
eISBN 978 1 78450 054 2

Colour Coding for Learners with Autism
A Resource Book for Creating Meaning Through Colour at Home and School
Adele Devine
Illustrated by Quentin Devine
ISBN 978 1 84905 441 6
eISBN 978 0 85700 812 1

of related interest

Talking with Your Child about Their Autism Diagnosis
A Guide for Parents
Raelene Dundon
ISBN 978 1 78592 277 0
eISBN 978 1 78450 577 6

The Ice-Cream Sundae Guide to Autism
An Interactive Kids' Book for Understanding Autism
Debby Elley and Tori Houghton
Illustrated by J.C. Perry
ISBN 978 1 78775 380 8
eISBN 978 1 78775 381 5

A Parent's Guide to
AUTISM DIAGNOSIS

*What to Expect and How
to Support Your Child*

Dr Sophia Mooncey
and
Adele Devine

Illustrated by Quentin Devine

Jessica Kingsley Publishers
London and Philadelphia

First published in Great Britain in 2022 by Jessica Kingsley Publishers
An Hachette Company

1

There are supplementary materials which can be downloaded from
https://library.jkp.com/redeem for personal use with this programme, but may not
be reproduced for any other purposes without the permission of the publisher.

Disclaimer: The information contained in this book is not intended to replace the
services of trained medical professionals or to be a substitute for medical advice.
You are advised to consult a doctor on any matters relating to your health, and
in particular on any matters that may require diagnosis or medical attention.

A CIP catalogue record for this title is available from the
British Library and the Library of Congress

ISBN 978 1 78775 424 9
eISBN 978 1 78775 425 6

Printed and bound in Great Britain by TJ Books Limited

Jessica Kingsley Publishers' policy is to use papers that are natural,
renewable and recyclable products and made from wood grown in sustainable forests. The logging and manufacturing processes are expected
to conform to the environmental regulations of the country of origin.

Jessica Kingsley Publishers
Carmelite House
50 Victoria Embankment
London EC4Y 0DZ

www.jkp.com

For the children who have inspired and taught us.

This book is dedicated to the wonderful children we have met, the 'Louisas', 'Harrys' and 'Yusufs' who have been on this journey, supported by the constant love and care of their parents and families. These young people have made and continue to make good progress and are a source of inspiration to our practice. They teach us and give us the understanding that a diagnosis of autism is filled with difference and hope. With the appropriate support and positive attitude these children will continue to blossom and thrive to become valuable members of our society. Our work continues to lead them onto bigger and better things.

Contents

Part 4: Education

Part 5: The Journey Continues

Acknowledgements

This book is dedicated to the many children we 'know' who have been on their diagnosis journey supported by the constant love and care of their parents and families. They continue to teach us and will be a source of hope and inspiration for other families. We recall their personal triumphs and 'wow' moments with much pride. Working with parents and their children at such a crucial time has been an absolute privilege. We hope this book will honour each of them by providing a source of honesty and hope, making the journey a little less overwhelming and frightening for other children and parents.

We are grateful to those families who have allowed us to share case studies and personal reflections.

We thank our colleagues and professionals who have volunteered their precious time and expertise by reading and writing parts of this book:

Dr Helen Davies BSc (Hons), PsychD, CPsychol, AFBPsS, paediatric clinical psychologist. Helen gives advice on behavioural issues that may arise and strategies that families can use.

Rachael Gartland BSc (Hons), PG Cert, MRCOT, specialist paediatric occupational therapist. Rachael explains the sensory difficulties that autistic individuals experience and how to manage them.

Neha Makwana BSc (Hons), MMedsci, MRCSLT, MHCPC, MASL-TIP, highly specialist speech and language therapist. Neha addresses speech and language and communication aspects of autism.

Clare Walker BA (Hons), QTS, DipED, Deputy Head Teacher, Portesbery School. Clare has a wealth of experience providing practical support and advice to families.

And so many others.

We thank Quentin Devine (Adele's husband) for his patience in listening to our combined ideas and creating the illustrations in a style that we are both so happy with.

Special mention to Vikki Hardy (PA to Sophie) for all of her incredible work from start to finish.

Particular thanks to Dr Mumtaz Mooncey (Sophie's daughter) for her valuable editing.

We thank our teams at Portesbery School, Spire Healthcare and Luton NHS for their dedication, constant smiles and positivity despite working through the most difficult situations during the global Covid-19 pandemic.

We would like to say a huge thank you to our own wonderful families and the friends who have constantly supported us. To our husbands and our inspirational children who have enriched our lives.

Loving gratitude for our wonderful parents for their unconditional love, their support and ambition for us to reach our potential. They all believed in us and the book wholeheartedly when we started our writing journey. Sadly, during the writing of this book we have both lost our individual, non-conformist and brilliant dads and Sophie has also lost her dear loving mum. Such difficult and devastating times, further complicated by the Covid-19 pandemic. It is sometimes during the darkest times that we discover our own inner strength and resilience.

We thank Jessica Kingsley Publishers for their understanding, patience, support, creativity, dedication and their incredible attention to detail.

Finally, we thank you for reading this book and for supporting an autistic child or children to succeed and celebrating their potential.

We have both learnt a lot from each other and complemented our skills to make your journey one of hope and optimism.

Note: In this section, Sophia Mooncey is referred to as Sophie, the name used by her family and friends.

Introduction

'We didn't want you to diagnose Henry with autism – we wanted you to tell us that he was fine. Or perhaps a tiny, little bit autistic and that he would grow out of it.'

(Henry's Mum)

Your child may be autistic?

Emotions suddenly rise: intense fear, denial and possible grief. These are the feelings that parents may experience when the word 'autism' is mentioned. Is this the beginning of doom and despair? A life overtaken by anxiety and struggle? No, this is not the case. You have the potential to adapt your skills to support your child to achieve their full potential. Your child can develop into a confident and happy young person, but you will have to learn to understand that your child sees the world differently.

This book guides families and key workers through the journey from the moment concerns arise. It provides guidance and information throughout the assessment process and implications of a diagnosis. There is, in addition, a chapter that focuses on the roles of speech and language therapists, clinical psychologists and occupational therapists, written by professionals from these three areas of expertise. They offer useful advice on meeting children's needs and support for families. The chapter can be downloaded from https://library.jkp.com/redeem using the voucher code KFMSQRC. This book does not replace clinical evaluation or advice from experienced professionals but supports your understanding of the process.

A diagnosis of autism is not a dark hole that you fall into and cannot get out of. In fact, some autistic individuals have strengths which can be academic or may be creative and enable others to see the person beyond the diagnosis.

Autism in children appears to have increased, as prevalence data confirms, but varies from country to country, depending on the source of data collection, the age of the children and the definition of autism.[1] CDC data collection refers to data collected from 11 communities across the United States in 2016. The data refers to 8-year-olds as it was considered that most children are identified by services at this age. However, more children were being diagnosed at an earlier age in 2012 compared to 2008. These estimates are based on the ADDM (American Autism and Developmental Disability Monitoring) network data.[2] In the UK the estimate is 1 in 100 children.[3]

There are some self-professed experts, both in the educational field and the family arena, who will be ready to point out to you their concerns about your child having possible autistic behaviours. If you have questions, it is important to seek a professional opinion. There is strong evidence that early support equals better outcomes. What we would say is: try to remain calm and level-headed and continue to support your child. There are other conditions which may appear similar to

1   Chiarotti, F. and Venerosi, A. (2020) 'Epidemiology of autism spectrum disorders: a review of worldwide prevalence estimates since 2014.' *Brain Sciences 10*, 5, 274.

2   Shaw, K.A. *et al.* (2020) 'Early Identification of Autism Spectrum Disorder Among Children Aged 4 Years – Early Autism and Developmental Disabilities Monitoring Network, Six Sites, United States, 2016.' *CDC Surveillance Summaries 69*, 3, 1–11.

3   BMA (2020) 'Autism spectrum disorder.' Accessed on 10/04/21 at www.bma.org.uk/what-we-do/population-health/child-health/autism-spectrum-disorder

autism and these will need to be excluded in order to confirm a diagnosis. Regardless of this, each child is unique and an individual. No two children will present with the same behaviours or difficulties. Studies have shown that identical twins who may be identical in many ways will be different in their behaviours and personalities.[4] If one identical twin has autism, the chance of the other twin having autism is around 80–90 per cent. In non-identical twins it is 0–10 per cent.[5] Siblings of autistic children are also more likely (10–15%) to be diagnosed as autistic.[6] This is why it is important to gather as much information as possible from different settings (home and school). NICE (National Institute for Health and Care Excellence) recommends a multidisciplinary approach in order to obtain evidence and consensus regarding difficulties in various skill areas before a diagnosis can be confirmed.

CASE STUDY
Personal experience: Dr Sophia Mooncey

As a child growing up, you love and respect your parents. They are wise and wonderful, they love and nurture you, something you take for granted. As you mature into adulthood, you may see your parents differently and begin to question some of their views and parenting behaviours.

Over the years, working in neurodevelopment, I have come to realise and understand that my father's eccentric and obsessively controlling behaviours may have been explained by autism. He was an extremely bright and ambitious man, with rigid views which my dear mother tolerated throughout their lives. Socially, however, my father was direct, to the point of rudeness at times (much to our embarrassment when we were old enough to appreciate it!), but we knew no different. I have since also seen autistic traits in extended family members and some have been diagnosed with autism. I am certain that if my father had been assessed, he would have been diagnosed with autism. Although we did struggle with some of

4   Johnson, W., Turkheimer, E., Gottesman, I.I. and Bouchard Jr, T.J. (2010) 'Beyond heritability: twin studies in behavioral research.' *Current Directions in Psychological Science 18*, 4, 217–220.

5   Bailey A., Le Couteur, A., Gottesman, I., Bolton, P. *et al.* (1995) 'Autism as a strongly genetic disorder: evidence from a British twin study.' *Pychological Medicine 25*, 1, 63–77.

6   Constantino, J.N., Zhang, Y., Frazier, T., Abbacchi, A.M. and Law, P. (2010) 'Sibling recurrence and the genetic epidemiology of autism.' *American Journal of Psychiatry 167*, 11, 1349–1356.

my father's rigidity and social awkwardness on a regular basis, my siblings and I remain forever grateful to our parents for their ambition and support to encourage us to achieve our potential.

Family members can have certain characteristics which may be similar, but we are all unique, we learn to accept differences. My husband has to tolerate some of my cranky behaviours too! We have four wonderful children, each with their uniqueness. They help us to see the beauty in the world. We appreciate that there are challenges in life, but as a family we can overcome them and learn from life's lessons. With love and support we can celebrate individuals for who they are.

. . . .

CASE STUDY
Personal experience: Adele Devine

Many years ago I was lucky enough to attend some training led by Professor Tony Attwood (a clinical psychologist known worldwide for his knowledge of autism). As he described some typical traits of autistic girls, I related to nearly everything he said. As a child I was an extremely picky eater. I was happiest in my own company playing with my dolls or with animals. I have had the same amazing best friend since I was five. As I got older, I loved reading and writing and was a natural when it came to acting. I recall my father expressing concern that I wouldn't be able to learn the part of Rosalind in *As You Like It*. Rosalind, with 685 lines, is Shakespeare's biggest female role. The next day I walked into his study, handed him the play and said, 'Test me.' I had learnt the entire part. My father was amused and pleased but not overly surprised. He was an actor with a passion for Shakespeare and knew most of Shakespeare's plays and sonnets by heart.

Reading more about the pattern in abilities in autistic girls was enlightening:

> Teenage girls with Asperger's Syndrome can also develop a fascination with classic literature such as the plays of Shakespeare and poetry. Both have an intrinsic rhythm that they find entrancing and some develop their writing skills and fascination with words to become a successful author, poet or academic in English literature.[7]

---

7   Tony Attwood (1999) 'The pattern of abilities and development of girls with Asperger's syndrome.' Accessed on 12/03/2021 at www.tonyattwood.com.au/books-by-tony-m/archived-papers/80-the-pattern-of-abilities-and-development-of-girls-with-aspergers-syndrome

I love working as early years lead at Portesbery School for children with severe learning difficulties and autism. If I won the lottery tomorrow, I would still choose to work at Portesbery. The children I teach fill me with joy with their everyday 'wows' and are constantly teaching me and developing my understanding. We ensure that they have the routine, structure and happy atmosphere that they need. There is no unnecessary 'adult chat' creating verbal clutter. I can feel anxiety or joy in others with a sort of 'hyper-empathy'. This has helped me to understand the importance of supporting and reducing the anxieties of parents as well as the children in our school. I see the visuals in school in the same detail as some of the children and know how important it is to get them right. In fact, I took this to an extreme in recreating and ordering them for my first book *Colour Coding for Learners with Autism*.[8] What a labour of love that was! My colleagues at work are wonderfully understanding and many have said in passing that they would diagnose me autistic. I do believe I am autistic, but I have not sought a diagnosis.

When my husband Quentin was a child, he recalls his mother trying repeatedly to get him to speak by saying his name over and over, obviously hoping he would repeat it back. He didn't start speaking in the way his older brother had. He would stand banging his head on the kitchen door repeatedly. He recalls sometimes sitting and staring at the sun whilst eating orange peel. Aside from the orange peel, he was a very fussy eater. He still hates the sound of other people eating, which is a shame as I have a love of eating crunchy salads. As Quentin grew older, it became clear he was a natural artist. He could draw anything or anyone perfectly. As an adult, he has used his artistic talents in his career. He sees things in a unique way and creates artworks people stare at, trying to work out how they are even possible. Search 'Quentin Devine' and you will see this... He also believes that he is autistic, but like me he has not been diagnosed.

We have three unique, wonderful and very bright children who will one day have their own stories to share. They have taught us a lot, added to my personal experience, and given me a lot more insight into the realities of home life. I recall a small child once asking me, 'Am I autistic?' My answer was 'I think so – yes.' Next they asked, 'Are you autistic?' My answer was 'I think so – yes.' Next they asked, 'Is Daddy autistic?' Again, my answer was 'I think so – yes.' And finally, 'Is Nana autistic?' to which I answered, 'No

---

8   Published by Jessica Kingsley Publishers in 2013.

she's not.' They smiled at that, nodded approval and bounced off happy. End of discussion. Our children grew up with the word 'autism' being mentioned, with books on autism everywhere. Autism has been very much a part of all of our lives, a part of our story, and we would never change that.

．．．．．．．．．

Professionally we have experience in assessing and supporting children and families where a child may be autistic. We would like this book to help families understand the strengths, the difficulties, the joys and, at times, the heartache that comes with a diagnosis. We would also like to help you navigate the various pathways involved in reaching a diagnosis, implications of the diagnosis and support for your children, young persons and your family.

We hope the book will be useful for families who do not know how to approach the frightening journey to find out if their child is autistic. It also provides valuable information for carers and teachers of these children. The format helps to provide useful, practical advice, alerting you to warning 'red flag' signs and tackling issues that may arise. More importantly, it should not overwhelm you but help to guide you through the process with useful and practical advice.

You will be faced with many challenges and be presented with differing opinions and advice from different people, both professional and non-professional. We hope to make the path less painful and tortuous so that the ride is less bumpy, but also to empower you with skills and knowledge so that you are able to make informed decisions for your children.

We have also included comments and suggestions from families whom we have supported and cared for over the last decade. This may help you to understand that you are not alone – many families have travelled this path and will continue to do so.

Some information may be more specific for the United Kingdom; however, the general information is relevant to all individuals across the world. The medical and educational support may vary in different countries, but the book is intended to give an overview with general advice and support that is relevant for all families beginning this journey.

We wish you and your families the best for your journey and support for your child. We hope that you will find this book as helpful as it has been for us to write it.

Part 1

· · · · · · · ·

PRE-DIAGNOSIS

There is an additional chapter discussing professionals and support and extra resources that can be downloaded from https://library. jkp.com/redeem using the voucher code KFMSQRC

CHAPTER 1

Concerns, Fears and Challenges

'We went to toddler groups, and each child that came in developed quicker than she did. She didn't really play or talk and she had such meltdowns that she would head bang hard objects.'

(Parent reflection)

Imagine this scenario. You are picking up your delightful little bundle of joy from nursery. Your child is about 15 months old and has been in the nursery since the age of 10 months. The key worker asks if you have time to discuss your child's progress. You've had a long day at work and assume this is routine. You get out your diary and put in a time that is convenient for you, the key worker and the nursery manager. On the day of the meeting you are hoping to get an update on your child's progress, but the key worker and the manager look uncomfortable and uneasy. They have 'concerns'! Immediately you start having palpitations. They start off with the positives: 'Your child is a happy little one who is settling into the nursery. However, we have noticed a few areas where development is not in line with "the norm".' This immediately rings alarm bells. You have a discussion and ask many questions and they hint to you that they think your child's social development is different. This is the bombshell!

As a parent, and indeed a first-time parent, you hope and assume that everything your child does will fit within 'the norm'. You take for granted some of the cute, quirky behaviours and think they will be a phase that the child outgrows. This may well be the case in some children, but it is the persistence of unusual behaviours, including restricted and repetitive behaviours, which can be of concern. Along with that, social and communication difficulties may conjure a different picture. In your mind you think about this and you say, 'No...no, this cannot be possible, my child is doing well. My child is happy and content, enjoys playing and is not demanding, keeps occupied and is not distressed.'

Here are some thoughts which may run through your mind:

Facts

- He/she is my child and I know him/her best.
- There is a wide range of child development – surely my child still fits into that 'norm'.
- I have had no concerns so far about my child.
- Nursery staff are experienced in seeing a wide range of childhood development.

Opinions

- This is the opinion of my child's key worker and may not reflect true difficulties.
- My child is shy so will behave differently in the nursery.
- What gives nursery staff the right to suggest I seek a diagnosis for my child?

Self-reflection

- I know my child better than anyone else and everything seems fine.
- Maybe as an outsider they see things differently.
- What should I do, who do I talk to and how do I support my child if needed?

All of the above will have raced through parents' minds when they are confronted with this situation. This one statement, 'We are concerned about your child', opens up an ocean of unknowns with numerous questions. Where does one start? The easiest answer is Google. Google 'autism' and you will get multiple hits, thousands of links – in fact, over a million!

'I felt like a rabbit caught in the headlights.'

(Parent reflection)

'I recall standing outside our son's bedroom and crying. I just felt so overwhelmed and frightened.'

(Parent reflection)

Steps you might take

- Wait and see and not take any action. (My child will grow out of this phase.)
- Go home and speak to your partner to decide what to do next.
- Google information on child development.
- Speak to friends or family who are professionals in health and education for further guidance.

*Steps you **should** take*

- Try not to panic!
- Allow your acute reaction to settle and think about things logically.

- For a preschool child, speak to your health visitor.
- Consider speaking to your doctor (your GP – general practitioner or primary care physician).
- Arrange another meeting with your child's carer and the SENCo (special educational needs coordinator) of the nursery or childcare setting.
- Identify any areas you think are of concern and think about what the nursery has highlighted.

Possible concerns that may have been identified by carers

These may be about the child's behaviour, their play or even eating.

Toddlers behave in many different ways and go through many phases, some fun and some difficult. The difficult behaviours are mostly a phase and as the child matures their behaviour changes. Some possible 'red flag' behaviours are described below.

Your child may have struggled and not wanted to leave you when you dropped him/her off at the nursery. This is not unusual and is part of the attachment process, and separation from the primary carer may be difficult. It becomes an issue if this continues for a long period of time or if the child does not settle within the first 15–20 minutes of arriving at nursery.

Once the child is settled in the nursery, there may be concerns about the child's interaction with the carers or the other children. Once children feel secure in a setting, they will develop a bond with their carers and look to them for comfort in times of need. If a child does not develop this relationship, carers will express a concern.

Tantrums or 'terrible twos' are part of children's development. Terrible twos can occur at any time between 18 and 30 months and this is the stage in development when a child's physical and intellectual development is progressing at a rapid rate. The child's ability to express themselves may not be as well developed as their understanding, causing frustration and behaviour outbursts. Furthermore, at this stage toddlers start exerting their own views and this can be challenging. This is usually because the toddler's emotional skills, as well as their speech and language and motor skills, are still developing and they can become frustrated, resulting in behaviour outbursts.

The terrible twos can include screaming, shouting, hitting, kicking or throwing themselves on the floor. Studies have indicated that in 75 per cent of children these usually last less than five minutes.[1] They are common in both boys and girls.

Signs that indicate that the terrible twos may not be in line with normal developmental progress include the following:

- A tantrum lasting more than 20 minutes.
- Frequent tantrums during the course of the day (at least more than half a dozen).
- Tantrums where the child tries to injure themselves.
- Inability of the child to calm down or soothe themselves.
- Tantrums which include hitting and injuring others such as parents or carers.

Other indications to seek support may be the child becoming withdrawn, violent, not making eye contact and not engaging in play. Fortunately, as the child grows, the terrible twos will reduce and ultimately the toddler will outgrow these, mostly by the age of 3–4 years, once again depending on the child.

It is important to understand why children react in these ways and to try to find triggers for their behaviours. For example:

- Identify whether the child is having a tantrum or meltdown. If it is a meltdown which is triggered by sensory overload or excessive demands, there will be no goal expectation from the child.
- Remove the child from the audience.
- Distract the child from the activity which is causing agitation.
- Try incentives – for example, encourage good behaviour through a positive reward system.
- Once the tantrum is over, try to understand their feelings.

Autistic children who have difficulty in communication or are non-verbal can also exhibit self-injurious behaviours (SIB). SIBs are a

---

1   Potegal, M., Kosorok, M.R. and Davidson, R.J. (2003) 'Temper tantrums in young children: tantrum duration and temporal organisation.' *Journal of Developmental and Behavioral Pediatrics 24*, 3, 148–154.

complex pattern of repetitive and rhythmic behaviours that cause physical harm to the individual and can occur in 30 per cent of autistic children. Common examples of these behaviours are head banging, hair pulling, biting or picking skin. SIBs have been linked to dopamine and serotonin in animal studies. An interesting theory is the opiate hypothesis, which suggests these behaviours are addictive, causing release of opiates which can produce a feeling of euphoria. It has been found that children who are better able to communicate resort to fewer SIBs, so the key to supporting a child with these difficulties is improving their communication skills.

Your child may be withdrawn. The carers may indicate that your child is not showing an interest in the other children and playing on their own. Parallel play, or playing alongside others, is part of normal development. Children may show an interest in others even if they may not directly play with another child. For example, they may be interested to see what another child is doing, try to share toys or indeed even smile at other children. If a child is withdrawn and not engaging in any of these activities, once again this may be a worrying sign.

Play is a very important part of development. Children learn through play, and as parents we play with our children intuitively. The staff may have concerns about your child's play skills and social interaction.

Social stages of play

Parten's stages of play (1929) described play as having six stages.[2]

Type of play	Age	Description of play
Unoccupied play	Birth to 3 months	The first stage is between birth to 3 months, where a baby is too young to engage in play and instead watches and observes.
Solitary play	Up to 2 years	The next stage is up to 2 years, where toddlers usually engage in solitary play – they enjoy playing with things but are not always aware or interested in what other children are doing.

---

2   Adapted from https://childdevelopmentprograms.ca/elearning-modules/the-power-of-play/story_content/external_files/Developmental%20Milestones%20of%20Social%20Play%20and%20Sharing.pdf

Spectator/ onlooker	2–3 years of age	This is when a toddler starts looking at other people's behaviours and showing an interest but does not join in. Common between 2–3 years of age.
Parallel play	2–4 years of age	As they get older, above 2 years of age, children engage in parallel play. They will play close to other children and may mimic their actions. Often this is the beginning of complex social play and is seen in 2–4-year-olds.
Associative play	3–4 years of age	Between 3 and 4 years, they have associative play – that is, they start showing an interest in other children and engaging with others. Play is not usually organised.
Cooperative play	4–6 years of age	By the age of 4 years, most children are able to engage in cooperative play – that is, a 'to and fro game', listening and joining in with others and having imitative or imaginative play which may involve some simple rules. This is the beginning of teamwork. It is commonly seen at 4–6 years of age.

Play is an important part of development and this is crucial for brain development – particularly the prefrontal cortex, which is the area involved in regulating emotions, planning, and solving problems. Research at a university in Alberta has looked into the role of play and brain development, which reported that play helps build new connections in the prefrontal cortex and is also important for social interaction.[3] It is very important to engage in play with your child as much as possible because these are the early developmental stages of social communication, emotional intelligence and understanding.

Joint attention sharing

Joint sharing of attention is an important milestone where a child will learn to engage with adults, either verbally or non-verbally, and will show an interest in what the other person is doing. During

3   Bell, H.C., McCaffrey, D.R., Forgie, M.L., Kolb, B. and Pellis, S.M. (2009) 'The role of the medial prefrontal cortex in the play fighting of rats.' *Behavioral Neuroscience 123*, 6, 1158–1168.

toddler group or nursery sessions, children will usually engage in story time or rhyme time and be interested in what is going on. Some children will not show an interest and indeed not even want to sit and engage in the activity. This does not necessarily mean that the child is autistic as there may be other reasons why the child is not focusing. Young children have a short attention span and they may be interested in something else, or they are not able to sit for that period of time to engage or they are just generally inquisitive or curious about what is going on around them. Generally, the pattern or trend of these behaviours needs to be observed, as a one-off behaviour does not indicate autism.

Another example of 'joint sharing' is when the adult will point to an object or picture and expect the child to look at what is being indicated. Children who are unable to display this joint attention sharing may be on the autism spectrum. However, once again, remember that no single feature is diagnostic of autism.

Pointing

Pointing can be used by a child to share something of interest – for example, a puppy or an animal or a funny picture that they may have seen. Children should be pointing with their index finger by the age of 18–24 months.

There are two types of pointing:

- *Protoimperative pointing:* If a child wants something, they will point towards an object for need (e.g. if they would like a biscuit when they are hungry). Autistic children may either hand or finger point to objects that they have a need for. At times they may use a parental hand to guide the parent to the object they may want.
- *Protodeclarative pointing:* When a child wants to share an experience, they will point (e.g. to an aeroplane or a dog). Autistic children will very rarely point to share interests as this does not fulfil a need for the child.

Response to name

Babies usually respond to their name by the age of 6–7 months. They will turn their heads and understand that they are being called. This is an important developmental milestone. Children who are not aware of their names or do not respond to their names being called by the age of 1 year need further evaluation. It may be that the child's hearing is an issue, but it could be a marker of autism. This is not to say that just because a 1-year-old does not respond to their name they are autistic. There may be other developmental reasons. However, it is an important marker, particularly if there are other signs such as poor eye contact, limited imitative or imaginative play, or difficulty in communication or joint attention sharing. Researchers at the MIND institute in California in 2007 found in their study that a baby not responding to their name by the age of 12 months was suggestive of a developmental delay such as autism.[4]

To summarise – in the nursery the following signs would be of concern in the child's development:

- Lack of response to name when being called.
- Joint attention sharing where the baby does not shift their gaze from people to objects or engage in shared activities.
- A child not imitating others' facial expressions or not trying to copy gestures.
- A lack of emotional responsiveness.
- Not engaging in pretend play.

These signs are *not* diagnostic and further assessments need to be carried out as there can be many causes for children not reaching their milestones as expected. Be alert and aware and seek support early.

Your concerns

You may have concerns about your child around 12–18 months of age. You may notice that your child is not communicating as you would like. The child may be non-verbal or have delayed speech

---

4   Nadig, A.S., Ozonoff, S., Young, G.S., Rozga, A., Sigman, M. and Rogers, S.J. (2007) 'A prospective study of response to name in infants at risk for autism.' *Archives of Pediatrics and Adolescent Medicine 161*, 4, 378–383.

development, show no interest in others, have poor eye contact, not respond to their name, have limited facial expressions or gesturing or prefer to be in their own company. They may have some unusual repetitive behaviours such as flapping or spinning, sensory sensitivities or intense interests.

Areas of difficulty that need clarification for possible assessment for autism would be in social communication, interaction and unusual behaviours.

Communication

As already mentioned, difficulties with communication could be lack of engagement or interaction. More concerning features would be:

☐ No tuneful babble, pointing or gesturing by 12 months of age
☐ Inability to say single words by the age of 18 months (non-verbal)
☐ Inability to put two words together to form simple phrases by 24 months
☐ Repetitive use of words or phrases
☐ Echolalia or echoing of words or phrases the child hears[5]
☐ Any regression or loss of skills such as speech or communication

Social impairment

☐ Poor eye contact, avoidant or poor in quality
☐ Lack of interest in peers and others
☐ Poor empathy
☐ Lack of imitative or imaginative play
☐ Poor joint sharing of attention or interest
☐ Lack of pointing or response to name
☐ Lack or delay in social behaviours such as clapping and waving
☐ Insistence on lining up toys or cars[6]

---

5   This is an important step in normal speech development as children learn by copying. By the age of 2 years children start using their own phrases as well as using some echoing. However, by the age of 3 years most children use echoing minimally.

6   This alone is not a diagnostic feature of autism. Most children learn through play, and lining up is part of normal development. They may line up objects in size order, or by shape or colour. If the child is fixated on order and play is not varied, this may be of concern.

Unusual patterns of behaviour

☐ Difficulties with change in routine and rigidity in behaviours
☐ Motor mannerisms such as spinning, flapping or stimming[7]
☐ Difficulty with sensory issues
☐ Disordered play or minimal interest in toys

Other signs

☐ Using a made-up language or words
☐ Limited use of language (selective mutism)
☐ Referring to self as 'you', 'she' or 'he' after the age of 3 years
☐ Social impairment, inability to join in with peers in play
☐ Preferring to be a 'loner'
☐ Being overwhelmed by sensory stimuli
☐ Display of extreme behaviours such as screaming and shouting
☐ Poor appreciation of personal space

IQ

Autistic children do not always have a low IQ or intellectual disability as previously thought.

A study from the SNAP (Special Needs and Autism Project)[8] found:

- 55 per cent had an intellectual disability (IQ <70).
- 16 per cent had moderate to severe disability (IQ <50).
- 28 per cent had average intelligence (IQ 85–115).
- 3 per cent had above average intelligence (IQ >115).

---

7   Motor mannerisms are repetitive actions and don't appear to have a purpose, apart from possible enjoyment for the child. Some are common in many children, such as jumping up and down when excited. Children with autism might flap hands, spin in circles or rock. This may increase when the child is anxious or uncomfortable. Stimming (self-stimulatory behaviour) can be common in anyone and may include hair twirling or nail biting. Autistic individuals may spend more time stimming and be unaware that they may be disruptive or risk hurting themselves. At times, stimming can provide sensory soothing for the child.

8   Charman, T., Pickles, A., Simonoff, E., Chandler, S., Loucas, T. and Baird, G. (2011) 'IQ in children with autism spectrum disorders: data from the Special Needs and Autism Project (SNAP).' *Psychological Medicine 41*, 3, 619–627.

Children with a lower IQ are more likely to present with difficulties before the age of 5 years. Children with a higher IQ are more likely to be missed in the early years.

Regression

Regression can be seen in up to 20–25 per cent of children[9] and this usually occurs between 15 and 21 months of age. You may notice that your child was developing normally up until about 18 months and then they stopped talking or playing, avoided eye contact and became more withdrawn. They may have started showing some unusual behaviours, such as flapping, spinning and rocking. Their habits may have changed – for example, eating and sleeping have become more difficult.

Regression is also seen in other childhood conditions. The cause in autism is unknown and includes loss of language and social skills.[10]

9   Bradley, C.C., Boan, A., Cohen, A., Charles, J. and Carpenter, L.A. (2016) 'Reported history of developmental regression and restricted, repetitive behaviors in children with autism spectrum disorders.' *Journal of Developmental Behavioral Pediatrics 37*, 6, 451–456.

10 Nouf Backer Al Backer (2015) 'Developmental regression in autism spectrum disorder.' *Sudanese Journal of Paediatrics 15*, 1, 21–26.

CHAPTER 2

Childhood Development

'Whilst she could whiz through puzzles for older children, she couldn't point to toys that she wanted or ask me for a drink.'

(Lucy's Mum)

Is this autism or something else? As we are well aware, childhood development has a wide range of 'normal'. It is impossible to compare one child to another even though they may be exactly the same age. We start by outlining what babies and young children are expected to be able to do and when. And then we move on to list milestones that a child may not have achieved that might suggest developmental delay.

Areas of childhood development can be divided into five main categories:

1. *Gross motor skills:* The very first sign is head control. A baby will start to support their head from around 6–8 weeks. As their

neck muscles develop more strength they will progress to holding their head independently for longer periods of time.

The next milestone is the ability to sit with support at approximately 4–7 months.

Sitting independently usually occurs between 6 and 9 months.

The next major milestone is crawling. Babies normally crawl between 9 and 11 months. Commando crawling is a variation of crawling where the child will not progress from their elbows to their palms and will crawl on their elbows, resembling commandos in action. Some children may never crawl and prefer to bottom shuffle. This can be a normal stage of development. It is sometimes seen in babies who have poor muscle tone.

Once your baby can weight-bear, they will learn to pull to stand and start cruising (moving by holding onto furniture).

The normal milestone for walking is between 12 and 18 months but depends on many factors.

Toddlers rapidly learn to move faster, start running and become little daredevils!

2. *Fine motor skills:* These refer to the ability to use the smaller muscles of the body in order to control fine motor behaviours. The earliest fine motor skill is your baby holding your finger in the palm of their chubby little hands! This then progresses to grasping objects and toys and more fine motor control such as the pincer grasp. Fine motor skills are also important in the development of self-care skills such as feeding and dressing.

3. *Self-care and social skills:* A brief note on food preferences. As part of normal development, babies learn to develop taste preferences at around 9–12 months.[1] It is best to introduce a wide range of tastes and textures by 12–15 months of age. Dislike or rejection of foods can begin from about 14 months. Around 2 years of age, toddlers may develop a neophobic response, meaning they may reject new tastes. This usually peaks at 24 months and gradually diminishes by 8 years of age.

4. *Vision:* Vision is important for the development of other skills.

---

1   Schwartz, C., Issanchou, S. and Nicklaus, S. (2009) 'Developmental changes in the acceptance of the five basic tastes in the first year of life.' *The British Journal of Nutrition* *102*, 9, 1375–1385.

For normal eye contact to take place the child must have no impairment in the visual pathway. Provided this is normal, the child should be able to give good eye contact. You may remember your baby looking towards your face while feeding in the early months. This then progresses to some social interaction with cooing and smiling. Vision is also important in sharing interests such as books and toys.

5. *Speech, language and hearing:* The earliest memory you may have of your baby making a noise is crying when they are hungry or need something – this is a basic survival instinct in all animals. Humans have the ability to communicate with their voices, and babies will start babbling and making cooing sounds from the age of 4–6 months. As your baby grows, they become more interactive and from 9 months of age they will start to make simple sounds such as 'mumma' or 'dadda'. From the age of 18 months onwards, your toddler will increase their vocabulary and start to string between two and four words together to form simple phrases. Speech and language continues to develop and by the time they attend preschool they will be able to have simple conversations with you and sing nursery rhymes. It is important to note that normal hearing is important for speech and language development.

Overview of speech milestones

By 3 months of age

- ☐ Smiles and makes cooing sounds
- ☐ May recognise your voice and be soothed
- ☐ Develops different cries for different needs

By 6 months of age

- ☐ Babbles and makes gurgling sounds
- ☐ Uses voice to express pleasure or displeasure
- ☐ Pays attention to music
- ☐ Responds to changes in parent's voice

By 12 months of age

- ☐ Says a few words such as 'mumma', 'dadda'
- ☐ Imitates sounds – e.g. animal sounds
- ☐ Recognises names of everyday objects – e.g. 'teddy'
- ☐ Understands and may follow simple instructions

By 18 months of age

- ☐ Recognises names of familiar people and objects
- ☐ Vocabulary increases up to ten single words
- ☐ Follows simple directions with gestures

By 24 months of age

- ☐ Uses simple two-word phrases
- ☐ Vocabulary increases to over 50 words
- ☐ Answers simple questions
- ☐ Speech mostly understood by parents and carers

Hearing and language

Hearing is important for the development of normal speech and language. There are many causes for hearing impairment, which may be either congenital or acquired. Knowing the family history of hearing loss is important in order to rule out any familial causes of hearing loss. In children a common cause of acquired hearing loss is glue ear, which can occur at any time but is more common over the winter months and is associated with upper respiratory tract infections.

Self-care and social skills

Self-care skills refer to the ability of the child to learn to feed themselves, dress and undress, and to toileting skills.

Toilet-training is an important milestone, beginning with day-time dryness (day-time dryness is attained around 18–24 months, but some boys may not achieve this until 3 or 4 years of age[2]) and progressing to night-time dryness. Bowel control is usually acquired by 3–4 years of age, but some autistic children develop a fear of opening their bowels on a potty or toilet. This may be related to rigidity in behaviours or sensory difficulties. Although they may be dry and in pants, some children will request a nappy/diaper to open their bowels. Some studies have found a higher incidence of constipation in autistic children (33%).[3]

Developmental delay

Developmental delay is an umbrella term used to describe any difficulties a child may experience in the early years. This could be either a global developmental delay, which means that delayed development is present in all skill areas, or a delay in a particular area.

There are some milestones that parents may notice have not been attained by their child or that have been delayed. These may be signs of developmental delay and are *not* specific to autism.

For example:

2 months of age

- ☐ Does not smile at you
- ☐ Does not respond to loud sounds
- ☐ Does not bring hands to mouth
- ☐ Poor head control

4 months of age

- ☐ Does not smile at people
- ☐ Does not make cooing noises
- ☐ Does not watch things as they move around
- ☐ Does not take things to their mouth or fix and follow faces

---

2   Schum, T.R. *et al.* (2002) 'Sequential acquisition of toilet-training skills: a descriptive study of gender and age differences in normal children.' *Pediatrics 109*(3):E48. doi: 10.1542/peds.109.3.e48

3   Peters, B., Williams, K.C., Gorrindo, P., Rosenberg, D. *et al.* (2014) 'Rigid-compulsive behaviors are associated with mixed bowel symptoms in autism spectrum disorder.' *Journal of Autism and Developmental Disorders 44*, 6, 1425–1432.

6 months of age

- ☐ Does not roll over
- ☐ Does not laugh or make baby sounds
- ☐ Appears stiff
- ☐ Appears floppy like a rag doll
- ☐ Does not show much affection
- ☐ Has difficulty taking things to their mouth
- ☐ Does not make vowel sounds

9 months of age

- ☐ Does not respond to their name
- ☐ Does not recognise familiar people
- ☐ Does not look when you point (no shared joint attention sharing)
- ☐ Does not transfer toys from one hand to another
- ☐ Does not babble
- ☐ Does not sit with support
- ☐ Does not weight-bear on legs with support

1 year of age

- ☐ Does not yet crawl
- ☐ Does not stand when supported
- ☐ Does not say single words like 'mumma' or 'dadda'
- ☐ Does not wave or clap
- ☐ Does not point to things
- ☐ Loses some of the skills that they once had

18 months of age

- ☐ Does not yet have the ability to walk
- ☐ Does not learn new words
- ☐ Does not have at least six single words
- ☐ Does not look for the carer or parent when they are left on their own
- ☐ Does not point to objects
- ☐ Loses skills

2 years of age

☐ Does not have the ability to use two-word phrases
☐ Cannot carry out self-care skills such as using a fork or spoon, or everyday actions like using a phone
☐ Does not follow action songs or nursery rhymes
☐ Does not follow simple instructions
☐ Does not walk steadily

3 years of age

☐ Does not have clear speech
☐ Does not speak in sentences
☐ Does not follow simple instructions
☐ Does not use imaginative or pretend play
☐ Does not show interest in other children or play with toys
☐ Does not show eye contact
☐ Loses skills

4 years of age

☐ Does not have the ability to jump or run
☐ Does not have the ability to use a pen or scribble
☐ Does not take an interest in imaginative play
☐ Does not respond to other children or show an interest in other children
☐ Does not have the ability to use the toilet
☐ Does not follow commands
☐ Does not use 'me' or 'you' correctly
☐ Does not speak clearly

5 years of age

☐ Does not show a wide range of emotions
☐ Does not respond to others' conversation or commands
☐ Does not play with a variety of toys or games
☐ Does not have the ability to give their first and last name

☐ Does not have the ability to use grammar, plurals and tenses appropriately

☐ Does not have the ability to perform basic self-care (brush teeth, wash hands, get undressed without help)

☐ Does not have the ability to draw basic pictures

☐ Shows extreme behaviours, such as aggression or withdrawal

CHAPTER 3

Brief Guide to Differential Diagnoses

'Since our youngest has been diagnosed, our eldest has also received a diagnosis. The more we learnt about autism, the more things clicked into place. Both our children are completely different, with totally different needs, but they have a fun relationship and our eldest shows his brother the most extraordinary amount of patience.'

(Parent reflection)

Differential diagnosis is the means by which healthcare professionals consider a patient's symptoms and history, together with physical examination, to distinguish between a particular disease or condition. In, this chapter, we look at conditions involving developmental delay which may present like autism. Clinicians will consider these conditions in their assessment and suggest further tests if necessary, depending on their findings.

Developmental disorders

- *Speech and language disorder or specific language disorder:* Children with speech and language delay may be able to compensate for their lack of speech and language by using gestures and non-verbal communication. In addition, they will not lack the imaginative play and interaction with parents. These children may have isolated speech and language delay and no difficulties with communication and interaction.

- *Global developmental delay:* This means there is developmental delay in all areas of development, including speech and language, communication, motor skills, fine motor skills, and social and interactive skills. There are many causes for developmental delay, such as prematurity, maternal antenatal substance misuse, chromosomal abnormalities.

- *Chromosomal abnormalities:* Examples are conditions such as Down syndrome and fragile X syndrome, but there are many others. Some may be rare and occur randomly because of mutations.

- *Intellectual disability or learning disabilities:* Children who struggle with learning or have immaturity in their learning can present with delay in their social communication skills. However, their non-verbal interaction, peer interaction and some imaginative play may be preserved.

- *DCD (developmental coordination disorder):* This condition includes difficulties with social communication skills, attention and concentration skills with some hyperactivity and clumsiness or dyspraxic symptoms. These children could present difficulties similar to those of autistic children. If these skills do not improve over time, they may require further assessment, including input from the occupational therapy team.

Sensorimotor difficulties

There is increasing evidence to suggest that children on the autism spectrum are at increased risk of having developmental delay, particularly in the sensorimotor domain. Landa and Garrett-Maya[1] have shown that fine motor difficulties in early childhood lead to a significantly increased risk of developing autistic difficulties around the age of 36 months. This shows the variability in motor difficulties that can be present in autistic children. A study by Hannant *et al.*[2] aimed to identify whether children on the spectrum had significantly greater difficulties in their coordination and motor progress as well as their sensory difficulties. It showed that children on the spectrum did have significant fine motor difficulties, sensory issues and receptive language delay compared to children with similar IQ and age. Fine motor difficulties were mainly with manual dexterity and balance, which impacts on coordination. The child's response to sensory stimuli was studied: some children sought increased sensory activities (e.g. tactile behaviours or strong tastes), whereas others avoided sensory input (e.g. tactile sensations such as hugs, or they preferred bland tastes).

Movement disorders which may be stereotypic

Some hand/finger mannerisms or twitches, tics or tremors may resemble unusual movements which could be interpreted as 'stimming behaviours'. However, they could be associated with underlying neurological disorders and this should be considered – for example, Tourette's syndrome or other neurological problems.

Neurobehavioural disorders

- *Anxiety:* Children who are extremely anxious may present as being very shy and have difficult social interaction. These children may present as autistic; however, there may be a mood disorder associated with the anxiety.

1   Landa, R. and Garrett-Mayer, E. (2006) 'Development in infants with autism spectrum disorders: a prospective study.' *Journal of Child Psychology and Psychiatry 47*, 6, 629–638.
2   Hannant, P., Cassidy, S., Tavassoli, T. and Mann, F. (2016) 'Sensorimotor difficulties are associated with the severity of autism spectrum conditions.' *Frontiers on Integrative Neuroscience*, 17 August. https://doi.org/10.3389/fnint.2016.00028

- *Attachment disorders:* Children who have experienced a traumatic or chaotic early life (ACEs or Adverse Childhood Events) or those who have not bonded well with their carers may develop social communication difficulties as a result of attachment issues and this may resemble autism. At-risk infants are those whose mothers misused substances in pregnancy or developed postnatal depression.

- *Attention deficit hyperactivity disorder (ADHD):* ADHD is not usually diagnosed in preschool children but in school-aged children. A child who has ADHD may also struggle to interact socially because of their chaotic and aggressive manner.

- *Developmental regression:* Autism can present in young children who have been developing normally until the age of 18–24 months. At this stage, despite the fact that the child has acquired language and has been socially interactive, they may suddenly regress or plateau in their development. Conditions which may cause regression are, for example, Rett syndrome, a chromosomal condition commonly seen in girls.

- *Other neurological conditions:* There are a range of other neurological conditions, including genetic syndromes and epileptic-type disorders which may need to be considered. In some cases, there may be clinical signs present, such as unusual skin conditions or physical features.

- *Selective mutism:* Some children develop this condition, which means they will choose to speak in certain settings only. A study by Steffenburg *et al.*[3] found that 63 per cent of the children with selective mutism also met the criteria for autism or a developmental disorder.

- *Severe hearing loss:* Severe hearing loss will impact on the child's ability to listen to instructions and be aware of things going on around them, and may cause delay in speech and language development. It is always very important to have hearing tested in these children.

- *Severe visual impairments:* A child who is partially sighted or has difficulty focusing on objects may appear to have poor eye contact and struggle with joint interaction and shared play.

3   Steffenburg, H., Steffenburg, S., Gillberg, C. and Billstedt, E. (2018) 'Children with autism spectrum disorders and selective mutism.' *Neuropsychiatric Disease and Treatment 14*, 1163–1169.

- *Child abuse:* A child who has been abused may present similarly to an autistic child, due to reluctance to engage with people. Often a fear of adults can present as autism.

It is important to remember that neurodevelopment is very complex and to identify concerns early so that appropriate support can be given.

Signs and symptoms which a paediatrician may observe and require further investigations include:

- Head size that is bigger or smaller than expected according to the growth chart.
- Any unusual facial features.
- Abnormalities in tone – the child appears floppy or stiff.
- Unusual birthmarks.
- Failure to thrive – a child who is not growing despite having a good diet may have an underlying medical issue.
- Seizures.
- An enlarged liver or spleen – on examination this may indicate a metabolic abnormality.
- Any neurological deficit – this could indicate underlying neurological or metabolic issues.

CHAPTER 4

Is This Autism?

'At the time of diagnosis, as with most parents, we felt a mixture of
sadness, worry, guilt and relief that some support would be on the way.'

(Pierre and Aurelie's parents)

Autism may be described as a complex neurodevelopmental condition
which is seen in individuals of all ethnicities, cultures and intellectual abilities. Children with possible autistic difficulties are being
increasingly identified. This could be because of increased awareness
and understanding of autism. It has resulted in services being overwhelmed by referrals (both an increase in number of referrals leading

to increased waiting times for assessment and diagnosis as well as for therapeutic service provision).

The prevalence of autism is thought to be 1 in 100 children in the United Kingdom.[1] The United States report 1 in 81 school children have some form of autism.[2]

Autism was initially described in 1943 by Leo Kanner, a psychiatrist in the United States, but also by Hans Asperger, a paediatrician who in 1944 described similar findings in children in Austria.[3] In their studies of young children they noticed similarities in some of the behaviours.

The common features were as follows:

- They had a specific or restricted interest in a variety of topics.
- They had an obsessive desire for sameness, and difficulty with change.
- They had an exceptional ability to learn by rote memory.
- They were preoccupied with toys or objects or particular parts of them and focused on detail.
- Some of them had specific areas of ability.

Subsequent to these observations, various psychologists and scientists have investigated autism. Further studies in 1979 by Lorna Wing, a paediatrician who had a daughter with severe autism, and Judith Gould, a clinical psychologist in London, observed more and more children having complex difficulties associated with social communication and interaction. Wing and Gould pioneered work in the field of autism, and Wing founded the NAS (National Autism Society) in the UK. At that time, in the 1970s, Wing and Gould identified children who lacked pretend play and had common social difficulties.[4] Further studies in 1993 by Christopher Gillberg, Professor of Child and

---

1   Baron-Cohen, S., Scott, F.J., Allison, C., Williams, J. *et al.* (2009) 'Prevalence of autism-spectrum conditions: UK school-based population study.' *The British Journal of Psychiatry 194*, 6, 500–509.
2   Safer-Lichtenstein, J., Hamilton, J. and McIntyre, L.L. (2021) 'School-Based Autism Rates by State: an Analysis of Demographics, Political Leanings, and Differential Identification.' *Journal of Autism and Developmental Disorders 51*, 7, 2271–2283.
3   Baron-Cohen, S. (2015) 'Leo Kanner, Hans Asperger, and the discovery of autism.' *The Lancet 386*, 10001, 1329–1330.
4   Wing, L. and Gould, J. (1979) 'Severe impairments of social interaction and associated abnormalities in children: Epidemiology and classification.' *Journal of Autism and Developmental Disorders 9*, 1, 11–29.

Adolescent Psychiatry, and Stephen Ehlers in Gothenburg described the prevalence as being more common, presenting in 36 out of 10,000 young people.[5] These studies may suggest that autism is increasing in prevalence across the globe. The incidence may vary in different parts of the world. Worldwide estimates are that 1 in 160 children have autism.[6] In the United Kingdom there are 700,000 people who have been diagnosed with autism.[7]

Sometimes people use the expression 'We all have autistic tendencies', but what does this mean? Does it mean we all display certain restrictive repetitive behaviours, obsessive compulsive issues, or awkwardness in social situations? Of course, if we look at ourselves as individuals, we may have some quirky habits or behaviours, but they do not make us autistic. A common condition, obsessive compulsive disorder (OCD) may resemble some of the features of autism (see Chapter 21). Mostly we are able to control them and not allow others to see them. These behaviours should not stop us from doing everyday activities. In some cases they may take over our thoughts and actions, and then intervention is required.

Classification of autism has changed over the years. The first classification of autism was included in the *Diagnostic and Statistical Manual of Mental Disorders* (*DSM-III* 1987) which described autism. Prior to that, these conditions were called childhood schizophrenia (*DSM-II* 1952). These criteria were revised in 1994 in the *DSM-IV* manual and continued to be in use until 2013. A triad of difficulties would have to be fulfilled to consider a diagnosis of autism. In 2013 the *DSM-5* criteria were once again revised and are widely used to confirm a diagnosis of autism.[8]

The diagnosis and understanding of autism have changed dramatically in the past 25 years. Autism was considered uncommon before the 1990s, with a prevalence of approximately 0.6 per cent. The annual incidence for autism in the UK was found to have risen five-fold in

5   Ehlers, S. and Gillberg, C. (1993) 'The Epidemiology of Asperger Syndrome.' *Journal of Child Psychology and Psychiatry 34*, 8, 1327–1350.

6   World Health Organization (2021) 'Autism spectrum disorders.' Accessed on 09/04/21 at: www.who.int/news-room/fact-sheets/detail/autism-spectrum-disorders

7   BMA (2020) 'Autism spectrum disorder.' Accessed on 09/04/2021 at: www.bma.org.uk/what-we-do/population-health/child-health/autism-spectrum-disorder

8   American Psychiatric Association (2013) *DSM-5*. Washington, DC: APA.

the 1990s.[9] There are many reasons for the rise in the diagnosis of autism, such as improved diagnostic criteria, and increased awareness and understanding of the condition. In the last century, the 'autistic stereotype' was a 'male with lower intellectual ability'. We now know that although the sex ratio is 4:1 for males: females, autistic girls present differently and often are diagnosed much later in childhood or even adulthood.[10] It is estimated that autistic children constitute approximately 1.5 per cent of the general population. Of these autistic individuals 70–90 per cent do not have general intellectual difficulties.[11]

Theory of mind

Simon Baron-Cohen put forward the 'theory of mind' hypothesis in 1985.[12] 'Theory of mind' refers to an individual's ability to put themselves in somebody else's shoes and understand their thoughts and feelings. This allows the person to see things from their point of view and try to understand how they are feeling. Autistic children may struggle with theory of mind and find it difficult to understand and predict other people's behaviour or emotions.

There are milestones in a child's life when these abilities develop, but in autistic children they may not be observed.

- At around 14 months a toddler will learn joint attention sharing – that is, they are interested not only in objects but in the person who is sharing the activity with them.
- A 2-year-old will start to engage in pretend play.
- A 3-year-old has the concept that things that are seen may not necessarily predict what lies beneath them.
- A 4-year-old is able to understand when others have a belief

9   Taylor, B., Jick, H. and MacLaughlin, D. (2013) 'Prevalence and incidence rates of autism in the UK: time trend from 2004–2010 in children aged 8 years.' *BMJ Open 3*, 10. doi: 10.1136/bmjopen-2013-003219

10 McFayden, T.C., Antezana, L., Albright, J., Muskett, A. and Scarpa, A. (2020) 'Sex differences in an autism spectrum disorder diagnosis: are restricted repetitive behaviors and interests the key?' *Review Journal of Autism and Developmental Disorders 7*, 2, 119–126.

11 Lord, C., Elsabbagh, M., Baird, G. and Veenstra-Vanderweele, J. (2018) 'Autism spectrum disorder.' *The Lancet 392*, 10146, 508–520.

12 Baron-Cohen, S., Leslie, A.M. and Frith, U. (1985) 'Does the autistic child have a "theory of mind"?' *Cognition 21*, 1, 37–46.

that is not true. They understand deception, whereas autistic children will assume that everybody is telling the truth.

- By the age of 9 years, they will be able to understand when they have hurt somebody's feelings and be able to recognise more complex facial expressions and non-verbal gestures.

Lack or delay in acquiring these skills may indicate lack of empathy.

Newer research has refined this theory to include strengths of the child as well as areas of difficulty.[13]

Empathising–systemising (E–S) theory

A new concept has been put forward by Simon Baron-Cohen called the empathising–systemising (E–S) theory.[14] This looks at both aspects of an autistic child – that is, those areas which are lacking in the child, as well as those that are strengths in the child. The E–S theory examines two main features in an autistic person. The empathising element is the lack or difficulty in empathy, which may explain social communication difficulties. The systemising component of the theory explains the child's repetitive behaviours, specific interests and rigidity about change. The child's ability to systemise things also supports the theory of attention to detail and memory that individuals on the spectrum can display.

Examples of systemising are as follows:

- *Social:* Insistence on playing the same game with the same rules.
- *Environmental:* Resisting changes around them – for example, objects having to remain in a particular place or lining up of toys.
- *Spatial:* These are obsessions about routes and directions, where some children may wish to always take the same route when going to school, for instance.
- *Natural:* Repetitive questioning about everyday occurrences, such as asking over and over again, 'Is it a school day today?'
- *Sensory:* Sensory difficulties with tastes and textures. Insisting on sameness and rejecting anything different.

13 Baron-Cohen, S. (2008) 'Theories of the autistic mind.' *The Psychologist 21*, 112–116.
14 Baron-Cohen, S. (2009) 'The empathising-systemising theory of autism: implications for education.' *Tizard Learning Disability Review 14*, 3, 14 July.

- *Motoric:* Spinning, flapping and other behaviours.
- *Collectable:* Specific interests in collecting objects or books. A typical example is collecting stones or dinosaurs. A child who loves to make lists or go through shopping catalogues.
- *Numerical:* Obsessions with numbers relating to timetables or maths.
- *Motion:* Watching repetitive actions such as the spinning of a washing machine.
- *Mechanical:* Taking apart toys or gadgets and putting them back together.
- *Vocal:* Echoing or making up repetitive phrases.
- *Systemising:* Repeated watching of the same programme or reading the same book over and over again.
- *Musical:* Singing or playing the same tune repetitively.

Various theories have been suggested to explain autism. The theory of mind refers to 'mind-blindness', which was first described by Simon Baron-Cohen.[15] The theory of mind has been investigated in detail over the years since it was first put forward by Simon Baron-Cohen and his colleagues in 1985. It is thought that children develop theory of mind (the ability of the child to understand another person's beliefs, ideas or feelings) between the age of 3 and 5 years. Lack of this ability impacts on the child's social communication and development.

Many years ago, autism was thought to be a result of poor parenting, which may still be mentioned by some people. This was the 'refrigerator mother theory' in the 1940s, which has been discredited.[16] It was used to label mothers of autistic children, who were 'blamed' for being cold towards their children. Thankfully this is no longer considered valid in most countries. Autism is now a recognised neurodevelopmental condition, which has many possible causes. No single specific cause has been identified.

When your child is diagnosed with autism, you will want to try and find a cause. However, a specific cause is rarely identified. Autism is thought to be multifactorial – that is, many factors may contribute

---

15   Baron-Cohen, S., Leslie, A.M. and Frith, U. (1985) 'Does the autistic child have a "theory of mind"?' *Cognition 21*, 1, 37–46.

16   Cohmer, S. (2014) 'Early infantile autism and the refrigerator mother theory (1943–1970).' *The Embryo Project Encyclopedia*, 19 August, https://embryo.asu.edu/handle/10776/8149

to autism – genetic predisposition as well as environmental factors. It is, however, important to note that autism can coexist with other medical conditions such as ADHD, dyspraxia, epilepsy or mental health problems.

Your new baby

The joy and miracle of parenthood begins with euphoria and elation. A newborn baby comes into this world innocent and beautiful. However, this little baby does not come with a handbook entitled 'How to Take Care of Me'.

The love and excitement that fills parents' hearts is indescribable and immeasurable. Their hopes and aspirations are that this beautiful little baby will grow up to have a happy, healthy, normal life. We do not look to the future at how this baby will develop into a child, young person and adult. Each step is a milestone in their achievements and a pleasure of the moment. We celebrate their achievements and are saddened by their disappointments. As parents we have to hold their hands over obstacles and hurdles. We comfort and encourage them every step of the way, especially when they need encouragement and support. We as parents don't know when these hurdles will appear. As parents walk the path of parenthood and look out over the horizon, the path is smooth with green grass and beautiful flowers along the way. However, when they are met with a concern about their baby, there is a hump on the road like a speed bump which can catch us unaware, give us a jolt and perhaps increase our heart rate. However, we can overcome this and we settle down as our heart rate drops back to normal.

Life is an experience of learning through the challenges we face and learning to focus on positive goals. Once you overcome these, you will be able to accept and deal with life's challenges. As a parent these are your experiences; no one can take away those feelings, but with support they can be eased and the pain managed. Each child is different and no one list of instructions will suit all children.

CHAPTER 5

The What, Why, Where and When of a Diagnosis of Autism

'As someone working in education, I was fortunate enough to know the process from the other side, and to see the benefits that having a diagnosis can have.'

(Maryam's Dad)

What? What is autism?

Autism is a complex condition of varying severity that can present at any stage in a child's life. The most severe forms will present early; for those with high intellectual ability who are able to 'mask' and cover their difficulties, it may present later. There is no one specific age when the diagnosis is made. It is also important to note that there is no age when autism cannot be diagnosed. We have heard parents say to us that when they have made enquiries they are told an assessment cannot be carried out until a child is above 3 years, or in some areas over the age of 5 years! There are no rules or guidelines as to when is the best time to assess a child for autism. What we do know about autism is that difficulties should be identified early and support should be sought as soon as possible. Evidence points to the benefits of early diagnosis so children can be 'taught' skills before they become rigid in their ways of behaving. Parents know their child best and if they have concerns, these should be addressed.

Difficulties in autism include social communication interaction difficulties, with restrictive repetitive behaviours and/or sensory sensitivities. This is according to the *DSM-5* criteria which are influential internationally. These criteria need to be fulfilled in order for a diagnosis to be made. Depending on where in the world you live, the pathway for seeking a diagnosis may be different. Even within the same country, service provision for autism diagnosis will vary.

It is a traumatic time for families as not all autistic children are the same and the prognosis cannot be predicted. Some children may remain non-verbal throughout their lives, whereas others will learn to speak over time. Others may have no difficulty with speech and language development and are very articulate.

Why? Why is my child autistic?

There is no definitive answer. Despite research into this area over the last several decades, no specific cause has been identified. Most experts in the field say it is a combination of genetic and environmental factors, whilst there may be a familial predisposition in some cases.

Genetics and autism

Research on whole genome analysis has found more than a hundred genes may be responsible for contributing to autism.[1] Multiple genes have been implicated on various chromosomes (e.g. chromosomes 2

---

1   Rylaarsdam, L. and Guemez-Gamboa, A. (2019) 'Genetic causes and modifiers of autism spectrum disorder.' *Frontiers in Cellular Neuroscience 13*, 385.

and 7, and 16 and 9); however, a specific gene has not been identified for autism.

The most common variant associated with autism is the duplication 15q syndrome.[2] This is still being researched extensively to increase the understanding of genetics and autism.

There are some chromosomal anomalies or syndromes associated with autism[3] such as:

- *Fragile X:* Affects mostly males and is a common cause for intellectual disability. Autism occurs in 20–50% of males with Fragile X.
- *Rett syndrome:* X-linked disorder affecting girls and presenting with developmental delay, seizures and autism in 25–40 per cent of cases.
- *Tuberous sclerosis:* Autosomal dominant condition causing intellectual and behavioural difficulties, with epilepsy. Autism is seen in up to 40 per cent of cases.
- *Other syndromes:* They include Down's, Prader-Willi and Angelman syndromes.

In conclusion, there is no single test which can confirm autism and a diagnosis is made ideally in a multiprofessional clinic, considering specific criteria which are internationally recognised and included in the *International Classification of Diseases (ICD)* or *Diagnostic and Statistical Manual (DSM)*. The latest versions are *ICD-11*[4] and *DSM-5*[5].

2   Urraca, N., Cleary, J., Brewer, V., Pivnick, E.K. *et al.* (2013) 'The interstitial duplication 15q11.2-q13 syndrome includes autism, mild facial anomalies and a characteristic EEG signature.' *Autism Research 6*, 4, 268–279.

3   Ornoy, A., Weinstein-Fudim, L. and Ergaz, Z. (2016) 'Genetic syndromes, maternal diseases and antenatal factors associated with autism spectrum disorders.' *Frontiers in Neuroscience 10*, 316.

4   World Health Organization (2022) *International Classification of Diseases, 11th revision (ICD-11)*. Available at https://icd.who.int/en

5   *American Psychiatric Association (2013) Diagnostic and Statistical Manual of Mental Disorders, 5th edition (DSM-5)*. Washington, DC: APA.

When? The age that children can present with difficulties is variable

In the most severe and extreme cases, during infancy the baby will not acquire a social smile or may not be engaging, will not give you eye contact, will not respond to your peek-a-boos or your smiles and will be content on their own. Others will present with speech and language delay and will not engage socially unless they desire something. Some may present with behavioural difficulties as they find the world around them overwhelming. Senses can be over-stimulated or under-stimulated, causing distress to the child.

Later presentations can be in the form of non-conformity to social norms, behavioural difficulties and emotional or psychiatric disturbances.

This makes identification of autism difficult as it can present at different times of childhood development with a large variety of presentations. There is no specific age when children will present with difficulties suggestive of autism.

Regression

Some may develop normally up until the age of 18 months to 2 years in terms of motor skills and speech and language development; then things suddenly change. It is this regression in development that was described in (then Dr) Andrew Wakefield's theory on the link between the MMR (measles, mumps and rubella) vaccine and autism.

Wakefield's paper published in *The Lancet*[6] raised the profile for a possible cause for this condition. Many families whose children had shown regression around the age of 18–24 months have also linked the MMR vaccine as a potential cause for their child's autism. Subsequent research has shown that there is *no* evidence to support the link between the immunisation and development of autism.[7] There are children who have never been immunised with the MMR who present

---

6   Wakefield, A.J., Murch, S.H., Anthony, A., Linnell, J. *et al.* (1998) 'Ileal-lymphoid-nodular hyperplasia, non-specific colitis, and pervasive developmental disorder in children.' *The Lancet 351*, 9103, 637–641. Retracted article.

7   DeStefano, F. and Thompson, W.W. (2004) 'MMR vaccine and autism: an update of the scientific evidence.' *Expert Review of Vaccines 3*, 1, 19–22.

with autistic behaviours. This has resulted in pockets of outbreaks of measles and mumps, sometimes with life-threatening consequences.[8]

Where? Where do I go when my child has been given a diagnosis of autism?

Where does a parent go? The option of modern technology leads to autism being typed into the search engine. Within 0.6 seconds, over 237,000,000 hits for autism will appear on your screen. How does a parent decide which sites will give the most accurate and reliable information on autism? Some parents read blogs or follow others on Facebook. Other avenues are support from friends and family who have experience of autism, either personally or professionally. Whichever route is taken, facts about autism can be overwhelming. Where do you start? A useful start would be information from experts such as Tony Attwood, a psychologist in Australia, who is internationally renowned for his work on autism and Simon Baron-Cohen, a distinguished clinical psychologist and director of Cambridge University's Autism Research Centre UK.

It may be helpful to take one step at a time in understanding the condition. A good start is with ABC:

- *Accept:* Learn to accept the difficulties but be grateful about the positives.
- *Believe:* Believe that things can improve with support.
- *Carry on:* Advocate for your child and nurture their strengths.

It will take time for the information to sink in. That's normal. Try to remember the following:

Dos

- The diagnosis does not change your child.
- You cannot change some things, but you can change yourself.
- Take time for yourself.

---

8   www.gov.uk/government/news/measles-outbreaks-across-england

- Think about the rest of the family and be there for them.
- Seek early support to do the best for your child.
- You are not alone.

Don'ts

- Don't become negative.
- Don't forget the beautiful baby you fell in love with.
- Don't look at your child as having a disability.
- Don't blame yourself or feel guilty.
- Don't look for a cure.
- Don't expect quick solutions.

Part 2

· · · · · · · ·

DURING DIAGNOSIS

CHAPTER 6

Supporting Evidence

'I think by the time of diagnosis, most parents have some idea that autism is at play. My son was diagnosed when he had just turned 3.'

(Amit's Mum)

A diagnosis of autism is based on gathering information about the child and clinical assessment. The team of clinicians will carry out a thorough assessment including a developmental history, observation and examination of the child. The confirmation of the diagnosis requires robust evidence to justify the diagnosis. Most practitioners will request this information prior to the consultation. It is important that accurate information is obtained from families as well as teachers or carers of the child. Some services will base their recommendations for accepting the child for an assessment on the information provided.

If autism is suspected, an early assessment should be carried out.[1]

Commonly used classifications for diagnosing autism

- *Diagnostic and Statistical Manual of Mental Disorders (DSM-5),* Criteria for 299.00 Autism Spectrum Disorder.[2]
- *International Classification of Diseases 11th Revision (ICD-11),* Autism Spectrum Disorder 6A02.[3]

DSM-5: Diagnostic criteria for 299.00 autism spectrum disorder

These criteria for autism diagnosis were revised in 2013, changing the criteria from three symptoms to two ('triad' to 'dyad'):

1. Difficulties in social communication and interaction.
2. Repetitive behaviours, also known as restricted repetitive behaviours (RRBs) or sensory difficulties.

The core of the social and behavioural presentations in autism can vary, depending on intellectual ability and the presence of other genetic or syndromic disorders.

It is important to note if there are any associated difficulties such as:

- Intellectual impairment.
- Language impairment.
- Medical or genetic causes.
- Any other comorbid conditions.

This classification also helps to identify the type of support that may be required by the child: level 1, 2 or 3 (1 being minimal, and 3 substantial support).

The *DSM-5* criteria include various changes from the *DSM-IV* criteria and combine the previous four diagnoses in autism, namely:

---

1   Baird, G., Cass, H. and Slonims, V. 'Diagnosis of autism.' *BMJ 327*, 7413, 488–493.

2   www.DSM5.org

3   https://icd.who.int/en

- Autistic disorder.
- Asperger's syndrome.
- Pervasive developmental disorder (not otherwise specified in PDD-NOS).
- Childhood disintegrative disorder.

The biggest change has been the use of an umbrella term, 'autism spectrum condition', for the four previous separate diagnoses. Autism can be viewed as a spectrum difficulty without differentiating Asperger's syndrome as a different entity. Previously Asperger's was thought to be a milder form of autism, with less stigma attached to it, often giving parents false reassurance about the child's needs. The working group for *DSM-5* confirmed that there was no consistent biological feature that distinguished Asperger's from autism.

The *DSM-5* criteria aim to combine the difficulties in different areas to simplify diagnosis. They combine the social and language deficits into one domain and include social communication and interaction difficulties. In addition, individuals should also display restrictive and repetitive behaviours in order to qualify for a diagnosis. Should the child not have any repetitive behaviours, they may receive a diagnosis of 'social communication disorder'. Conversely, if a child presents with RRBs but social communication difficulties do not meet the *DSM-5* threshold, a diagnosis of 'stereotypic movement disorder' may be applied.

This description is to provide some understanding of the ways clinicians will confirm a possible diagnosis. It is *not* intended for parents or others to self-diagnose their children. This is *DSM-5* in its simplest form, an internationally recognised set of criteria clinicians use to diagnose the child or young person. There are also other diagnostic criteria such as the *ICD-11 International Classification of Diseases*.

ICD-11 criteria

The *ICD* criteria refer to difficulties in three domains:

- The child's skills in social communication.
- The ability of the child to interact socially.
- Any unusual patterns of behaviour.

These difficulties need to be apparent before the age of 3 years and various criteria need to be met before a diagnosis can be confirmed.

Assessment tools

The diagnosis of autism requires skills, expertise and experience. Clinicians need to use evidence-based criteria to confirm a diagnosis. This is a challenge in itself as there is no single test or tool that is the benchmark.

Various assessments or tools have been devised. A well-recognised test is the ADOS-2 (Autism Diagnostic Observation Schedule) published by Western Psychological Services (WPS) in 2000 and available in 15 languages. This is considered to be the gold standard for diagnosing autism, but it is not always necessary – it depends on the child's presentation and whether there are obvious autistic difficulties giving sufficient evidence for a diagnosis.

The ADOS was co-developed in the 1980s by Dr Catherine Lord and Sir Michael Rutter. It includes structured as well as semi-structured tasks involving the child and the examiner. There are other standardised tests and questionnaires which can also be used to gather evidence and confirm a possible diagnosis of autism. The clinicians will decide what best suits children and families to provide information.

Other questionnaires include:

- M-CHAT (Modified Checklist for Autism in Toddlers).
- CAST (Childhood Autism Spectrum Test).
- SCQ (Social Communication Questionnaire).
- SDQ (Strengths and Difficulties Questionnaire).
- ADI-R (Autism Diagnostic Interview – Revised).
- DISCO (Diagnostic Interview for Social and Communication Disorders).
- 3Di (Developmental, Dimensional and Diagnostic Interview).
- BOSA (Brief Observation of Symptoms of Autism).

The BOSA requires a mention, particularly as this book has been written partly during the Covid-19 pandemic. An ADOS assessment is difficult to use with social distancing and is considered invalid if masks are used, as facial expressions cannot be observed. International experts have been concerned about this predicament and Catherine Lord and her team devised the BOSA to address this.[4] Online training was offered to clinicians to administer the test virtually or in a clinical setting with social distancing.

A survey carried out by the NAS (National Autistic Society in the UK) was reported by Baird *et al.* in 2012.[5] One of the questions explored was what parents wanted from a diagnosis of autism. The responses were as follows:

- A clear pathway before and after diagnosis.
- Better access to specialist services.
- Reduced waiting time.
- An improved multidisciplinary team approach.
- Increased awareness of other medical or mental health conditions associated with autism.

---

4   www.semel.ucla.edu/autism/video/brief-observation-symptoms-autism-bosa-training
5   Baird, G. (2012) 'What did parents want? National Autism Society Parent Survey.' Paper presented at conference: Autism spectrum disorder: from clinical practice to educational provision, 12–13 January 2012.

CHAPTER 7

Educational Input

'I cried when I went to look around an SEN school for our son. The school was beautiful and the children seemed so happy, but the guilt I felt for "limiting his choices in life". I wish I could go back and tell myself then that we weren't limiting his choices; we were giving him the best possible chance at reaching his full potential.'

(Parent of S)

Educational input is very important for two main reasons. First, children and young people spend a large proportion of their waking time in school; and second, observations and assessments by educational staff provide insight into the child's functioning outside the home. This is useful not only for clinicians but also for parents. The information clinicians request prior to the assessment may be in the form of specially designed questionnaires. These can be completed by the child's class teacher in primary school or by the teacher who knows the young person best in secondary school settings. At times there is a collaborative response, where staff have liaised with different teachers to complete the information required. Sometimes we receive feedback from all subject teachers, which is also helpful (it makes for lots of reading but is useful!).

Additional information that parents can provide are previous annual school reports. Also useful is feedback from parent–teacher consultations and information about extra-curricular activities the child may be attending.

Parents are sometimes disappointed at the depth and quality of information sent by school. Quite often this is because the SENCo, the special educational needs coordinator, has completed the request. The SENCo may not know your child well or may have done only a brief classroom observation. In some cases, we ask for further input and request extra information, such as observation in the playground or at lunch time. Where there may be other concerns such as speech delay, fine motor difficulties or ADHD symptoms, one of the multidisciplinary clinicians may go into school to carry out an observation, which is always helpful. In preschool children, a home observation can also be useful, especially if it is reported that the child is very anxious and presents very differently at school.

There are some health services in different parts of the UK where an educational psychologist's assessment is mandatory as part of the diagnostic pathway. This may cause a delay in the assessment process as the number of children who can be seen by an educational psychologist each term is finite. Multidisciplinary assessments do not always have a rigid protocol and depend on the needs of the child. For example, a preschool child with delayed speech may initially be seen by a speech and language therapist/speech pathologist, or a child with learning difficulties may be seen by an educational psychologist.

The focus remains on the needs of the child and that is paramount in our assessments. We aim to support families and help them overcome any difficulties they experience in getting appropriate support.

How diagnosis can improve educational provision

Getting the 'autism' diagnosis can help schools access additional funds for more support or staffing to help them to meet the needs of your child. It might be that a child needs high levels of support and a staff member nearby at all times. A mainstream classroom can have 30 or more children with one teacher and one teaching assistant. A child diagnosed with autism could enable a school to request funding for an extra member of staff to support their learning. The diagnosis will inform teachers and staff and provide a clear direction. This will enable them to meet the child's needs more effectively. In England a child with a diagnosis may be able to get an education, health and care plan (EHC) in place, which is a detailed legal document outlining the child's diagnosis, individual needs and targets for future learning. This plan is prepared with parents or guardians and will involve any professionals involved such as health professionals, speech therapists, occupational therapists or physiotherapists and teachers who have worked with your child. Having the diagnosis and legal documents such as the EHC plan can open the door to more support and understanding for your child. The EHC plan can also include therapies required by a child, such as speech therapy, and may specify how much speech therapy input should be provided weekly, monthly or termly.

Should parents look at other schools?

If a child is not coping in a mainstream preschool, if they are not yet speaking or interacting in a similar way to children of their age and if autism is a potential diagnosis, it is worth parents looking at what provision is available within driving distance. Looking at what's available doesn't mean that a child won't attend the local infant or primary school. But looking at alternatives and keeping an open mind will mean that parents know what provision is available and can start thinking about their own preferences. A discussion with the child's teacher and SENCo is always helpful.

Communication with teachers

It is important to establish good communication with your child's key worker or teacher from the start. Children are known to behave differently at home and at school. Discuss any concerns you experience with your child at home. If you have a worry, then let them know, but do this by email, phone call or a little note. You do not want these conversations to take place at drop-off and pick-up times while your child is standing and listening. Even if they do not understand all the content, they will pick up on voice tone and anxieties. It may be that you have concerns before they do. If this is the case, be open with them and ask them if they will gather evidence, write observations or video the child.

Play

The early years foundation stage (EYFS) is centred around learning through play. The classroom is set up with lots of motivating activities so that the children can move around the room exploring the different play areas on offer. They will be learning to negotiate, cooperate and communicate through access to role play, dressing up and interactions with key workers and other children. There will be opportunities for sensory and physical development such as arts and crafts, climbing equipment and bikes. There will be opportunities for structured times as a group when the focus will be on listening, turn taking and developing skills for cognition and learning. Focus on social and emotional development is important and promotes the child's ability to express and manage their feelings, and develop their empathy and understanding of others' feelings. In any good early years setting, there will be so much on offer and so many exciting opportunities for learning.

But what if your child does not enter the room and travel around accessing these activities? What if they stand by the door or just choose to do one thing, such as sand play? These behaviours are fine at the start as a child establishes themselves and gets their bearings, and they should be allowed the time they need; but these are things to look out for if they are ongoing. If a child remains in one area and focuses on one activity, they will not be accessing all of the learning opportunities on offer. It could be a sign that they are uncomfortable, but it could also be that they don't know that they can move on. We must not assume that a child knows our unwritten, unexplained rules. If they are staying with the same activity, their logic might be, 'I like doing this. I will stay here.' A visual schedule showing that they need to access all areas could be all that they need to understand and explore a bit more. If they are standing by the door all day, their logic might be, 'If I stand here, Mummy might come to the door and we will go home.' They might climb on tables or windowsills because they just feel like climbing and need to learn what it is okay to climb on. Maybe they cast the sand onto the floor rather than build sandcastles because that's what they believe they should do. The child needs redirection and structures in place to teach them a way to do what they enjoy in an acceptable way. It is so important that the adults supporting them don't tell them off as this can actually reinforce the behaviour.

Eye contact

Lack of eye contact seems to be one of the most known characteristics a self-professed autism expert can become fixated on. If your child does not like making eye contact with people, don't be tempted to insist on eye contact, or let others try to insist on it, as this will actually redirect your child away from paying attention to the learning activities on offer and heighten their anxiety. Lack of eye contact is something to be discussed out of earshot. Don't be alarmed by it. It is not an area of learning to focus on early in the child's educational journey. The focus must be on building their trust, and making them comfortable, confident and happy. Your child must know that they can be themself. Making eye contact may cause distraction and discomfort and should not be insisted on when there are so many other things they are learning to cope with and adapt to.

The essentials for learning

A few years ago, the teachers at Portesbery School got together to discuss what we consider to be the essentials for learning. Nathan Aspinall, the head teacher, asked if Quentin and I could present all the teachers' ideas on a poster. We now display this poster in every classroom and share it with staff who join the school.

The foundations required for learning to take place are written as roots, and these roots are essential for growth.

The foundations are planning, routine, structure, knowledge, trust, the environment, communication and visuals. The grass represents differentiation (ways of supporting different learning styles and ability), thus enabling each child to feel they can succeed. The stalk of the flower represents independence. It is vital to create structure to enable children to learn to be independent. They don't have to constantly seek reassurance or need adults to do things for them. They need to learn that they can have a go. This independence may not come naturally but can be learnt with the right support. Each of the petals represents the things you will see in place during any great lesson.

- *Personalisation:* Different strategies in place to support individual children.
- *Engagement:* Activities designed to engage all the children and spark their interest.
- *Teamwork:* A staff team working seamlessly together, reducing the need for speech.
- *Assessment:* A teacher with excellent knowledge of each child's abilities and possibilities.
- *Listening:* Attentive listening from learners and teachers.
- *Structure:* Familiar, repetitive routines and predictable and clear ways of doing things.

For a flower to grow we also need the rain, which represents meeting sensory and physical needs. It is vital to meet these needs if we are to help the autistic child feel comfortable and safe. Sensory issues must be understood and accommodations put in place to support the children – for example, sensitivity to sounds, lights, smells or textures, or physical needs such as the need for movement or personal space (see Chapter 12).

Finally, we have the sunshine. Represented as rays of the sun are the words 'warmth', 'smiles', 'happiness', 'resources', 'fun' and 'praise'. The relationship with staff and teachers is included here, which is so vital to a child's happiness.

Think of all those wonderful quotes about education. Good education is about making children feel happy, connected and excited to find out and investigate. The greatest teachers may appear more like fellow learners in the classroom. Enter a great teacher's classroom and you will feel the atmosphere they have created almost at once. A great teacher may not let you linger or chat if there are students present.

They will be fiercely protective of their learning environment, and the individual needs of students will be a priority.

So, when considering education or a child's learning at any stage, think about the essentials for learning. They should be in place. These essentials are the tools that will help your child to learn.

CHAPTER 8

Diagnostic Pathways

'I requested my health visitor refer us after my son stopped talking at 18 months, I was very lucky that because of my years working in childcare she took my concerns seriously and referred us straightaway.'

(Omer's Mum)

There are various pathways used by different health services to assess autistic children, depending on the age that the child presents and on their difficulties in different skill areas.

Gathering information

Clinicians may request further information and details on developmental milestones and information from other carers or settings such as nursery or preschool. This will provide further understanding of the child's behaviours, including social communication and interaction in the educational setting.

Depending on the child's difficulties, referrals can be made to appropriate professionals. For example:

- If there are general developmental concerns, the health visitor may be the person who will monitor the child and provide advice and support to the family.
- If a child has delayed speech, then a speech and language therapist (SLT) assessment may be the first port of call.
- If there are any mobility concerns, the child may need to see a physiotherapist (PT) or an occupational therapist (OT).
- For a child with multiple concerns, ideally a multidisciplinary assessment (MDA) would be recommended.

There are some children who do not present with concerns in the early years. This may be for a number of reasons, including lack of behavioural or learning concerns. Some children on the spectrum enjoy a structured environment and follow rules and routines well. Girls especially are good at masking their behaviours outside the home. Meltdowns may be experienced once the child comes home and may be the result of anxiety or frustration. The assessment process in these cases remains similar.

Assessment

The assessment involves a paediatrician and at least one other professional such as a SLT, OT, PT, psychologist or early years education team member. Initial consultation normally consists of an information-gathering appointment where a detailed history is taken of the child's difficulties. At the same time, the child will be observed in the consulting room whilst they are playing with toys that will be set up in an age-appropriate manner. Following the initial assessment, a diagnosis is unlikely to be made without a follow-up assessment. Sometimes a school observation is carried out if more information is needed. This can provide useful observations of, for example, play skills and peer interaction. The child is made to feel comfortable during the assessment, and clinicians make every effort to ensure that the environment does not feel intimidating. The aim is to help families be completely at ease and prevent them feeling overly anxious about the assessment. Toys are available for the child to play with and some interactive activities such as blowing bubbles can be used to engage the child. This assessment provides a snapshot of the child's play and interaction skills.

Diagnosing autism can be complex because of the variable age of presentation and diverse presentation. It is important to ensure that as much information as possible is available and the following assessments are carried out:

- Full developmental and medical history.
- Medical examination.
- Family history.
- Developmental assessment.
- Routine testing of vision and hearing, particularly if speech is delayed.
- Blood tests and investigations as indicated.

Specific tests such as brain scans and brain wave tests are not recommended for diagnosis unless there are clinical symptoms of an underlying medical condition.

CHAPTER 9

This Is Autism

'I guess I knew deep down but I always hoped I was wrong and that he would all of a sudden catch up.'

(Leeroy's Mum)

Confirmation of a diagnosis of autism for your child may have been something you were expecting or it may come as a complete surprise. The implication of the diagnosis will affect your entire family. It will change the way you parent your child, and you may encounter difficulties and have to support your child in many ways. It is important, as parents, to allow yourselves time to accept the diagnosis, seek support and also take time for self-care.

Professionals in health and education will give you a better understanding of the child's needs and tailor support for your child.

> 'Really understanding the whole process was a huge help. There can be a lot of stigma and cultural bias involved, particularly with family members of older generations, so having a good sense of the current landscape was very useful. It was useful to understand that sceptical friends and family weren't being rude, they just weren't experienced in this landscape. Seeing a full report and diagnosis helped them to understand.'

(Harvey's Dad)

Autism is not a disability, a disease or a disorder; autism is a condition. It is a difference that enables autistic individuals to see the world through a different lens. It is usually described as a spectrum with mild difficulties at one end and severe difficulties at the other. However, it is important to know that it is not linear. Difficulties in autism can best be described as differences on a colour wheel. Their strengths and weaknesses will vary as they do on a colour wheel. Autistic individuals can be very literal and have their own rule book. They do not want to blend with normality; they want to nurture differences and aspire to their goals, which can lead to great things.

Communication is key, not only in supporting your child but in enabling them to communicate. Various methods are used, depending on the child's ability, ranging from visuals and pictures to Social Stories™.[1]

Disability or difference?

Society is full of diversity. Genetics plays a major role in shaping the individual, but the environment also has a role in psychological development.

Our DNA defines who we are as individuals. Chromosomes come together and become the blueprint of our physical features, our learning and our thinking. This influences our personality. In our daily

---

1   See www.carolgraysocialstories.com

interactions we will come across some people who are extroverts and others who are introverts.

Adults who have been diagnosed with autism will say autism is not a disorder or disability but a difference: a difference in the way an individual sees the world, reacts to the world and relates to the world. This has an impact on those around them. With maturity, individuals, particularly girls, develop insight into their differences. They have learnt to cope with simple social scenarios and managed to integrate socially – on a superficial level at times. With the onset of adolescence and puberty come the complexities of social dynamics, interaction and relationships. At these stages, children may begin to question themselves and their differences.

Autistic young people sometimes feel that they are invisible or not seen. This in itself can cause emotional distress. They may feel broken, or that they have 'failed' at friendships, that their quirkiness and obsessions can make them appear odd. Autistic individuals are unique but may not fit the box of a neurotypical society.

There are many articulate autistic people, including young adults who may have received a diagnosis of autism in adulthood and are very positive. For many, a diagnosis of autism can come as a relief: they are able to understand why they feel different, but insist they are not 'weird' or 'broken'. They do not want to fit stereotypes, as stereotypes can imply limitations.

A diagnosis of autism can change perspectives and enable an individual to realise that they are unique and have different strengths. Neurodiversity is becoming more acceptable in society and should be promoted. The 'awkward' young person is able to flourish and become a valuable member of society.

A brief mention here of the myth that autistic individuals are gifted or talented. Research indicates that only 10 per cent of autistic individuals have exceptional abilities and they are the ones we see in the media. It is these individuals who seem to have superpowers and have the ability and determination to pursue their interests. They are sought after for their skills by universities and the science and technology industries. Famous people who have been thought to be autistic are musicians, such as Mozart and Beethoven, scientists, such as Einstein, and creative artists and entrepreneurs like Bill Gates. They are inspirational. Another example is Elisabeth Wiklander, a talented cellist for the London

Philharmonic Orchestra who had a late diagnosis of autism. Since her diagnosis, Elisabeth has shared her story and celebrated her 'differences'. She has come to understand that society is a rich tapestry and that everyone has a place. Despite awareness of autism, there remains a stigma and prejudice.

The 10 per cent of the autistic population who have exceptional ability may use their remarkable aptitude for creating extraordinary ideas. One such example is Satoshi Tajiri, a young Japanese man on the autism spectrum. Satoshi grew up with a special interest in collecting bugs – he was nicknamed 'Doctor Bug'. As his interests changed, he went on to produce the Pokémon series. Pokémon has become a worldwide phenomenon which is extremely popular with many young people and even some adults!

Many children have special interests and go through phases. In the early years, they may include dinosaurs or Thomas the Tank Engine or princesses. Sometimes these interests become obsessions or evolve into other interests. Some may be lifelong. These interests can sometimes take over the autistic person's life and they will want to share their passion with others, often not appreciating that others may not have such enthusiasm in those areas.

It is important to be understanding and not be offended by comments from autistic individuals.

CASE STUDY
Clear your clutter! Dr Sophia Mooncey

I recall in my clinical practice during a consultation with a teenager who was struggling with difficulties in accepting injustices. He came into my 'consultation' room and went on to ask me how I could work on a table which looked messy! However, I explained to him that I had just seen a younger child and that there were toys, pens and paper lying around the room. This was not really messy, but clearly not how he saw things. So, the next time I saw this young individual, I made sure that my desk was free of clutter, tidy and neat so that there were no distractions!

• • • • • • • • •

CASE STUDY
Identity checks: Adele Devine

I recall a little girl who would look at everyone's ID labels as they came into class and insist on redoing their hair so that it matched the photo. If your hair was down in the photo, she would want it down. I would tell new staff to think very carefully about how they had their hair when their ID photo was taken. It was important to the child that the ID matched the reality.

* * * * * * * * * *

Gender and autism

Sex and gender impacts on the behavioural presentation and recognition of autism.[2] Autism has been portrayed in, and reinforced by, the media as a male characteristic, with films like *Rain Man* (1988). The film won four Oscars, including best actor for Dustin Hoffman who played Raymond, an autistic young man with a superb memory. This brought autism into the wider public eye; however, it also portrayed a person who was extremely gifted or talented in a particular skill, in this case memory-recall and numbers, despite having poor social skills.

A more recent media portrayal of an autistic person was the character Sheldon Cooper, a theoretical physicist in the television series *Big Bang Theory*. He is an exceptionally bright character with a genius-level IQ. This character was not specifically written to portray an autistic person, but Sheldon's characteristics and mannerisms suggest this.

Contemporary series include autistic boys such as Sam in *Atypical* experiencing the world as an autistic teenager. Viewers see the world through Sam's eyes and can understand his view of the world, relationships and interpretation of social situations. It makes for interesting viewing and the creator Robia Rashid consulted with experts at UCLA's Center for Autism Research when she wrote the scripts. The series addresses teenage issues such as dating and relationships in teenage autism in a realistic way. Sam's obsessive interest in penguins also reminds viewers that special interests can be drawn on to engage the autistic individual.

---

2   Lai, M-C. and Szatmari, P. (2020) 'Sex and gender impacts on the behavioural presentation and recognition of autism.' *Current Opinion in Psychiatry 33*, 2, 117–123.

Differences between the sexes

Over the past ten years, autism has become increasingly recognised in girls, who may not present with difficulties in their early years. The ratio of autistic boys to autistic girls is 4.5:1. The Centers for Disease Control and Prevention (CDC) in the United States in 2014 confirmed that the incidence of autism in males was 1 in 38 and in females 1 in 167. A large study at the University of Cambridge[3] examined sex differences in autism. They found that typically females were more empathetic and males were more systems-orientated. In autistic people these differences were reduced. Systemising individuals were found to get jobs in STEM disciplines (science, technology, engineering and mathematics).

The presentation of autism in girls led to the creation of a new character, Julia, in *Sesame Street*. Julia is a young autistic girl with special skills in drawing.

Without applying gender stereotypes, we have observed that given a choice, girls will tend to choose dolls and more imaginative play, mimicking everyday behaviour such as feeding and changing them. Boys on the other hand, will be drawn towards vehicles such as trains and cars and engage in rough and tumble play. Despite the gender differences and type of play, there will always be exceptions.

Boys tend to present earlier because they may display more obvious unusual behaviours and are less likely to try and fit in with their peers. Girls, on the other hand, are not easily noticed as they are better at observing and copying behaviours or 'camouflaging'. Girls are said to be good at masking behaviours – that is, at observing and imitating social mannerisms. They learn to master behaviours that are expected responses, which may not come to them naturally. These girls may be described as model students at school but explode when they get home as they cannot continue the charade! This can lead to anxiety and emotional conflict, which may need support. Girls are often better at facial recognition, understanding and carrying out pro-social behaviours. Pro-social behaviours are behaviours that are of benefit to others, such as sharing, helping, volunteering and cooperating. Autistic girls are often found to be very nurturing and caring towards younger

---

3   Greenberg, D.M., Warrier, V., Allison, C. and Baron-Cohen, S. (2018) 'Testing the empathizing–systemizing theory of sex differences and the extreme male brain theory of autism in half a million people.' *PNAS 115*, 48, 12152–12157.

children. They come across as kind and caring, even though autistic individuals are usually said to lack empathy.

There are various papers and evidence to indicate that 'social camouflaging' is a characteristic of girls in autism. Tony Attwood, an expert in autism, coined this phrase in 2006–2007.[4] He described 'camouflaging' as a coping mechanism. This mechanism facilitates friendships, avoids being bullied and protects the person from humiliation.

Eating disorders in autism require a mention and can be seen in both girls and boys. It may be the sensory sensitivity to food that affects the diet or issues with body image.[5] This can be further complicated by repetitive behaviours, such as obsessive calorie counting or exercising. Studies suggest that many young people with eating disorders may have underlying autistic behaviours.[6] Some use the term avoidant/restrictive food intake disorder (ARFID), which includes picky eaters and food avoidance.

Another topical subject is gender dysphoria.[7] Gender issues may be more prevalent in autistic individuals and may be a way to remove the person from their autistic shell and find a new identity. It is very important that this is managed sensitively and no decisions should be undertaken lightly. Psychological support is extremely important to manage these young people's anxieties and emotional conflict.

There are many books on autistic girls.[8] Interestingly, many of the books are written by young autistic women, many of whom were diagnosed as young adults. The books describe the journeys of these young women who often felt socially awkward, unable to engage on a deeper level with their peers, and felt different. This can result in social isolation and withdrawal and it is important that we do not miss the opportunity to identify them.

---

4   www.tonyattwood.com.au/index.php?Itemid=181&id=80%3Athe-pattern-of-abil-
    ities-and-development-of-girls-with-aspergers-syndrome&option=com_con-
    tent&view=article
5   Huke, V., Turk, J., Saeidi, S., Kent, A. and Morgan, J.F. (2013) 'Autism spectrum disorders
    in eating disorder populations: a systematic review.' *European Eating Disorders Review*
    21, 5, 345–351.
6   Dell'Osso, L., Carpita, B., Gesi, C., Cremone, I.M. *et al.* (2018) 'Subthreshold autism
    spectrum disorder in patients with eating disorders.' *Comprehensive Psychiatry 81*, 66–72.
7   Warrier V., Greenberg, D.M., Weir, E., Buckingham, C. *et al.* (2020) 'Elevated rates of
    autism, other neurodevelopmental and psychiatric diagnoses, and autistic traits in
    transgender and gender-diverse individuals.' *Nature Communications 11*, 3959.
8   Kearns Miller, J. (2003) *Women from Another Planet? Our Lives in the Universe of Autism.*
    Bloomington, IN: AuthorHouse™.

Different stages of life bring on different challenges, and in girls particularly, puberty can be challenging. Body changes and onset of periods can be frightening. Autistic girls can have sensory issues and struggle with the sensation of sanitary pads or tampons. It is important that these are managed sensitively, particularly in terms of personal hygiene and emotional support.

In conclusion, autistic girls have come to the fore in the last decade, and social media is full of young girls who have blogs or YouTube clips of how they were diagnosed and how late the diagnosis was. The ultimate question is, does the diagnosis make any difference? A diagnosis can be a relief to the young girl as she is then able to understand her behaviours and to appreciate that she is not the only one who struggles with social issues and the challenges that lie ahead. It also takes away the guilt and worry that may be caused by feeling different.

Difference is a gift and must be celebrated.

Part 3

POST-DIAGNOSIS

CHAPTER 10

Comorbidities and Implications Associated with Autism

'Don't be afraid to ask questions. No question is silly if it will ease your concerns.'

(Parent reflection)

Comorbidities: What other conditions can occur with autism?

'We found out two years ago that he has a non-hereditary genetic condition called Syngap1 Syndrome which explains his motor and coordination difficulties – and this visible disability definitely helped with a quick diagnosis.'

(Parent reflection)

With greater awareness and identification of autistic children and growing interest in autism, research has found that autistic individuals can have coexisting medical conditions.[1] Simonoff *et al.*[2] reported that in their study of 112 autistic children they found that 70 per cent had one other condition and 40 per cent had at least two other conditions.

- Learning disability may be present in 40 per cent of autistic people, compared to 1 per cent of the general population.[3]
- Epilepsy can develop in up to 17 per cent of autistic children.
- ADHD can be seen in up to 29% of autistic children.
- Dyspraxic difficulties or poor fine motor skills can be present in autistic children. Developmental coordination disorder of childhood (DCD) is considered by some to be similar to autism. The motor difficulties can impact on social skills and ability to concentrate and fidgetiness. The term DCD is sometimes used synonymously with dyspraxia.
- Behavioural problems can be significant in up to 40 per cent of children.
- Psychiatric disorders such as depression and anxiety may occur with an incidence of 15 per cent.
- Eating difficulties are more common in autistic children.

---

1   Bauman, M.L. (2010) 'Medical comorbidities in autism: challenges to diagnosis and treatment.' *Neurotherapeutics 7*, 3, 320–327.

2   Simonoff, E., Pickles, A., Charman, T., Chandler, S., Loucas, T. and Baird, G. (2008) 'Psychiatric disorders in children with autism spectrum disorders: prevalence, comorbidity, and associated factors in a population-derived sample.' *Journal of the American Academy of Child and Adolescent Psychiatry 47*, 8, 921–929.

3   Autistica (n.d.) 'Learning disability and autism.' Accessed on 09/04/21 at www.autistica. org.uk/what-is-autism/signs-and-symptoms/learning-disability-and-autism

- Bowel problems such as diarrhoea, constipation and abdominal pain can occur more frequently in autistic children. Constipation may be behavioural, whereas diarrhoea may be caused by inflammation of the bowel.[4]
- Sensory sensitivity to noise, light, touch, taste and smell can impact on an autistic child's behaviour and everyday life.
- Sleep difficulties are more common in autistic children.

The impact of autism has long-term implications as it is a lifelong condition. These individuals may require support in different areas ranging from health and educational support to self-care and social skills. Countries across the world have different support plans for autism. The Autism Act 2009 states that the government has to have a strategy for improving the lives of autistic adults. At the time of writing, the strategy is under review with the intention that it should cover children as well as adults.[5] The United States[6] and New Zealand[7] both have frameworks for supporting autistic individuals.

What parents can do

'Having a proper diagnosis makes a huge difference. My daughter is able to explain herself to others, and also to understand that she perceives the world differently. Rather than thinking that she's odd, or a failure, or weird, she has ways of explaining things. This process has enabled her to own her ASD [autism spectrum disorder] and to be proud of it.'

(Julie's Dad)

The ultimate goal in supporting autistic children should be to improve

---

4   Harvard Medical School (2015) 'The autism-GI link.' Accessed on 09/04/21 at https://hms.harvard.edu/news/autism-gi-link

5   See www.gov.uk/health-and-social-care/autism

6   Myers, S.M. and Johnson, C.P. (2007) 'Management of children with autism spectrum disorders.' *Pediatrics 120*, 5, 1162–1182.

7   Ministry of Health (2016) *New Zealand Autism Spectrum Disorder: Guideline Summary* (2nd edn). Accessed on 09/04/21 at www.health.govt.nz/system/files/documents/publications/nz-asd-guideline-summary-aug16-v3.pdf

their quality of life, optimise the child's independent functioning and promote emotional wellbeing.

There are three phases:

1. The first stage is assessment for possible diagnosis. The pathway will depend on local protocols. In the UK these are described in the National Institute for Health and Care Excellence (NICE) guidelines.[8] These are evidence-based guidelines developed by a working party of professionals and experts in the field.
2. The second phase is the outcome and follow-up. If a diagnosis of autism is confirmed, it is important that your child is supported both at home and at school. The support should extend to all aspects of the child's life including the home, school and leisure activities.
3. The third phase to consider is the transition to adulthood. As your child grows into a young adult, it may be daunting to think of the future. Perhaps it is best to see how your child is developing, acquiring new skills and learning to be independent. It is very important that transitions are carefully planned and implemented.

Transition

Support for young people can be variable post-diagnosis. If your child does not have any specific medical needs, they may be discharged from paediatric follow-up. Support would continue through education and autism support teams. There are also voluntary sector groups or charitable trusts that provide support for families and schools.

Adolescent transition can be challenging. The Royal College of Nursing[9] can support young people and guide them to appropriate services.

If there are coexisting medical conditions such as ADHD, these young persons will be followed up by the relevant medical professionals (paediatricians or child and adolescent psychiatrists).

---

8   NICE (2011, updated 2017) Autism spectrum disorder in under 19s: recognition, referral and diagnosis. Clinical guideline 128. Accessed on 09/04/21 at www.nice.org.uk/guidance/cg128
9   www.rcn.org.uk

Implications of a diagnosis of autism

Confirmation of a diagnosis may be the end of one journey but the beginning of a new path towards learning and living with autism. There will be new achievements as well as new challenges, but that creates the fabric of our being.

Autism and anxiety

Research indicates that at least 40 per cent of autistic individuals will experience anxiety at some stage in their lives.[10] Quite often, anxiety is the presenting symptom in young people who may have underlying neurodevelopmental difficulties such as autism. This is referred to in the literature as 'diagnostic overshadowing'.[11] Many theories have been put forward for the causes of anxiety but the most significant one is around understanding one's emotions or alexithymia. In autistic individuals this can be blurred by difficulties of emotional dysregulation, sensory processing difficulties, restrictive repetitive behaviours and intolerance of uncertainty. Emotional acceptance can help autistic individuals reduce anxiety.

The brain is a complicated organ and when the individual encounters sensory input it processes and predicts responses. The ability of the brain to suppress expected stimuli and amplify unexpected stimuli alerts the person to events. A mismatch between expectation and unexpected events can cause anxiety. It is very important to understand and be able to identify anxiety in young people so that they can learn to manage it.

Quite often the anxiety presents as defiance or reluctance to do something without the child being able to give a reason. For example, a child not wanting to go into the assembly hall may suggest that the child is nervous or defiant. The trigger may be a noisy and crowded hall. There are many psychological support strategies available:

10　Autistica (n.d.) 'Learning disability and autism.' Accessed on 09/04/21 at www.autistica. org.uk/what-is-autism/signs-and-symptoms/learning-disability-and-autism

11　Mason, J. and Scior, K. (2004) '"Diagnostic overshadowing" amongst clinicians working with people with intellectual disabilities in the UK.' *Journal of Applied Research in Intellectual Disabilities 17*, 2, 85–90.

- CBT (cognitive behavioural therapy) helps to alleviate some of the anxiety and improve emotional wellbeing.[12]
- CUES (Coping with Uncertainty in Everyday Situations) in the world, is another strategy.[13]
- MBT (mindfulness-based therapy). Mindfulness is the ability to be aware, accept and be non-judgemental about behaviours.[14]
- Some young people with anxiety are managed by using a 'sensory processing toolbox' where sensory items are used to calm their nervous system.[15]

Parental stress

There is evidence to indicate that parents of children with neurodevelopmental delay and other difficulties experience a higher risk of stress.[16, 17] This also applies to children who have autism.[18]

Parental stress is reduced when children are able to function independently.[19] It is important to find time for self-care. It may be watching Netflix or going for a run!

---

12 NICE (2013) Autism spectrum disorder in under 19s: support and management. Clinical Guideline 170. Accessed on 09/04/21 at www.nice.org.uk/guidance/cg170/chapter/1-Recommendations#specific-interventions-for-the-core-features-of-autism

13 Rodgers, J. (n.d.) CUES. Accessed on 09/04/21 at https://research.ncl.ac.uk/neurodisability/ourstudies/recentlycompletedstudies/cues/#:~:text=Overview,can%20be%20a%20significant%20problem

14 Ridderinkhof, A., Bruin, E.I., Blom, R. and Bögels, S.M. (2018) 'Mindfulness-based program for children with autism spectrum disorder and their parents: direct and long term.' *Mindfulness 9*, 3, 773–791.

15 Autism Speaks (2013) 'Study finds sensory integration therapy benefits children with autism.' Accessed on 14/07/21 at https://www.autismspeaks.org/science-news/study-finds-sensory-integration-therapy-benefits-children-autism

16 Baker, B., Blacher, J., Crnic, K.A. and Edelbrook, C. (2002) 'Behaviour problems and parenting stress in families of three-year-old children with and without developmental delay.' *American Journal of Mental Retardation 107*, 6, 433–444.

17 Dumas, J.E., Wolf, L.C., Fisman, S.N. and Culligan, A. (1991) 'Parenting stress, child behavior problems, and dysphoria in parents of children with autism, Down syndrome, behavior disorders, and normal development.' *Exceptionality 2*, 2, 97–110.

18 Davis, N.O. and Carter, A.S. (2008) 'Parenting stress in mothers and fathers of toddlers with autism spectrum disorders.' *Journal of Autism and Developmental Disorders 38*, 7, 1278–1291.

19 Estes, A., Munson, J., Dawson, G., Koehler, E., Zhou, X-H. and Abbott, R. (2009) 'Parenting stress and psychological functioning among mothers of preschool children with autism and developmental delay.' *Autism 13*, 4, 375–387.

Eating

Eating is a very important physiological process as it enables babies and children to grow, develop and function physically and cognitively. Parents like to ensure that children are always well fed, no matter how old they are! It is an extremely frustrating situation when parents find that despite children being offered a variety of foods, they remain limited in their intake. This is striking in autistic children. They have very specific food preferences and despite parents' culinary abilities the child will be resistant to even tasting foods that they are not familiar with. This preference for foods can be for a variety of reasons. As children develop and grow into adolescence, and indeed adulthood, they become more adventurous and their palates enjoy different tastes. This is where autistic children differ as their sensory sensitivity does not allow them to learn to accept new tastes and textures.

Autistic children can be described as 'selective eaters'.[20] This may be because of their sensory sensitivity, when they are not accustomed to the different appearance of the food, the colour, the texture, the smell or the temperature of food on offer. Food will need to be presented in a way the child is familiar with. This will determine whether the child is willing to put the food in their mouth.

It is important that a child's nutrition is well balanced, and the government guidelines of 'five a day' fruit and vegetables apply to all individuals. This plan is very difficult to implement with children who are extremely faddy in their eating. Autistic children may choose to eat only foods of a particular colour, for instance, or carbohydrates or beige foods. Some children do not want to eat green food and this is a cause of concern to parents and clinicians. It is important that all children have a balanced diet to include the main food groups: proteins, carbohydrates and fats as well as essential vitamins and minerals. This promotes both physical and cognitive development. There have been various studies looking at the nutritional intake of autistic children. It is difficult to compare the eating habits of autistic children with those of children who do not have autism. The general opinion is that autistic children tend to be fussier than non-autistic children because

---

20 Cermak, S.A., Curtin, C. and Bandini, L.G. (2010) 'Food selectivity and sensory sensitivity in children with autism spectrum disorders.' *Journal of the American Dietetic Association 110*, 2, 238–246.

of their sensory needs. They may display 'tactile defensiveness' in areas including taste, smell and touch.[21]

Food selectivity is not an unusual phenomenon in children and many children will go through phases of being fussy with food. Selective eating can cause nutritional disorders, not only in terms of deficiencies but also obesity,[22] and autistic children who prefer one particular type of food may overeat that food.

'Neophobia' has been used to describe the fear of new foods. This can relate to any fussy eater but particularly to autistic children where the child is unable to accept any new foods if they look, taste, smell or feel different.[23] Other issues can impact on the food intake of autistic children. One that has already been mentioned is sensory sensitivity. Others include behavioural difficulties which may impact on eating, family mealtimes which may not suit the autistic child, and parental opinions on eating.[24] It is important to address these eating behaviours as they could continue into adolescence and adulthood and impact on the child's growth and physical wellbeing. An interesting book that addresses these issues is *Can't Eat, Won't Eat: Dietary Difficulties and Autistic Spectrum Disorders*.[25]

An MDA is useful in managing children with food selectivity and difficult eaters. This would include a dietician or nutritionist to manage the dietary intake, an OT to support the sensory difficulties and a psychologist to manage the behavioural approach.

Some autistic children struggle with the way food is presented on a plate. They may refuse to eat foods that are touching each other as they prefer to eat foods separately. Others may not tolerate foods mixed with sauce or gravy, as they prefer dry foods because of their sensory sensitivity. Every child is different in their tolerance of food

21   Attwood, T. (2015) *The Complete Guide to Asperger's Syndrome*. London: Jessica Kingsley Publishers.

22   Ho, H.H., Eaves, L.C. and Peabody, D. (1997) 'Nutrient intake and obesity in children with autism.' *Focus on Autism and Other Developmental Disabilities 12*, 3, 187–192.

23   Dovey, T.M., Staples, P.A., Leigh Gibson, E. and Halford, J.C.G. (2008) 'Food neophobia and "picky/fussy" eating in children: a review.' *Appetite 50*, 2–3, 183–193.

24   Cermak, S.A., Curtin, C. and Bandini, L.G. (2010) 'Food selectivity and sensory sensitivity in children with autism spectrum disorders.' *Journal of the American Dietetic Association 110*, 2, 238–246.

25   Legge, B. (2008) *Can't Eat, Won't Eat: Dietary Difficulties and Autistic Spectrum Disorders*. London: Jessica Kingsley Publishers.

tastes and textures. There are also of course autistic children who will eat anything and everything!

As previously noted, a healthy, balanced diet is extremely important and food selectivity is therefore a major issue in autistic children. It is difficult to manage, but with multidisciplinary support it can improve over time and ensure that the autistic child is well supported nutritionally.

Other disorders associated with eating may arise in the adolescent or teenage period, including eating disorders for other reasons such as rigidity in thought or behaviour, and body dysmorphia. An MDA is recommended for managing these young people as once again nutrition must be optimal in order for puberty and growth to progress. Other conditions are classed together under the acronym ARFID. This is a relatively new diagnosis according to the *DSM-5* criteria and was previously labelled as 'selective eating disorder'. It can impact on growth and is different from anorexia and bulimia in that it does not cause any distress regarding body image. However, the restrictive pattern of food intake can still affect growth and nutrition.

Sleep

There are many aspects of a child's behaviours that can have an impact because of the child's underlying autistic characteristics. These can affect both eating and sleeping and cause parents, who often spend a lot of time encouraging the child to eat well and get a good night's sleep, concern. Sleep is very important for development of learning and other skills. When children are not sleeping through the night, other family members will usually miss out on sleep too. Sleep hygiene measures should always be tried to establish a routine before bedtime.

Ten ways to ease bedtime

- The same routine and order – for example bath, pyjamas, teeth, toilet.
- Same time to go to bed (before overtiredness becomes an issue).
- Same number of stories.

- Social Story™ [26] about bedtime.
- Tucking in tight.
- Relaxing music or meditation.
- Blackout blinds or curtains.
- A hall light on (if requested).
- Same firm, calm responses.
- Reward for staying in bed.

It is important to note that weighted blankets are not recommended. Some families favour weighted blankets for sleep, but evidence from a randomised, controlled study conducted by Professor Paul Gringas and team concluded that weighted blankets did *not* improve sleep in children with autism.[27] Sleep is a time when our body recovers and rests. It is a temporary state which allows our body's physiological functions to 'catch up'. It allows our bodies to attain homeostasis (stability) and carry out important functions such as growth and restoring cellular functions. Sleep helps improve cognitive function, behaviour and many everyday activities. Sleep is a complex process and much research continues into patterns of sleep and the effects of sleep deprivation. There is research to evidence the importance of sleep for rest, recovery and improving academic performance as well as improving mood.[28] The amount of sleep an individual requires varies and depends on the age of the child. Babies, as we know, require more sleep than adults:

- Newborn babies sleep for most of the day. They require 14–17 hours of sleep.
- In infancy, babies require 12–15 hours of sleep.
- Toddlers require 10–13 hours of sleep.
- Thirteen-year-olds require 9–11 hours of sleep.

Reduced levels of sleep can lead to increasingly challenging behaviour.

---

26 https://carolgraysocialstories.com
27 Gringras, P. *et al.* (2014) 'Weighted blankets and sleep in autistic children—a randomised controlled study.' *Pediatrics 134*, 2, 298–306.
28 Vassalli, A. and Dijk, D-J. (2009) 'Sleep function: current questions and new approaches.' *The European Journal of Neuroscience 29*, 9, 1830–1841.

The literature suggests that 40–80 per cent[29] of children on the spectrum have problems with sleep, which may manifest in different ways:

- *Prolonged latency:* Children take a long time to fall asleep – in some cases hours.
- *Fragmented sleep:* Children wake up frequently during the night – they have disturbed sleep.
- *Shortened sleep:* Children don't need a lot of sleep and are early risers.
- *Daytime sleepiness:* Children experience daytime sleepiness, which can impact on behaviour and learning.

Importance of sleep

Essential physiological functioning occurs during sleep, and it may be argued that the most important of these is growth in children. Disrupted sleep can affect growth hormone secretion.

- *Physical health:* A good night's sleep restores energy and helps us to function better.
- *Cognitive development:* A good night's sleep helps with memory.
- *Mood regulation:* Lack of sleep can result in behaviour difficulties.

Physiology of sleep

Sleep is regulated by the circadian rhythm, which alerts our brains to when it is time to go to sleep. This is regulated by various factors, including the amount of light perceived by the eyes, which in turn is interpreted by the brain. In addition to the environment which controls the light and dark aspects, there are hormones (mainly melatonin) which are released from the brain to initiate sleep. There are other hormones which also regulate sleep. Orexin is the hormone which is released when it is time to wake. Other hormones such as cortisol, GABA and glutamate can also have an influence on the circadian rhythm. This rhythm has a cycle of 24 hours.

---

29 Vassalli, A. and Dijk, D-J. (2009) 'Sleep function: current questions and new approaches.' *The European Journal of Neuroscience 29*, 9, 1830–1841.

Sleep is not a uniform process throughout the night and is made up of several cycles, each lasting approximately 90 minutes. During those 90 minutes there are four stages of sleep including NREM (non-rapid eye movement) sleep and REM (rapid eye movement) sleep. NREM sleep makes up the first three phases of the cycle.

- *Stage 1:* This is the drowsy phase and usually lasts a few minutes.
- *Stage 2*: Brain waves slow down and the muscles begin to relax. This lasts between 10 and 25 minutes.
- *Stage 3:* This is the slow wave sleep which is critical for the body to repair itself and restore function and growth. It boosts immunity. There are some theories that deep sleep contributes to insightful thinking, creativity and memory. This stage lasts between 20 and 40 minutes.
- *Stage 4:* The final stage of sleep is REM sleep. This is when dreams usually occur and it is thought that REM sleep is important for cognitive function, creativity, memory and learning. This stage lasts between 10 and 60 minutes.

Sleep hygiene

This refers to the steps leading up to sleep. A good routine is helpful for the child and avoids the need for demands at bedtime. Having a calm environment and 'down time', as some parents call it, and getting a good pre-sleep routine, are important.

Factors that are important prior to falling asleep are:

- *Light:* The brain releases melatonin in response to darkness, so subduing the light in bedrooms or using red light is thought to enhance the release of melatonin.
- *Reducing screen time:* This is very important as blue light from screens is interpreted by the brain as daylight.
- *Down time:* Relaxation and calming activities such as warm baths, story time, etc.
- *Avoiding caffeine and eating too late.*
- *A goodnight hug and a kiss.*

Children on the spectrum can suffer from anxiety. This can result in fatigue, tiredness and physiological signs such as rapid breathing, rapid heart rate, tensing of the muscles and general distress. Individuals with OCD may have compulsive behaviours before going to bed that impact on their ability to fall asleep. Autistic children can have rituals which need to be completed prior to sleep. These factors as well as others, such as mental health difficulties, can influence the person's sleep cycle.

Melatonin

Melatonin is a natural hormone that is released by the pineal gland in the brain, which is controlled by signals from the suprachiasmatic nucleus (SCN) located near the hypothalamus. Release of melatonin is influenced by the amount of light that enters the retina (at the back of the eye). This in turn sends signals to the SCN and results in the release of melatonin. This is why it is very important to have subdued lighting[30] in the bedroom prior to going to sleep. There is evidence to indicate that children on the autistic spectrum, as well as children with other neurodevelopmental and neuropsychiatric disorders, have poor release of melatonin. The circadian rhythm is out of synchronisation and the melatonin is not secreted. Exogenous melatonin – that is, melatonin that is taken orally – has been found to be useful in initiating and maintaining sleep.[31] This is an option that can be explored with your clinician. Although melatonin is available over the counter in some countries (e.g. the United States), in the UK it is a prescription-only medication prescribed by specialists.

Screen time and gadgets

Given the widespread use of modern technology, the effects on people of screen time and gadgets have become subjects of interest and substantial research. As noted in the previous section, studies indicate

---

30 Gringras, P., Middleton, B., Skene, D.J. and Revell, V.L. (2015) 'Bigger, brighter, bluer – better? Current light-emitting devices – adverse sleep properties and preventative strategies.' *Frontiers in Public Health 13*, 3, 233.

31 Gringras, P., Nir, T., Breddy, J., Frydman-Marom, A. and Findling, R.L. (2017) 'Efficacy and safety of pediatric prolonged-release melatonin for insomnia in children with autism spectrum disorder.' *Journal of the American Academy of Child and Adolescent Psychiatry 56*, 11, 948-957.e4.

that the blue light emitted from electronic gadgets appears to hamper the release of melatonin. This blue light sends alerting signals to the brain and keeps the individual awake.

The National Sleep Foundation carried out a survey and found that 95 per cent of people use some kind of screen, be it computer, tablet or phone, at least a few nights a week in the hour before bedtime. Screens should ideally be switched off two hours before bedtime, which can be very difficult. Studies have indicated that children who have electronics in their room tend to sleep less well than other children. Lack of sleep can exacerbate core symptoms of autism, as well as affect academic function and mood dysregulation.

Orexin (also known as hypocretin)

This is another hormone which keeps us awake. It is a neuropeptide produced by the hypothalamus and is important for wakefulness. It has the opposite effect of melatonin. This chemical is thought to excite different areas of the brain to keep us awake and cause wakefulness. It also regulates appetite and arousal.

Monitoring sleep

Parents may be given questionnaires to complete or be asked to keep a sleep diary. The most commonly used questionnaire is the Children's Sleep Habits questionnaire, which can be modified for autism. There are two versions, the preschool and the school version, and it is like completing a sleep diary.

Medical factors which can influence sleep are comorbid symptoms of ADHD, anxiety, epilepsy and headaches. It is also known that other conditions can influence sleep, such as gastroesophageal reflux disease, where there is increased reflux that causes discomfort when lying down and sleeping, and obesity which can cause sleep apnoea and difficulty in falling asleep.

If the lack of sleep is impacting on the child's general wellbeing (physical, emotional and cognitive), it is imperative that therapeutic action is taken, and the use of melatonin is very useful. The Autism Treatment Network recommends that all autistic children should be screened for sleep difficulties and four main questions need to be asked:

- Does the child fall asleep within 20 minutes?
- Do they still sleep in the parental bed?
- Do they wake up in the night?
- Do they sleep too little?

If there are more than two factors, further intervention is required. Investigating other medical causes such as obstructive sleep apnoea and comorbidities is also relevant.

Top tips

- Avoid screen time.
- Good exercise during the day is very useful.
- Good sleep hygiene.
- Avoid eating or drinking just before bedtime and avoid caffeine for five hours before bedtime.

Sleepwalking

Sleepwalking (also called somnambulism), as well as other conditions such as sleep talking, usually occurs during stage 3 of the sleep cycle. Sleepwalking occurs in approximately 30 per cent of children between the ages of 2 and 13 years. It is not very common in autistic children.

Nightmares and night terrors

Nightmares and night terrors appear to be similar, but there is an important difference in that a child usually wakes up following a nightmare, but in night terrors they remain asleep and it is very difficult to communicate or speak to the child.

Night terrors usually occur during NREM sleep and commonly occur between midnight and 2am. Most children outgrow night terrors by the time they reach their teens.

Nightmares usually occur in REM sleep and the child will wake up stating that they have had a really bad dream.

CHAPTER 11

Evidence-Based Therapeutic Interventions

> 'We have been using PECS for four years now; at first it was a way for my son to request his favourite snacks or toys but I really believe it has opened the doorway to some speech for him. He now requests whatever he wants verbally but has retained the PECS sentence structure. Today he wanted to go out in the car for a drive and said "I want blue car please" – the only trouble is now I am simply unable to refuse a request.'

(Parent reflection)

Autism is a lifelong condition which cannot be cured. However, there are therapeutic interventions which can help support autistic children and adults so that they can achieve their potential and focus on their strengths. There is no recognised, standard treatment which applies to all autistic children as they will all have different skills. There are strategies to support communication such as Intensive Interaction, Attention Autism and PECS® (Pictorial Exchange Communication System; see Chapter 14).

There are strategies which help support learning and increase independence such as TEACCH® and strategies to support social and emotional needs such as Social Stories™ and the Zones of Regulation™ (See Chapter 13). Autistic children perform well with predictability, clear and visual structures, and routine and these strategies teach children to understand social scenarios. Furthermore, schools play a vital role in supporting your child. There are specialist teachers, trained in autism, who can provide specific supports such as social skills groups.

Local charities provide resources, information, training and support for children and families. There is of course a wide range of literature available for parents to access, as well as 'Google'. Professional support is available for difficulties that may be experienced by autistic individual experiences. Your clinician will signpost you to relevant support as needed. We have been very fortunate to have colleagues who have contributed to our book. Their expertise in their fields with advice and input can be found at https://library.jkp.com/redeem using the voucher code KFMSQRC.

Cures?

There are people and practices who claim that there are cures for autism. These may be diet or medication-based, or use alternative medicine. It is very important to understand that there is *no* cure for autism.[1] Autism can be managed and children can be taught to understand and learn life skills and social interaction skills. These help to improve quality of life for the children and their families.

Where there are coexisting medical diagnoses, medication does have a role – for example, to help support the child's sleep or anxiety, or their hyperactivity if they have symptoms of ADHD.

These interventions aim to reduce symptomatology, improve daily function and optimise educational access in order for the young person

---

1   Medavarapu, S., Lakshmi, L.M., Sangem, A. and Kairam, R. (2019) 'Where is the evidence? A narrative literature review of the treatment modalities for autism spectrum disorders.' *Cureus 11*, 1, e3901.

to achieve their maximum potential and integrate into society. Autistic individuals are all unique in their strengths and weaknesses, and support programmes need to be tailored to the child's individual needs. This is where the MDA is very important, as different professionals will have different support strategies for the child's health or education.

In the medical field, GPs or primary care physicians can give help and advice. For children under 5 years of age, a health visitor can give guidance.

Further specialised treatment and support is available from paediatricians and child and adolescent mental health services (CAMHS), including psychologists and psychiatrists if necessary. Allied professionals such as SLTs/speech pathologists and OTs can also support children's individual needs.

The following interventions can be considered and advice should be taken from your clinician or educationalist.

Behavioural interventions

Behaviour and communication are the mainstay for managing and supporting autistic individuals (see Part 4).

- *PECS® (Picture Exchange Communication System):* This is used with children who are pre-verbal or minimally verbal, and uses pictures for them to express their needs. This can be in the form of single pictures or, as the child becomes more proficient in using the system, it can lead to full sentences.
- *TEACCH®:* This is also a system which uses visually structured activities as part of the programme. The approach works on the skills and interests that children already have and it aims to build on them to promote development. Another highly structured programme delivered in a school or home setting. This method has shown some possible benefits.[2]
- *Assistance of technology:* Young children are very proficient in using electronic gadgets. Electronic tablets and communication boards can be very useful and children can become very good

---

2 Panerai, S., Zingale, M., Trubia, G., Finocchiaro, M. *et al.* (2009) 'Special education versus inclusive education: the role of the TEACCH program.' *Journal of Autism and Developmental Disorders 39*, 6, 874–882.

at communicating by using them. Those who are non-verbal may also be able to use a speech generating or communication device. This is referred to as 'facilitated communication'.

- *ABA (Applied Behaviour Analysis):*[3] Researchers are increasingly concerned about the possible damage caused by this kind of intensive intervention. There are many different types of ABA used in school settings or clinics. It is a style of teaching which is highly structured, repetitive and intensive. Initially put forward by psychologist Ole Ivar Lovaas in the 1960s, it is now receiving criticism. ABA has not had many randomised controlled studies to prove its benefits. There are areas where ABA is still being implemented.[4] *Note*: Many autistic people have spoken out and shared negative experiences about ABA, so please do your research if you are considering this approach for your child.

- *Other methods:* Some are gaining in popularity but most do not have adequate evidence-based data to support their use. Horse riding (also known as hippotherapy) is thought to stimulate social and motor development.[5] It is important to note that injury is a risk with this activity and should always be supervised. Dolphin-assisted therapy (DAT) has gained some popularity as it has been suggested that dolphins can help with human communication, but this is not scientifically proven. The relationship between humans and animals has a particularly special place in autistic individuals. Animal-assisted therapy (AAT) has been found to improve emotional wellbeing in autism.[6] There is limited evidence, however. Music therapy may be useful to improve behaviour and communication, but again there is limited evidence.

---

3   Virués-Ortega, J. (2010) 'Applied behavior analytic intervention for autism in early childhood: meta-analysis, meta-regression and dose-response meta-analysis of multiple outcomes.' *Clinical Psychology Review 30*, 4, 387–399.

4   Kirkham, P. (2017) '"The line between intervention and abuse" – autism and applied behaviour analysis.' *History of the Human Sciences 30*, 2, 107–126.

5   Bass, M.M., Duchowny, C.A. and Llabre, M.M. (2009) 'The effect of therapeutic horseback riding on social functioning in children with autism.' *Journal of Autism and Developmental Disorders 39*, 9, 1261–1267.

6   Burgoyne, L., Dowling, L. and Perry, I. (2014) 'Parents' perspectives in the value of assistance dogs for children with austism spectrum disorder.' *BMJ Open 4*, 6, 1–33.

Interventions by professionals

- *Speech and language therapy:* SLTs support children who have delayed speech and language for many different reasons. Some are specially trained and particularly skilled in observing, monitoring and supporting children who have poor social communication skills. They work intensively with young children in order to promote their social skills by using pictures, play and toys, and modelling behaviours. Many of the therapies focus on repetition and condition the child to learn behaviours.
- *Occupational therapy:* OTs specialise in fine motor skills as well as sensory integration. Some therapists undergo further training to specialise in sensory integration therapies. This speciality has been developed to support the sensory needs of children, as these difficulties can impact on everyday skills.
- *Clinical psychology:* Psychologists work with children and families to support behaviours, feelings and emotional difficulties, such as anger and anxiety. They provide therapeutic support but do not prescribe medication.
- *Social skills groups and training:* Education has an important role in supporting children who are on the spectrum. Teachers have a wealth of experience in supporting children with a variety of different needs. Social skills groups can be carried out in classroom settings not only for autistic children but for all the children in the class in order to promote understanding of social scenarios and skills. This can be beneficial not only for autistic children but for other children who may struggle with social communication and interactions.
- *Educational settings:* Specialist support can also be accessed from SENCos, educational psychologists (EPs) and autism teams.

Diet

Nutritional approaches have gained much publicity despite limited supporting evidence. Some desperate parents searching for a cure may turn to diet as it is within their control. There is no robust evidence to justify dietary manipulation to improve autistic behaviours.

- *Exclusion diets:* These eliminate major food groups from the diet, such as foods containing milk or dairy products. There is no robust evidence suggesting improvement of autistic behaviours following use of special diets. Exclusion diets are not recommended for autism management (unless a medical condition such as coeliac disease has been confirmed).

Parents may turn to the media or other families and be keen to try either exclusion diets or vitamin and fish-oil supplements. Neither have specific proven clinical benefits in autism. However, there are some anecdotal reports of improvement in autistic symptoms using exclusion diets. There is no scientific proof for the gluten-free, casein-free (GFCF) diets which some parents like to try.[7] Careful consideration is needed to ensure the child's nutritional needs are met. The diets of some autistic children may already be very selective because of sensory sensitivity to the taste or texture of foods. Sometimes, this may inadvertently cause nutritional problems and reduced bone density. Most clinicians would not advocate these approaches, as there are no large randomised controlled studies to support these interventions and further research is needed.

The Sunderland Protocol, based on a GFCF diet, has been tried by many families. This is not a cure for autism and does not take the place of behavioural and psychological support. The theory of this biomedical approach is that the gut in autistic children is 'leaky' and allows excess peptides (from poorly digested gluten and casein) to be absorbed into the blood and then to the brain causing autistic symptoms.[8,9] There have been some studies looking at blood biomarkers as well as urine peptides and these have been found to have some abnormalities in autistic individuals. Another theory is that the peptide groups from the casein and the gluten food products may have

7   Harrison Elder, J.H., Shankar, M., Shuster, J., Theriaque, D., Burns, S. and Sherrill, L. (2006) 'The gluten-free, casein-free diet in autism: results of a preliminary double blind clinical trial.' *Journal of Autism and Developmental Disorders 36*, 3, 413–420.

8   Winburn, E., Charlton, J., McConachie, H., McColl, E. *et al.* 'Parents' and child health professionals' attitudes towards dietary interventions for children with autism spectrum disorders.' *Journal of Autism and Developmental Disorders 44*, 4, 747–757.

9   Arnold, G.L., Hyman, S.L., Mooney, R.A. and Kirby, R.S. (2003) 'Plasma amino acids profiles in children with autism: potential risk of nutritional deficiencies.' *Journal of Autism and Developmental Disorders, 33*, 4, 449–454.

opiate-like characteristics which affect the nervous system, impacting on socialising and the nervous system. Despite the claims, the evidence for these 'cures' has not been substantiated and doctors do not recommend dietary manipulation, in line with NICE guidelines.

- *Probiotics and antifungals:* These have been tried to reduce the overgrowth of yeast and fungi thought to cause toxic effects if absorbed in the gut. No trials have yet been found to prove this theory.[10] Other vitamins and minerals, such as vitamin B6, magnesium and others, have been tried, again with no clinical evidence pointing to improved behaviours.

The biomedical approach may be offered in some clinics to investigate the micronutrients in a child's profile and there may be a temptation to pursue this route. There are many claims regarding cures for autism, and families who are desperate to find a cure for their child may be tempted. However, many interventions can be costly and difficult to maintain, without proven benefit. Expert medical advice must be sought.

Medication and recognition of coexisting conditions

It is important to recognise that autism can be associated with other medical conditions (known as co-morbidities). It is important that these are managed and not overlooked, for example:

- Mental health issues.
- Sleep difficulties.
- Other neurodevelopmental conditions such as ADHD.
- Medical conditions such as epilepsy.

Medication does have a role in treating some of the symptoms in autism, such as anxiety, sleep disorder or coexisting medical conditions (e.g. epilepsy). They do *not* treat the autism symptoms but may help

---

10   Strati, F., Cavalieri, D., Albanese, D., De Felice, C. *et al.* (2017) 'New evidences on the altered gut microbiota in autism spectrum disorders.' *Microbiome* 5, 24.

coexisting medical issues such as anxiety or ADHD. Medication can be useful to treat specific difficulties, for example:

- Risperidone has been commonly used with some children who display aggressive behaviours, extreme anxiety or self-harm. This is an antipsychotic drug which is used to reduce agitation, irritability and anxiety.
- ADHD medications such as methylphenidate (Ritalin) can be used with children who have comorbid symptoms of ADHD to help improve their attention, focus and impulsive behaviours.
- Anticonvulsant medication is used for autistic children who may have epilepsy.
- Other antipsychotic medication, tricyclic antidepressants and selective serotonin reuptake inhibitors (SSRIs) are used for mental health difficulties such as depression but are not routinely used in treating autism.
- Alternative medicine is used by some families who claim it is beneficial, but there is no substantial evidence-base for its efficacy.

Newer modalities of treatment with no proven benefit

There is ongoing research into methods or drugs to improve the symptoms of autism. The following drugs have been suggested, but this book will not go into detail regarding these therapies. Please note that *none* is clinically proven or prescribed for autism. This is *not* clinical advice and any advice about medication must be discussed with your clinician.

- Oxytocin has been trialled to reduce anxiety in autistic individuals. Oxytocin is a neuropeptide which has an effect on behaviour and possible effect on some autistic symptoms. However, this requires further studies and research. Trials have used intranasal oxytocin with inconclusive results.[11]

---

11 Guastella, A.J., Gray, K.M., Rinehart, N.J., Alvares, A.J. *et al.* (2015) 'The effects of a course of intranasal oxytocin on social behaviors in youth diagnosed with autism spectrum disorders: a randomized controlled trial.' *Journal of Child Psychology and Psychiatry 56*, 4, 444–452.

- Immunoglobulins have been considered by some in treating autism, as an association has been found with immune function and development. It is not proven to be beneficial and extreme caution is required.[12]
- Immunoglobulin therapy – a few small studies have indicated that there may be a connection between the immune system and autism. Intravenous infusion has been tried in very small studies and has not shown beneficial results. Extreme caution is advised as it is not recommended in clinical practice.[13]
- CBD purified oil is being investigated to reduce anxiety and aggression in autistic children. CBD oil has been trialled in animal studies on mice to examine the effect on anxiety and reducing behaviour outbursts. The safety and efficacy of CBD requires further research and is not currently recommended.[14]
- The drug bumetanide is undergoing trials at Cambridge University.[15, 16] It is a diuretic and, in animals, has been found to affect the function of a neurotransmitter GABA (gamma amino butyric acid). It was found to alter the GABA switch (excitatory-inhibitory switch) and reduce some autism symptoms. Further research is needed and it is not in clinical use for autism.

Access to health

It is vital to ensure that autistic young people have access to health and educational resources regardless of their intellectual ability or other comorbidities or diagnoses. These could be any of the following depending on the needs of the individual:

---

12 DelGiudice-Asch, G., Simon, L., Schmeidler, J., Cunningham-Rundles, C. and Hollander, E. (1999) 'Brief report: a pilot open clinical trial of intravenous immunoglobulin in childhood autism.' *Journal of Autism and Developmental Disorders 29*, 157–160.

13 Plioplys, A.V. (1998) 'Intravenous immunoglobulin treatment of children with autism.' *Journal of Child Neurology 13*, 2, 79–82.

14 Fleury-Teixeira, P., Viegas Caixeta, F., Cruz Ramires da Silva, L., Pereira Brasil-Neto, J. and Malcher-Lopes, R. (2019) 'Effects of CBD-enriched *cannabis sativa* extract on autism spectrum disorder symptoms: an observational study of 18 participants undergoing compassionate use.' *Frontiers in Neurology 10*, 1145.

15 Zhang, L., Huang, C-C., Dai, Y., Luo, Q. *et al.* (2020) 'Symptom improvement in children with autism spectrum disorder following bumetanide administration is associated with decreased GABA/glutamate ratios.' *Translational Psychiatry 10*, 9.

16 Santosh, P.J. and Singh, J (2018) 'Drug treatment of autism spectrum disorder and its comorbidities in children and adolescents.' *BJPsych Advances 22*, 3, 151–161.

- Specialist care and educational provision.
- Training and support for all professional staff responsible for looking after or caring for these individuals.
- Advice regarding any functional adaptations required in the home or school.
- Managing challenging behaviours.
- Treating coexisting conditions.
- Access to leisure activities.
- Support for families and carers.
- Good transition planning for any changes, such as transition to secondary school, higher education or adulthood.
- The differing needs of puberty.
- Consideration of sensory difficulties and adapting the environment.
- Support from local agencies including charities such as National Autistic Society (www.autism.org.uk).
- Emotional support for siblings and parents.
- Offering life skills development for young people to become independent.

Part 4

EDUCATION

CHAPTER 12

Anxieties and Sensory Issues

'The noise of the vacuum cleaner really terrified him. We had to keep it in the garage and could only use it when he wasn't in the house. I think it was the noise, but also seeing it suck things up and just not understanding what was going on.'

(Parent reflection)

Imagine being on a fast-moving, overcrowded underground train. As the train lurches and rumbles, people are all getting squashed together. It's a hot day and there is a stench of sweat in the air. You can feel the breath of a stranger on your neck and the sound is repulsive to you, but you can't get away from it. Someone is coughing loudly and you can see the tiny germy droplets of their spittle in the air. The lights are flashing like a horror movie. You are wearing a very uncomfortable, tight-fitting jacket and a high-neck jumper with scratchy wool and there is no room to move to remove a layer, so you are stuck like this. The feeling is getting worse by the minute. Add to this that you have no idea where you are going or how long this journey will last. The doors open and your instinct is naturally flight, but someone is holding your hand so tightly, not letting you escape. What would you do?

Now step off the train, breathe and think about being a small child in that situation. Flight, fight or freeze?

We can probably all relate to these feelings a lot more since the 2019 Covid-19 pandemic when social distancing, wearing masks and avoiding public transport were so normal, and coughing created so much anxiety. But even without a pandemic the autistic child could feel all this anxiety in so many of the situations other children cope well with. A trip to the supermarket, a restaurant or a preschool classroom could bring about the same feelings of anxiety and panic as that underground train. We can't judge how the child is feeling by our own experience, and the best way we can help them is by developing our empathy and tuning in. But we must also maintain our own perspective. We must be the anchor, the support, creating a sense of calm and trying to bring some order to a chaotic and overwhelming situation. But how?

Well, going back to that train, what are the things that support us on the Underground? There are many strategies in place which are there to help all those commuters navigate independently, stay on track and reach their destinations.

Think about all of the helpful colour-coded visuals and systems in place. There are colour-coded maps in the stations and on the walls so that commuters can count down the stops and be reassured that they are on the right train. The more times people embark on the same journey the less reliant they will become on these visuals; but if something happened and they needed to change trains, then they would look at the visuals for support. An autistic child might not need a visual when they are feeling okay and on a regular transition – for example, going from the car to the classroom – but what if they are feeling anxious? Maybe something changed on the way to school such as traffic lights being out of order or a road closed. That one different thing could create so much anxiety. Compare it to sitting on your regular train journey but seeing an unfamiliar station sign at the first stop. What thoughts might go through your head as anxiety bubbles? Am I on the right train? Am I going in the right direction? How will I get to where I'm meant to be going? Will I be late? What will the consequence be? So many, many thoughts from just one thing being different. When something changes, it can create a host of similar emotions in the autistic child. They may not be able to vocalise it though. They may just freeze. A short visual schedule such as a 'Now and Next' board with pictures to show what is happening 'Now' followed by what will be happening 'Next', can calm a child when they are feeling anxious and help them to stay on track. An alternative to this is to set a timer to show how long something will last.

CASE STUDY
Colour coding the way: Adele Devine
In our colour-coded classroom the schedule symbols and timetables are outlined in purple, behaviour symbols in orange and personal care symbols are aqua. We were using so many symbols and this system helped us create consistency. More importantly, because staff could find the visual more quickly, they were using them more. These symbols and systems are further explained in my first book *Colour Coding for Learners with Autism*.[1]

• • • • • • • • • •

Anxiety is catching
You may hear people say that autistic people lack empathy; but when it comes to picking up on others' anxieties, they can have a sort of hyper-empathy. The child will not understand that they are picking up on other people's feelings so will believe they are their own. This can be confusing and frightening. So, when an autistic child faces a new demand or change to routine, it is vital that they do not pick up on any anxiety from those around them. It's natural for parents to be highly anxious around the time of diagnosis and when their child transitions to school. They need to be aware that their anxiety will transfer to their child and the only way to manage this is to seek support and advice (out of earshot of the child). Call up the school to organise the transition. The child must not hear any anxieties a parent has. As a parent it's

---

1   Published in 2014 by Jessica Kingsley Publishers.

important to breathe and leave all that anxiety at home when first dropping a child at school. When one ability is missing others make up for it. Pre-verbal children may develop an ability to read people. This is the reason the autistic child may be drawn to certain adults. They just know when they are with someone calming who they can trust.

Settling the anxieties of parents and building a trusting relationship should all happen prior to the autistic child starting school. As the parent's anxieties reduce, the child becomes happier, more content and able to communicate. Diagnosis and school transitions can be frightening for parents and it is so important that they are supported during the transition with a lot of communication and care.

Modelling fears and anxieties

The autistic child may seem absorbed in their own thing, but they are constantly watching and learning. Imagine a parent with an absolute fear of something (let's say spiders). When Mum sees a spider she screams, grabs her child and runs out of the house and will not enter again until someone comes to the rescue and removes the spider. What will her child be learning? They will be learning that spiders are frightening; that you should scream and run when frightened (like Mum); that if Mum is frightened of something and responds irrationally, she could do that at any time with anything which is unpredictable and frightening in itself. We must be very careful what we are modelling to children.

Similarly, know that they may be listening and picking up on our spoken and unspoken language. Try to breathe, take a walk and work to reduce your own anxieties and protect children from being around others displaying anxiety.

Comfort items and motivators

Many children develop attachments to a certain cuddly toy or special blanket. When they need to get to sleep or are unwell, we give them these things to soothe them and help reduce anxieties. If the autistic child has a comfort object, it can be a good idea to keep it close at hand and also leave it with them if they are being cared for by someone else. Maybe they have a special blanket, their most comfortable clothes or a small toy dinosaur. One way to help soothe your child when anxieties arise is to have to hand that comforting or motivating thing that will help. Think of it as being armed and ready. We must try to plan and stay a step ahead.

If a child has a specific item they need to settle, make sure you get spare items the same and swap them in and out so that they all get equally worn and look and feel the same. Maybe it's a blanket or a toy bunny or a little pillow. Whatever it is, as soon as you notice the attachment, try to get some spare items in reserve.

Comforters are items that can help a child feel safer and more in control and will help set them up to succeed. In time they will learn that the situation is manageable and their need for comfort items can reduce significantly.

Where's my routine?

Routine helps us all. We know the alarm goes off at the same time on a workday. We naturally set our own order, which works well for us. Our routines help us feel more in control and set us up for the day.

Before we realise it, we have put in place numerous routines with our children. Even if we have a tendency to go with the flow once we have children, the need for routine increases. Routines are very important to children and can be vital for helping the autistic child feel safe. Routine makes the day more predictable, which makes it more relaxing. When a child is in a state of high anxiety and panic, they will not be able to learn and they will try to control things.

If your child is finding something challenging, then think about their routine. Have you changed it? If so, it will take time to adjust and they will not simply switch to a new rhythm. They need time, they need a reason and they need to experience the new routine again and again before they will be able to relax and feel restored.

Our children are watching and learning all the time and there are routines they will be aware of which we don't even know about. How we move about the house, the order we get things out for breakfast in the morning. So when something suddenly breaks this routine, it will send alarm bells out to the child. Think of it like the ripples when a pebble drops in the water or when a storm is coming. They know something is up and their anxiety begins to build.

The most important thing is to be aware of how important routine is in making the child feel safe and enabling them to cope. Do have routines, but we must also help children learn that these routines can change a bit and it will still be okay. It's better to introduce this before setting another challenge. For example, change the routine when the only challenge you are setting is the new routine, rather than changing the routine and then expecting your child to meet another challenge the same day.

CASE STUDY
Changing the routine of the school run

Sienna (4 years old) is starting school in September. She is very excited about it. Mum is not worried about Sienna starting school as she loved preschool and is ready for this next step. The concern is that Sienna's little brother Joe is autistic, and Mum expects that he will find the change in routine difficult. He has got used to walking to the preschool and leaving Sienna there, but the new school means a change to the morning routine. Anxiety builds as they get closer to the day. They leave the house as usual and Mum explains calmly that today is different because Sienna is going to big school. Joe tries to pull Mum and Sienna in the direction of the preschool. He does not hear Mum explaining. He just thinks they have got it wrong. If they get the route wrong, then anything could happen. It is like they are pulling the rug from under his feet and he needs to regain control. He will do anything to get them back on track. Joe is strong and determined. Sienna is distressed and cries, which makes Joe even more anxious. It is all going horribly wrong. Another mum steps in to help and takes Sienna to school. After a long time, Joe's meltdown ends. He still wants Mum to walk to the preschool. In order to pacify Joe, Mum walks the usual route and then they return home. Joe returns to the usual routine as if nothing has happened, but Mum feels devastated. The first day of the school experience with Sienna is gone forever. She will never have that photo, the smiles, the kiss goodbye…

· · · · · · · · · ·

What could Mum have done differently in the above scenario?

When we know the routine is going to change, we must introduce this gradually to the autistic child and when we are not under pressure.

If there is going to be a change to routine due to a change in school runs, then the best thing is to rehearse it several times before it actually happens. Are there any ways we can explain visually? Maybe use the school uniform? Sienna has a new school uniform. Take a photo of Sienna in her new uniform and use this to create a visual. You could draw a simple map to show Joe the new walk to school. Plan and prepare so that there is plenty of time for Joe to process the change. Show clearly and calmly what will happen before the actual day and walk it through together. It might also help to use a buggy (if the child is not too big), a comfort object or distractor.

What if we still think Joe won't cope well with the change this first day and there will be a battle? It's okay to seek support in these situations. Try to plan ahead. Is there another person who could stay with Joe so that you get to share that first walk to school with Sienna? Things which are easy for most parents can be a real challenge and it is okay to talk about them and seek support. If there are siblings, it's also good to let their school know that they have a brother or sister with an autism diagnosis as it will help the teacher have an understanding of their home life.

Using visuals

Visual cues can really help when a child is overwhelmed. Think of that underground train and how maps and being able to count down the stops help us to stay on the train until we reach our destination. Using a schedule or a 'Now and Next' board can really help explain what is going to happen next. It provides a sense of order and makes expectations clear. We can use schedules for the daily routine, but these can also be used for other routines a child finds challenging. We can have a schedule for washing hands, having a bath and washing hair. Showing the visual will not work like magic. If a child has an anxiety about hair washing, a visual schedule won't mean that they just think, 'Hair washing is okay', but it will help warn them of the expectation and show the steps in a calmer way than just suddenly covering their head in shampoo and bubbles. The visual routine also reinforces predictability and lessens anxiety.

Too busy

In recent times, due to the Covid-19 pandemic, the world has become maybe less busy as we remain in our homes. The guidance for social distancing, group gatherings and bubbles are all things that some adults have found difficult, but which others may have come to appreciate. The autistic child may be naturally inclined to prefer social distancing, being in their own bubble and feeling a sense of alarm when this is challenged. It is interesting how we have all been forced to walk this walk in recent times. Suddenly, things that would have been the norm in all of our lives, such as hugs, large social gatherings and shaking hands, are socially taboo. It has taken time to adjust and it will take time to adjust back. When will going to a party or social event feel completely normal again? The rules we have adjusted to provide us with the perfect way to empathise with the set of rules our autistic child may have chosen to live by. Playing alone may look unusual and alarming to us but makes total sense to our child. Why would they want to put themselves amidst a group of unpredictable, noisy children when they can create their own little ordered haven in a distant corner or dark den? Why be involved when retreating is so much more comfortable?

Too busy can be daunting and overwhelming and it takes time to adjust and acclimatise. The autistic child must be provided with this time. Think about how adults might respond to a cold swimming pool. Some will choose to jump right in and swim, some will edge in painfully and some will choose not to enter the pool at all. They make a choice based on their own experience, and whether they decide to get in the pool depends on what they will get out of it. What motivates them? We would never just throw an adult into a cold pool, yet we expect children to walk blindly into situations which they feel will bring them complete discomfort and distress.

Too busy can be overwhelming and can stop a child from accessing something they will in fact enjoy. Therefore, the best way to set the child up to succeed is to remove the people and let the child learn to feel comfortable with the space and the activity first.

CASE STUDY

Before T visited our school, we had many phone conversations with his mum. We knew T had cried a lot at his previous preschool and spent most of the time by the door waiting to be rescued. Large numbers of children made him anxious and he did not like to be separated from his mum. This experience had also made Mum anxious about how he would settle. We arranged T's settling-in time to be when the class would be out of the room in the school hall. I said to only bring T if it was going to be a good day for him – that is, he'd had some sleep and woken in a happy mood. I knew he liked Peppa Pig and had lots of Peppa Pig toys and books. We set up the classroom with a Peppa Pig theme so that he would have familiar and interesting things to explore. We had water play available too as this was another thing T liked. I met Mum at the door and T clung to her. Mum had a 'Now and Next' visual showing 'Caterpillar Class' and 'Choosing'. We were not expecting T to make a link with this visual yet but knew to get it in place early as he would understand it in time. I stayed a bit further away, said it was okay and we would wait, and I blew some bubbles. After a little while Mum and T started to transition towards me. We walked to class. It was quiet and there were familiar motivators around (all things Mum had told me he would like).

T entered class but was anxious as he still suspected he might be left. Mum went and sat down by the books (far from the door) and he went and sat with her. I went over to the water and started to quietly play. Then I went and sat in the home corner. T had been watching and went over to the water. He got completely involved in water play and had a big smile on his face. After a while I went and added some more water and he accepted me being near as I was adding another element to water play, whilst being quiet and predictable.

After a while the other children returned. The routine was snack-time and the table was set up and ready for them, and they went and sat for this. T continued to play with the water. We did not demand that he joined snack-time, but he could if he wanted to. T stayed for another half hour and then we showed him the five-minute timer and he left (a little reluctantly) with his mum.

I spoke with Mum on the phone afterwards and she could not believe how well he had coped and how happy and comfortable he had been.

T doesn't like 'too busy'. When we introduce something new, we still do it in such a way as to set him up to acclimatise. The first time he went to soft play, he was the first one in and then we let some quieter children join him. He learnt to love soft play and it became another comfort zone, and then we introduced more children. This was okay.

T has a little tent in class and sometimes when it gets too much, he goes in there to get a bit of space. He also likes to shut himself in a little egg chair we got from Ikea. It has a little roof he can pull down like a tent.

T is very settled and happy and transitions to class well. He mostly copes really well with 'too busy' as the busy children are a part of his comfort zone. They will never be predictable, but they are predictably unpredictable (just like T).

T would never have coped with walking straightaway into a busy class and first impressions mean so much to our children.

* * * * * * * * * *

Too noisy

Your child may be extremely sensitive to certain noises and you will soon learn what they are. Maybe it's the vacuum cleaner or hand dryers, dogs barking, babies crying. Their indicator may be subtle, such as withdrawal from the place or putting their hands over their ears, or it could be more extreme and dramatic. Think of a sound you really don't like, some noise that would really get to you. Now imagine that sound amplified and intensified, surrounding you with no end in sight. Next imagine another demand being placed on you, such as an important phone call. You're trying to listen with one ear whilst being bombarded in the other. Sensitivity to noise is personal, is very real, and can be painful and disturbing.

It also may not be the noise itself, but the unpredictable, uncontrollable nature of the noise – for example a dog barking or baby crying. It could also be a response to the feeling the sound gives them – fear or sadness. There are so many things to consider and our reaction must be empathic and supportive rather than frustrated or annoyed.

The response may not seem consistent. Maybe they are usually fine with the hum of the overhead lights, but all of a sudden they just can't cope with them. This can be due to some other thing and the light sound they usually cope with well starts seeming louder and louder.

Take a moment to tune in to the sounds around you. When you really tune in, you will begin to notice sounds that might not bother you at all. Now imagine upping the volume of those sounds so that they become a bit uncomfortable. Now go back to a moment when you were feeling really anxious (maybe you were running late for an important meeting or waiting for the phone to ring with bad news). When we are carrying lots of anxiety, we don't need lots of noise. When our heads are muddled and we are trying to sort out our emotions, we need calm and quiet. So sometimes a child might suddenly find a noise really hard to cope with because there is a lot of other stuff going on that they cannot understand or explain.

Some examples of difficult sounds:

- Chewing.
- Talking.
- Coughing.
- Balloons.
- Hand dryers.
- Hair dryers.
- Vacuum cleaners.
- Sirens.
- Fireworks.
- Electrics humming.
- Crying children.
- Dogs barking.
- Doors banging.

If you know that your child responds badly to certain sounds, then you will try to avoid it, but there are times when this can be impossible.

Ways you can support the sound-sensitive child

Think about whether there is a way to reduce or remove the noise. This sounds so obvious; but if it is at all possible, try to reduce the noise or remove some element that might be adding to it. Turn off the music or the TV, ask the chattering friend to talk another time, settle the crying baby or barking dog or remove them to another space.

Reduce all the verbal clutter. Noise intensifies noise, and talking (no matter how soothing) will only add fuel to the flames if a child is reacting to sounds. Stop the sound if it is possible; but if it is not, then create a visual explaining the noise. If you can provide a way to show the sound will finish, that might help too. If another adult tries to engage and advise you and this is not helpful, hand them an autism alert card (see Chapter 13).

- *Five-point scale:* Maybe your child will be able to use the five-point scale to visually explain to you how bad the sound is. The five-point scale allows a child to show just how bad something is, going from 1 (green) 'I am calm and relaxed' to 5 (red) 'I am going to explode.' Having a visual way to communicate and measure emotions can be so helpful in knowing what strategy to use to help.
- *Ear defenders:* These may be an option as they will reduce the impact of the sound, but not all children will accept wearing ear defenders. It is also important to note that they should not be used at all times as they will reduce the chances of your child hearing important sounds, such as spoken directions, human interaction, songs and music, as well as signals of danger such as alarms or traffic.
- *Visual volume control:* Using a visual volume control will help your child show the level of the noise and where it should be.
- *Access to a quiet space:* Create a sort of sensory bolt hole to which your child can escape. You can get pop-up dark dens or little tents.
- *Code words or signs:* Teach your child a way to communicate to you when it is getting too much. Rather than appearing rude by asking your elderly neighbour to stop talking to you, could there be a certain way that they squeeze your hand?

Anxiety intensifies and heightens our responses to everything, so it might be that a child can cope well with a noise on a good day, but responds differently on a bad day.

Another irony is that often our most sound-sensitive children can have the ability to create the most noise. They may not be aware that their own noise provokes the noise of others. Think of a room full of newborn babies sleeping peacefully in their cots and then that one decides to wake up and cry...

We must also be aware of the way in which noise reduces our ability to concentrate and when a child has communication difficulties, we want them to be able to hear important language and feel comfortable enough to develop interaction and play skills. Just because the other children are coping does not mean an environment cannot be improved. Make their space calm, uncluttered and happy and this will really bring out the best in them.

Sensory issues about wearing clothes

A child may only like wearing one type of clothing – for example, their pyjamas – or they may not want to wear clothes at all. Maybe they have learnt to tolerate clothes when they are outside but they remove them as soon as they get home.

This can cause so much frustration and anxiety. Why won't they wear clothes like everyone else?

Consider what they will wear. For example, if your child will only wear their pyjamas, could you get clothes with the same colour or texture?

CASE STUDY
Clothes off at home: Adele Devine

When we met E at his home visit, he was not wearing clothes. His lovely parents explained that he would wear clothes outside (because they had insisted on this), but as soon as he was in the house he removed them. They may have felt a bit self-conscious about this, but we reassured them that we are pretty much unshockable.

When E arrived at school, he was fully dressed and we didn't see any stripping in the first few days as he settled. In fact, he preferred to wear all the spare clothes in his bag, and his coat and hat too. Then the stripping started. It was always when he was somewhere enclosed – the soft play tunnel or in the little dark tent. The secret to stopping the stripping at school was to learn when it was likely and be really, really quick at stopping the first item of clothes coming off and then redirect E to something else fun to do.

If a child refuses to wear any clothes at all, or just certain clothes, and they don't have the language to tell us why, then it is up to us to try to work it out. Is it the feeling, the colour or the association? Is there any compromise we can reach?

'Wearing clothes…we are resolved to the fact we may have to move to a naturist resort at some point.'

(Parent of S)

School uniform

School uniform is a tricky one as you want your child to fit in and look the same as the other children. Make sure you get them to try the uniform before the first day so you are well prepared for any issue; but if you know that there will be an issue, then there are some simple things that you can do to help make the first try-on a success. Anything you can do to make it less scratchy and strange will help.

- Look at the school website and talk about the uniform and the school so they have lots of time to prepare.
- Buying a second-hand uniform can help as it will be softened by wear.
- Wash the uniform with your regular washing detergent if your child accepts other clothes with that smell.
- If there is one aspect of the uniform that is causing the problem, see if you can find a compromise.
- Speak to teachers about it, because they won't want uniform to cause anxiety or discomfort. They might be able to help too.

Tricky buttons

A child might be worried about wearing the school shirt because they wouldn't be able to do the top button after changing clothes. Other children have had this same issue. There are cheat versions with Velcro at the top. They are a good compromise.

Laces

Ask the school if you can get Velcro shoes while your child is still learning to tie laces. Learning to tie laces can be very challenging and frustrating. It might be a battle that can wait until they are a bit older. One cheat way to tie laces is to make two loops and tie them together in a knot. There are also cheat no-tie laces available, which are worth getting if it will reduce anxieties.

Changing

Changing for sports can cause the autistic child so much anxiety. If the changing creates anxiety, is there a way to compromise? Could they go to school in their sports clothes or change in a different space?

CASE STUDY
From comfort clothes to uniform: Adele Devine

When we arrived at N's home for our visit, she was wearing her pyjamas. Mum explained that N would only wear pyjamas, and I could see N was listening to this and would also be listening to my response. I smiled brightly at N and said that was absolutely fine. They were lovely pyjamas and of course I was happy for her to wear them to school if that would be more comfortable. I added that I sometimes wear pyjamas to school (this is true on some charity-themed days). I saw N smile at this. I think it was the moment when she decided she was going to like her funny new teacher. The home visit was a great success. We knew from Mum that N would probably find the separation difficult.

On N's first day Mum left once she knew she was comfortable. She said goodbye as agreed and made a swift exit. N had a quick cry and a cuddle and about ten seconds later she was happy and playing.

N got her top wet at the water tray and we were in the bathroom. I knew she had spare pyjamas in her bag, but thought I'd just see if she would wear something else. I offered her one of our spare school jumpers. I was expecting her to refuse and would have gone and got her spares. Demands will always wait until the children settle completely. N surprised me by putting the jumper on happily. Mum was a bit surprised to see her wearing a school jumper when she came to collect her. I explained that she had got her top wet so she chose something else to put on. She has worn the school jumper every day since.

Sometimes a child will suddenly decide that they will wear something new. Maybe it was being asked by someone new. Maybe N was at school so obviously a school jumper would be okay. Maybe she just really liked the jumper.

. . . .

Non-uniform days

It is a good idea to warn a child in advance if a non-uniform day has been scheduled. Many children enjoy these days. They are a way for schools to raise funds and it seems that they will always be a part of school life. Don't let this day creep up on you. Preparation is everything. Choose what they will wear together. If they don't want to dress up, that is okay too. Let them go to school in their usual uniform but send them with appropriate dress-up clothes in case they get to school and change their minds. There is no point in letting these days cause extra anxiety by insisting they dress up.

Many children enjoy these days and get a lot from them, but there are many children, parents (and teachers), who don't want to go to school in pyjamas or scratchy Christmas jumpers and that is their choice. It is completely okay.

CASE STUDY
Dealing with a different school day: Adele Devine

J was really, really anxious about Victorian Day at school. He didn't seem to mind the dressing up, but something was worrying him. J explained to his mum that the teachers had said they were all going to be super strict, just like in Victorian times. The other children probably realised that the teachers were having a little joke and they would still be their nice teachers, but J was frightened. Mum emailed J's teacher. When they arrived, she came and met him and bent down to his level and smiled. She said, 'It's okay, J. I am still the same teacher. See?' J was fine after that. He just needed reassurance that the scary teacher he had worried about wasn't going to be in his classroom.

Another day, the school had arranged to do a sponsored skip and told the children that they would be skipping all day so they could wear their sports clothes. J didn't want to go in that day. He explained to his mum that the teacher had said they would be skipping all day and he wouldn't like that. J had taken the teacher literally and imagined that he would arrive at school, start skipping and keep skipping until home time. He had imagined no lunch time, no sitting down and no toilet breaks. No wonder he didn't want to go in! It is so important to talk to the child and find out exactly what is bothering them about a different day. In this case, all the teacher needed to do was explain the schedule for the day and then J was okay.

* * * * * * * * * *

Wearing shoes

A child might refuse to wear shoes or only wear certain shoes. If they will only wear one type of shoe, I would recommend buying them some pairs that are exactly the same that they can grow into. Some children can be quite definite about the shoes they will wear. Shoes can be a frustrating and distressing battle. We know that children need to wear shoes to protect their feet. We know the looks they can get and the feelings of being judged and failing that can follow.

Your child is not the only one to refuse shoes or only wear one type of shoe. We have known many children with this sensory issue and whilst it seems like an impossible battle, it is something they can achieve with the right support. If they are not wearing shoes and starting school, then speak to the school about it. The school can give support for this. Given time, consistent expectations, adaptations and some compromises, your child will learn that wearing shoes is okay.

Tips to get a child to wear shoes

- Keep trying to get your child in shoes every day. Don't give up!
- Reduce language and use a 'shoes on' visual.
- Use a 'Now and Next' with Now – 'Shoes on', Next – 'Outside'.
- Get siblings or other children to model putting their shoes on.
- Introduce shoes into doll play or role play.
- Be consistent about where you expect shoes to be worn.
- Buy shoes with a motivating character or colour.
- Try to think of a compromise, such as sock shoes.
- When they do get shoes on, start walking and try to redirect them and shift focus to something else.
- Speak aloud the reason when putting your own shoes on.

CASE STUDY
New shoes, new strategies: Adele Devine

L would only wear his blue beach shoes at home and school. He would never wear any other type of shoe, but after years of shoe refusal it was good that he was wearing something to protect his feet. L was growing out of his beach shoes and Mum had bought a pair the next size up. L was refusing to wear them and we were concerned that the others could damage his feet. The beach shoes were the type that had little bobbles at the bottom. These had been worn down in his old pair. We used sandpaper to wear down the bobbles in the new ones and scuffed them about a bit so they were not such a bright new blue. We removed the other shoes. L didn't notice that the shoes were different until he had put them on. He noticed, but we distracted him with a toy rocket he loved and then a walk in the woods (a favourite activity). L knew what was going on, but we kept working on it until one day the old shoes disappeared and were replaced permanently with the new.

● ● ● ● ● ● ● ● ●

Sensory overload

Sensory overload occurs when one or more of the body's five senses become overstimulated and leave the person feeling overwhelmed. There can be any number of triggers.

Things that can cause sensory overload

- Going to a busy restaurant or school canteen.
- Busy shopping centres.
- A family gathering or party.
- The flicker and hum of fluorescent lights.
- Hand dryers in a public toilet.
- Radios or music being played loudly.
- The smell of perfume or cleaning products.
- Firework displays.
- The build-up to Christmas or other religious or public holiday.

Medical News Today lists the following as signs of sensory overload in children.

- Signs of anxiety, irritability or restlessness.
- Avoidance of specific places or situations.
- Closing eyes or covering the face.
- Crying.
- Sensitivity to sound and placing the hands over the ears.
- The inability to converse or connect to other people.

- Running away from certain places or situations.[2]

It is interesting how many of these signs are often seen as behaviours rather than being reactions and responses to sensory overload.

2   www.medicalnewstoday.com/articles/sensory-overload#symptoms

CHAPTER 13

Behaviour

'We still find the impulsive dangerous behaviours quite distressing, but as our child has evolved, so have we. We have become better at understanding what triggers him to run off, for example, and can plan our trips around this mostly. These behaviours seemed so all-consuming when he was little but are much more manageable now.'

(Parent reflection)

Our children get to understand us very quickly. The quicker they can train us, the more control they have. A little control is important to most children, but autism can take that need to control to another level altogether.

Imagine if you could not communicate by explaining your feelings. Imagine if you felt you were in a situation where all your control was being taken and you did not have a way to say 'Stop!' or question 'Why?'

Let us try to put ourselves in our child's shoes. What if someone you didn't know knocked on your front door, then barged past you and took your bag, then rummaged through to find your car keys, marched over to your car and got in the driver's seat. You watch in horror as they reverse, destroying a little wall you had built yourself and all the roses you had planted and cared for. The car is damaged, the wall is wrecked, roses destroyed and then they just drive off. Imagine the feelings – panic, anxiety, sadness or anger. There would be so many emotions if this actually happened. They could seem quite overwhelming. How might you react?

Now think about a situation when your child's behaviour might suggest that they are feeling like this.

When we are concerned by a new behaviour, the first thing we must do is try to unpick it and try to see through the child's eyes. Behaviour can be shocking, frustrating, alarming and upsetting to us, but it's important to keep all of these emotions in check when we are in the moment. Your first instinct might be to shout or scream or cry or, in some cases, laugh, but try really hard not to because the child will be looking for what your reaction will be. The behaviour might even be a way they have found to get that exciting reaction. Behaviour is communication and we must work out what the child is trying to communicate through the behaviour.

Key questions

- What are they communicating?
- What are they achieving?
- What are the triggers?
- Is there any pattern?
- Is there a compromise?

When faced with challenging behaviours, ask yourself the following questions:

If a child is…

- Climbing on furniture – is there something they are allowed to climb on instead?

- Refusing to follow transitions – where do they want to be?
- Trying to get to something – can they get it later instead?
- Not joining the group – could they join later?
- Leaving the group – what motivates them to stay?
- Not sitting when others do – is sitting essential to joining in?
- Throwing the toys – what toys motivate them to play?
- Staying in one area – what makes that area special?
- Not following the adult agenda – is the plan clear and achievable?
- Hurting other children – what reaction are they seeking?

Simple compromises or small changes to the way you do things, such as those suggested above, can make all the difference.

CASE STUDY
A tricky transition: Adele Devine

B had a good understanding of his visual timetable and was able to transition using a 'Now and Next' visual schedule.

We have transition boards outside all of the classrooms and B would match his symbol to the symbol on the board. When it was a transition he liked, he was brilliant. The issue was that when it was not so motivating, he would choose to go to the place he thought should be on the timetable.

Every Monday we have a dance session in the school hall, and this was not a session B enjoyed. He was able to take part but would sometimes use ear defenders if he found the noise too much.

But B had started to find the transition to the hall more frustrating. On the way, he walked past the room where we have a big trampoline, and B loved this more than anything. Instead of going to the hall he would stand looking through the window at the trampoline.

We discussed the behaviour at our team meeting. What was B telling us? He was clearly communicating, 'I would rather go on the trampoline than go to dance.' Was there a way to compromise?

First thing, I booked B a trampoline slot later in the day. He only needed ten minutes and it meant we would not be saying 'no', but 'not now'.

Then we had a think about the dance session and what he was finding difficult. The session did not always start right away, and often by the time it did he had lost interest and gone to find something better to do (usually climbing).

We decided to bring B in ten minutes later so that when he arrived it had started already. B understood our sand timers and we used them a lot, so we added a timer symbol to his 'Now and Next' schedule, so he could see that he only needed to stay in the session for ten minutes.

In the morning we followed our plan and made sure B had seen his visual schedule. He clocked the 'trampoline' symbol and smiled widely. B waited the ten minutes, then transitioned straight to the dance session and stayed ten minutes. He was brilliant! As time went on, we added another ten minutes and he coped with that too.

. . . .

Schedules

We all love our routines. In the days before you had children you may have had a lovely routine that helped set you up for the day. Maybe the routine went something like this: alarm, toilet, shower, dress, curtains, tea, feed cat, breakfast, teeth, make up, car. We learn our routine and stick to it because it works, and when one thing is missing, such as no water or no tea or missing cat, it can really throw us. But we are adults and we don't have a meltdown. We cope.

Our children love routines too. Routines help make them feel safe, comfortable and in control. Our autistic children can really love routines and it can be very helpful to provide a visual schedule for them. That way everyone knows the plan, and if there is an issue or a change in plan, the visual schedule can be a good way to show the plan. And for children who do not like demands it will reduce the verbal demand. Seeing the plan rather than hearing it makes it clearer and easier to process. The child might try to change the plan by removing symbols from the visual schedule, but being able to show what they want or don't want to happen is so much better than not being able to explain at all.

Individual behaviour support plans

All behaviour is communication, and if we are seeing the same behaviour on a regular basis, it is important to create a plan to ensure that a child is getting the same considered, agreed, consistent responses in all situations. A teacher may suggest writing an Individual Behaviour Support Plan. Please don't be alarmed by this. It can only be a helpful thing to know that there is a plan in place and support strategies that everyone agrees.

CASE STUDY
Finding a lunchtime compromise: Adele Devine

If Z's lunchbox was accessible, he would go to get it and eat the whole lot, so the staff had locked it away in a cupboard up high. Z was fixated on getting it back and we needed to think of a compromise because he was climbing and getting very cross. Could there be a compromise?

The next day, before putting the lunchbox away in the cupboard, we removed most of his lunch so there was just a snack and drink inside it. Z was not aware that we had done this.

We added a photograph of his lunchbox to his PECS® book, and when he went to climb to get the lunchbox he was shown the photo. Z was very good at using his photos and symbols to make requests and comment, so he knew what to do.

He took the photo and placed it on his sentence strip, making the sentence 'I want lunchbox', then he handed it to me. I opened the cupboard and gave him his lunchbox and he ate the contents. At lunchtime he was able to have the rest of his lunch with the other children. Everyone was happy.

. . . .

Now and Next boards

A 'Now and Next' or 'Now, Next, Then' board is a shorter, simplified version of the visual schedule. This may be a good introduction to using visuals with the child as it is brief and quick and useful for moving onto other things.

CASE STUDY
Using a 'Now and Next': Adele Devine

We have a rule at our school that the children need to wear shoes to access our outside area (unless they are in the sandpit or water play). This rule can take a while for the children to accept, but with consistent expectations and supportive strategies they do learn that we will not compromise on this. It is a rule.

One of the children wanted to go outside but was refusing to put their shoes on. A new member of staff was trying to get the child's shoes on without success. I went over to the child and showed him the 'Now and Next' visual. I said 'Now – shoes on, next – outside' while pointing to the pictures. The child paused to process this and then positioned his feet to allow the shoes to be put on with ease. The child had seen the visual many times and had learnt its meaning. Sometimes it's easier to follow a rule when it is a visual request rather than a verbal demand.

· · · · · · · · · ·

By using a 'Now and Next' there is less information for a child to process. The expectation is very clear, but rather than hearing too much language everything is depicted visually. Using a 'Now and Next' board can help show expectations and prepare children for transitions, which may reduce their anxieties. It will also keep your language simple, predictable and consistent and the symbols illustrate what you're are saying.

Using a visual also helps the adult feel more calm and in control. Using visuals can stop any unwelcome feelings being picked up and mirrored by the child. The autistic child may seem 'in their own little world', but that doesn't stop them picking up on the feelings of those supporting them. Supplementary visual materials can be downloaded from https://library.jkp.com/redeem using the voucher code KFMSQRC.

Transition boards

The symbols may also be used with transition boards. A transition board could be on the door to the garden for example and will have the symbol for 'garden' on it. These boards help the child link the symbols to the places they represent. They can also be used for matching symbols to if this helps the child to transition.

The child learns to remove the 'outside' symbol that is on their schedule or 'Now and Next' board and then goes to match it to the 'outside' transition board. By doing this they have made their way to where they should be without multiple verbal demands. They have also had time to process the request and a visual reminder as they go. We teach them to do this through modelling and then some gentle support and hand-over-hand help (if they are happy with this). We gradually fade out the assistance as they learn to complete this transitioning matching task independently.

A whoops!

No matter how much we all love routine and order, life will always throw us a whoops! You may have planned a lovely quiet morning with your child doing all the things they enjoy – breakfast, a walk to the park, cooking, then a snack – but then you get an unexpected phone call, a neighbour in need, or a sibling who has been sick at school and needs collecting right away. This is life, and unexpected changes to the schedule happen. We cope with this, but the autistic child can find a change such as this completely unfathomable and unreasonable. What would be an inconvenience to another parent is going to be an incredible battle.

So teach a child to recognise a whoops visual as soon as possible and reward them for coping well with a whoops! Teach them that seeing a whoops! means things are going to change, but that this is a part of life – it isn't you being unfair or purposefully ruining their day. Begin with something small and quick, and prepare in advance. Gradually build on this, and your child will learn to recognise the symbol and mentally prepare for a change of plan when they see it.

A whoops! does not have to be a bad thing. It's a powerful symbol if you know that a change to routine triggers your child's anxieties.

Why the rainbow outline and funny shape for this visual? We need this visual to be instantly recognisable at your child's worst moment. Imagine you had a terrible migraine coming on and your vision is blurring or you are travelling on a train at super speed. The colour and shape may be all your child sees and will help them see some order during their worst moments.

Wipe clean boards

One of the most useful, cheap and easy things to have to hand is a dry wipe board and pen. Keep one in the car, in your bag (if it will fit) and somewhere to hand at home. You can use the board to quickly draw a visual 'Now and Next' (no cutting out or laminating required). Don't worry about your artwork – the simpler, the better. If something unexpected comes up, you can react calmly and draw what you are expecting – for example, 'shoes on', then 'outside'. This will be so much more effective than lots of speaking. Using the visual and drawing a visual representation not only calms the child but reduces our own anxiety and frustrations. We must be calm and controlled no matter what. A dry wipe board can really help with this. Just keep pointing to it and saying 'shoes on' calmly. Maybe they will follow the instruction, but it's also possible that they won't; having the visual means everyone is clear on the expectation and that the demand or instruction is coming more from the board and pen than from a person, which may make it easier to accept and follow.

Think about when you attend training, or think back to being at school. When the trainer or teacher draws up a simple schedule showing the structure and when there will be a break, everyone relaxes a little because they know the plan.

Patterns and charts

If you are seeing a behaviour on a regular basis but are not sure of the reason behind the behaviour, then making a note of it each time might just reveal a pattern. Note the time, the behaviour seen, the antecedent (reason if known) and the consequence, each time it happens. Schools and residential settings will have ways of inputting this data to reveal these patterns in a more detailed flow chart, but this is not necessary for one child. You may not even need to wait for long before having that 'aha' moment.

CASE STUDY
Hunger game... Adele Devine

When a child close to my heart was 4 he would challenge me a lot. I'm grateful now that he taught me so much about how children can be at home and how exhausting and relentless things can seem when there is no handover and no supportive teaching assistant. He was developing my empathy, but at the time it was not fun. This child is brilliant, but wow how he loved to mix things up and knew every button to press. It was tough and I was not being the mum I'd imagined. I knew I should have the skill set to be able to manage this, so why was it so difficult? I realised I needed to use all the training I had, get some perspective and think of this child as one of the children in my class.

I created some charts, which would break things down hour by hour. What I noticed quickly from the charts was that at around 11am was when the behaviour kicked in. That's when we might see some hitting, kicking or throwing. There was a pattern and when I saw it I felt a bit silly. We introduced a snack time at 10am and this made such a difference. He was hungry, blood sugar low and he didn't know, but he was showing me through behaviour. The snack didn't make things perfect, but it really helped. Sometimes we are so caught in the moment and so exhausted as parents that we miss what should be obvious.

Every hour of 'being good' meant a sticker on the chart; and while he liked his dinosaur stickers, the power only lasted so long so we upped the reward. A set of stickers for the morning meant he could have something from the mystery box. The mystery box was filled with cheap little toy cars and dinosaurs individually and quickly wrapped in tin foil. He loved this reward and it worked. I remember someone questioning using rewards, but all the time he was learning to control the behaviour. He was also taking pride in getting all his stickers and the praise he got from Daddy when he returned from work.

'As parents every one of us can get caught in the headlights and freeze when it comes to our own children's behaviour. It's so important to stop, seek advice, look for those patterns and try a new strategy.'

(Parent reflection)

Time and timers

Imagine if there was no such thing as time or if you had no concept of it. If you were going to visit the dentist and thought a painful appointment could be five minutes but it could also be five hours. Imagine that you were travelling on a busy underground or subway train and didn't know if your journey would be 20 minutes or last the whole day. Knowing how long things will last enables us as adults to stay with things we don't like. It is the same for our children. Having a visual timer can really help your child to stay with things because they know the expectation and can decide if they can stay with the activity. You may be able to use your watch or a visual timer app to show your child the passing of time.

It's also important for your child to know when things are going to change. An egg timer can be a great visual way to show five minutes. Build using the timer into each day so that a child gets used to knowing what it means.

I remember once when our daughter had a playdate coming to an end. Her little friend was getting frustrated because she didn't want to go home. Her mum was waiting at the door and telling her to come and put her shoes on, and things were starting to escalate. It was going to be a battle and the tantrum was bubbling. I said, 'Let's give her five minutes.' The mum agreed, but the girl looked puzzled. So I then showed her a five-minute timer and she was fascinated. In fact, so much so that she took it away with her when she left happily after the five minutes. My friend said it was an amazing thing and her daughter loved the timer and it had stopped many meltdowns. The term 'five minutes' may mean nothing, but seeing sand go through a timer for five minutes is powerful, mesmerising and understandable.

Time timers are another useful resource to have if a child needs a visual representation of time. They look like a clock face and show the time left reducing gradually.

The countdown

We don't always have a handy egg timer and we don't always have five minutes. Holding up your hand and doing a calm quiet countdown can be another way to say something is finished using a visual and language your child can understand. Hold up your hand and count down from five, putting one finger down each time: '5, 4, 3, 2, 1, soft play is finished.' Then pause and give them a bit of time. This calm countdown will have given you some space to regain composure, breathe, and feel less anxious and more in control.

Be consistent

Remember that really soft teacher you once had in school who was probably a really nice person but had no idea how to control the class? She would say one thing and then not stick to it. There were no real set expectations or boundaries, and everyone quickly learnt this. Our children learn about us in exactly the same way. Every child has the ability to do this, no matter how much they seem to be 'in their own little world'.

If you say 'five minutes' and show it on the timer, then mean five minutes. If you say 'one more biscuit', then stick to it. If you count down, don't continue the activity...

Our children know just how to push us and create their own rules. We quickly learnt with one of our sons that if we did something once then his expectation was that it would happen every time. Think about how these things can happen. If you go to the supermarket and buy one of those magazines with a toy on once and do it again the next time you are in the shop, then your child will rightly expect you to do this every time. Expect a meltdown when you go to the shop and don't buy the magazine. If you buy a dinosaur toy in the toy shop for no reason other than wanting to treat your child but don't make it clear, then they could expect this every time; if you always go to the shops and then stop at their favourite fast-food restaurant, they will see this as a part of the routine. All of these treats can lead to future issues as our children learn when treats happen and want to keep these routines in place.

We can treat children, of course, but try not to let them establish a treat routine (unless you can be consistent with it).

When shopping, mix up the order of the shops you visit. It may help to tell your child or provide a visual schedule of shops. This might sound like a lot of work but it is a lot easier than having to wait out a meltdown. Buggies can be a wonderful help with early transitions, but always have in mind that there will be a day when your child is too big to lift or to put in a buggy. The sooner they learn to transition successfully when you are out and about, the better.

Know your child and how much and how long they will cope with outings and shops, and set it up so you can make it a positive. A quick stop at a local shop to buy bread and biscuits is a better starting point than a huge supermarket shop. We must try to set children up to succeed, and gradually build our expectations.

Autism alert card

You may sometimes feel self-conscious about your child's behaviour in public or if you have encountered input from members of the public. If this is the case, it can be helpful to carry an autism alert card or exclamation card. These cards can be bought as standard from autism organisations, or you can make your own personalised ones.

They will include a simple explanation about autism and will mean that if someone stops to question your child's behaviour or comment on your parenting, then you can present them with the card. Autism is not visible but can bring many challenges, and being out in public you might feel judged and out of your comfort zone. These cards can stop tempers from bubbling, rescue the need for too much language and help restore the peace sooner.

When we feel judged, it affects our reactions, but it's important that you don't assume that everyone is judging or thinking negatively. There are so many people with invisible disabilities, and awareness is improving. If you are in public and your child is having a meltdown and someone is staring, then assume that the stares are in admiration of the empathy, control and patience with which you are managing the situation.

Zones of Regulation™

The Zones of Regulation[1] is a systematic, cognitive–behavioural approach developed by occupational therapist Leah Kuypers and used to teach self-regulation by categorising feelings into four coloured zones.

One of the ways we use Zones of Regulation at Portesbery School is by providing each child with their own lanyard with symbols relating to the four zones. On one side there are the faces they might have, for example, in the blue zone, which includes feeling sad, tired, bored or sick. On the other side there are personalised ideas for what the child might do to support them if feeling this way – maybe get a blanket, go to a sensory den, go for a walk outside or tell an adult.

The zones can be a good way to teach a child to respond to their feelings in a controlled way before they become overwhelmed by them.

Social Stories™ and Comic Strip Conversations

Social Stories™ were first created by Carol Gray in 1991.[2] They can be a great support strategy for explaining confusing situations, prewarning and explaining upcoming changes. They provide a kind, concrete voice

---

1   www.zonesofregulation.com/index.html
2   https://carolgraysocialstories.com

and a calming, consistent way of explaining things. Comic Strip Conversations were also devised by Carol Gray. They can be used to unpick situations and work out the thinking behind a behaviour. Simple stick figures are drawn to represent the people.

Reducing language by using visuals

So many of the strategies we use to help autistic children stay on track are visual and there are many good reasons why they are so effective with many children.

How do visuals support?

- Explaining when a child is not able to understand.
- Allowing time to process (language can be impossible to process when anxious).
- Making language consistent, calm and clear.
- Reducing language (too much language can create more anxiety).
- They seem like less of a demand (the symbols rather than a person say to do it).
- They show we are respectful of the child's need to know and be truthful.
- A familiar visual also suggests a familiar structure, which will seem less frightening.

If a child's behaviour is challenging or anxiety seems to be bubbling, here is a summary of supports that might help them:

- Symbols for communication.
- Familiar routines/structure.
- An individual visual schedule.
- A 'Now and Next' schedule.
- Sand timers and symbols.
- Ear defenders.
- A quiet tent or space.
- A mini trampoline.
- A rocking horse or chair.
- Climbing equipment.

CHAPTER 14

Communication and Interaction

'If Lucy did speak in sentences, it was from phrases that she had heard from Peppa Pig.'

(Lucy's Mum)

We would like to thank Neha Makwana (highly specialist speech and language therapist) for her valuable input and edits to this chapter. A little boy is standing in a garden. He is watching a tiny droplet of rain on a leaf. He is loving how that individual droplet moves and shines.

We are watching through a window. We are in the house, warm and in our comfort zone. We could all stay where we are, happy, but our issue is that we know this boy isn't going to learn to interact, play and communicate unless we do something.

So, what can we do? Should we call the boy inside and try to persuade him to engage with toys and books? Should we set up an activity and lead him in and help him complete it, hoping he will learn that it is fun and interesting? We could try these things, but it's likely that the most successful approach will be to learn to love what he loves in that garden. If we go outside and really look at that droplet of rain and show the boy that we also see something unique and beautiful, if we smile at the feeling of the rain and lift our hands up to touch it (as he does), then maybe we will become a little bit more interesting. Once the boy notices, accepts and trusts us not to disrupt, then maybe he will become more comfortable, happy, engaged and playful.

Go quietly and look in the same direction as your child. Learn to love what they love and be in the moment with them in their comfort zone. There is no need to speak unless they speak. If they make little sounds or funny noises, then you might replicate them. Now we have the starting point for interaction, play and communication. The first step is to build the child's trust – to show them that we are not trying to change anything. We are just wanting to be in their space and enjoy what they are enjoying.

Maybe their interest is playing with leaves, jumping, flipping a card, spinning a wheel or maybe they know the name and detail of every dinosaur. Perhaps you are not so sure what interests them. There will be something that interests them though. Spend some time watching and see what this reveals. Finding a child's motivator can be like finding the key which may eventually help them to interact, play and learn.

We know why we need to communicate. We need to be able to say what we want, to get the things we want and need. Being able to share and explain our feelings is important to our emotional wellbeing. We also want to learn and to share what we have learnt with others. We know that communication is essential to our physical and emotional wellbeing. Most importantly, it enables us to interact and develop relationships. When a child struggles with communication, it can be disheartening and alarming. When a child doesn't seem to want to communicate with us, when they seem to be 'stuck in their own little world', what can we do?

There are so many strategies to develop communication, and there is no one approach which will work for every child.

A child with communication difficulties should see a speech therapist. It may be that your child is already having regular speech therapy or you may be waiting at this stage. As parents, our first point of call when we have any concerns is often 'Google' and there we find a minefield of information. A lot of this will be good information, but there will also be misinformation and exaggeration.

So, what we want to provide here is a bit of a filter to signpost you to what we consider some of the 'good' information.

One of the tools speech therapists may refer to when speaking about a child's speech is the language pyramid.

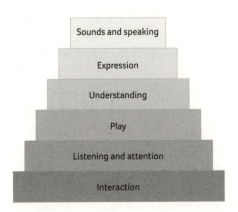

The language pyramid shows the foundations which need to be in place before speech. It provides a simple visual way to explain the rationale behind working on a child's interaction through strategies such as intensive interaction, then building attention through things that motivate and spark their individual interest or through Attention Autism[1] sessions; and then there is play, then understanding; and only after all these foundations are in place will we see expression and then speech sounds.

A speech therapist will suggest strategies appropriate to a child's current level of communication. Getting these foundations in place is so important.

Intensive interaction

In the early 1980s, Dr Dave Hewett OBE (Director of the Intensive Interaction Institute) was the Principal at what he describes as a 'very

---

1   https://ginadavies.co.uk

special, special school' in London. The school included many learners who for reasons including autism were still at the very early stages of communication. His team set about studying how all people develop communication during the early interactions in infancy.

Observe a mother interacting with a newborn baby. The baby does not yet have the language to have a conversation and yet they interact and bond through their facial expressions and movement. The newborn baby teaches the mother their pre-verbal language and they can enjoy these interactions. Then the newborn tires and the interaction pauses. It is very natural and child-led.

Hewett and his teaching team applied this research along with practice and 'trial and error' to develop an approach to develop communication through what would become known as 'Intensive interaction'.[2] They began to trial new ways to apply this knowledge and use it to develop interaction and encourage communication with students with severe learning difficulties and autism. 'Intensive Interaction works on early interaction abilities – how to enjoy being with other people – to relate, interact, know, understand and practice communication routines.'[3] Hewett explains that 'Intensive Interaction teaches and develops the "Fundamentals of Communication", attainments such as: use and understanding of eye contact, facial expressions, vocalisations leading to speech, taking turns in exchanges of conversation and the structure of conversation.'

CASE STUDY
Finding the way to play: Adele Devine

In our school we are lucky to have a room dedicated to sensory integration equipment, which is set up to help our students feel calm and organised and ready to learn. We call this 'sensory circuits'.

When we visited sensory circuits with J, he ran to a far corner. He had no interest in trying the equipment or engaging with anyone. The furthest corner seemed like a safe place and if anyone approached he would move away. He would be content as long as he was left in the corner, but there was no way he was going to join in.

---

2   For more information, see https://davehewett.com
3   www.intensiveinteraction.org/find-out-more/about-intensive-interaction

As the class got on with climbing up steps and balancing on benches, I went to the opposite corner at the other side of the hall far from J. He noticed this. J was shifting his weight from one foot to the other in his corner and I started to do the same in my corner. There was a little twinkle in J's eye. He had noticed I was doing the same as him. As the 'lesson' went on, J moved about three metres forwards. I did the same at the other end of the room. He then went back to his corner and I went to mine. He moved forwards and so did I. He decided to run and so did I. Eventually he was running across to my corner and passing me as I ran to his corner. He had the biggest smile on his face and we were having a wonderful connected time playing and running. We were interacting and he was noticing my potential to make things more fun for the first time. We were not doing sensory circuits, but we were making amazing progress with J's interaction, play and building communication skills through Intensive Interaction. That day I called J's Mum to tell her about this 'wow' moment.

In time, J's interaction developed and we introduced balloons and ball play. His engagement and confidence grew with the staff and other children.

After about four weeks, J was starting to use the sensory circuits. He was no longer in the corner. He was happier and more confident and willing to have a go.

Whenever I see J running about in the playground with a big smile lighting up his face, I remember that little boy who just wanted to stay in the corner.

. . . .

Building attention

Parents and professionals sometimes use the phrase 'stuck in their own little world' when talking about engaging with an autistic child. Some examples we have seen are a child who will spend hours sifting through sand, or lying on the ground and spinning the wheel of a toy car on repeat. We must not confuse this with a child who is able to self-occupy and completely engage in their own individual play.

Although children need to have time to do their own thing – and if this makes them comfortable and happy, that is okay – what we don't want is for the child to do this at all times, because whilst they are doing this they may also be zoning out a bit and not building those skills which are vital for them to learn to communicate.

So, what can you do? Initially, it is important to go quietly and join them for a bit. If they are sifting sand in a tub, get another tub and sift sand nearby. If they are lying down spinning the wheels of a toy car, go and get one and lie down somewhere nearby and spin the wheel in a similar way. Smile and enjoy what you are doing, and the child might find this interesting. You have to be interesting before they will want to pay attention to what you are doing.

Sprinkling flour, bubbles, water and mess making

Tune in to what a child enjoys and use this to gain and build their attention. Maybe they love cars; get a box of toy cars, build a ramp and send the cars down it one at a time. Maybe they love sprinkling flour; sprinkle some slowly from up above (be warned, this can be messy). Maybe they love water play; get watering cans and sprinkle from up high or blow bubbles in a tub of warm water and washing-up liquid. Do what they love and you will spark their interest and become a little bit more interesting. Suddenly they start to see that other people can be quite interesting too.

Attention Autism

Attention Autism is an intervention devised by Gina Davies (SaLT). It is a session that invites children to develop spontaneous communication through the use of visually based and highly motivating activities. Gina says in her training sessions that her primary objective is for the sessions to be fun and 'offer an irresistible invitation to learn'.

At the start of each session the person leading will depict what is going to happen by drawing a simple picture on a dry wipe board.[4]

Attention Autism sessions are highly motivating to children. They follow a set structure with a phase for each stage. The phase your child is at will depend upon their level of engagement and ability to sustain attention. This approach is highly effective for building and sustaining a child's attention, which is key to their progress with communication.

If your child is in an educational setting and needs to work on building attention, they will ideally be accessing this session at least

---

4   See https://ginadavies.co.uk for examples of this session in process.

a few times a week with a small group. If they are not, it is well worth suggesting. It is a highly effective way to build levels of engagement and help a child progress with communication.

For Stage 1 you will need a bucket, box or any other container filled with some things that will attract attention. Stage 1 is all about focusing attention. We write on a whiteboard '1' and then draw a bucket or whatever container we are using. The container is filled with highly motivating, attention-grabbing items. Some of the things children love most are a giant rainbow Slinky, balloon helicopters, a slinky wooden fish (we call this the slippery fish), a battery-operated yappy dog, any toys that dance or move about and any little wind-up toys. If a child is sound-sensitive, they might not like some of the noisy toys. Be aware and respectful of this and gauge by the child's responses how long things stay out of the bucket. The adult leader takes individual items out of the box and all adults respond with excitement and wonder as each item is produced. Language is repetitive, simple and consistent.

At stage two of Attention Autism, which is all about building the children's attention the adult leader will create something which is often big and visually appealing and often very messy. The children can't resist watching as paint, water, flour, feathers, tissue paper fall from above to create some amazing artwork.

There are lots of great examples on YouTube of creative Attention Autism sessions showing good practice.[5] Gina Davies also has a Gina Davies Autism Centre page on Facebook, which is worth following for inspirational ideas and updates.[6]

As a child becomes more interested and engaged in these sessions, they will sustain attention for longer.

CASE STUDY
Building and sustaining attention: Adele Devine

We knew from N's home visit that he liked plastic animals, dinosaurs and water play. He liked looking at books by Julia Donaldson (especially *The Snail and the Whale*) or lying in the little sensory room watching the lights projected on the walls. He was a quiet, soulful child and was very attached

5   Examples include Eggs, www.youtube.com/watch?v=Lose11EaRaM, and Traffic lights and zebra crossings, www.youtube.com/watch?v=rzbNF8lMNds
6   www.facebook.com/ginadaviesautism

to his lovely mum. Attention Autism or 'Box' was a session that happened every day at 11.30 as a part of the daily routine. At first N watched these sessions from a distance. Over time he started to join the group (sometimes he would be sitting on a big ball or the rocking horse) and staff would gradually edge him towards the group. He started to stay for Stage 1, when we would sing the familiar 'I've Got Something in My Box' song and take motivating items from the box.

One day, Stage 2 really grabbed his attention. Stage 2 activities are often quite big and messy. This particular time I was pouring paint onto a lazy Susan whilst spinning it on paper to make 'The World'. As I poured on the paint and spun the lazy Susan, N was completely engaged and excited. It was wonderful to see him like this. Such progress. The next day when we put out the chairs to set up the session, N came and sat down. N loves this session now and will usually come and sit. He can use a 'more' switch to ask for 'more' at Stage 1 and Stage 2. In class he is becoming more confident every day and he is a lot less quiet now. He is vocalising a lot more, exploring sounds in a way he never did before. He can still be soulful, but I would now add words like 'happy' and 'cheeky'. He still loves the books and the animals and rocking horse. The other day we were doing an Attention Autism session and N got up from his seat. We thought he might be leaving the group, but that was not his plan. He had seen that I was planning to make animal prints with potatoes for Stage 2. He walked over to the art table and got a bottle of blue paint and then came back and handed it to me. I used the blue paint on the potato and N sat watching and smiling.

N has been at school for a term now and we have seen amazing progress with his ability to sustain attention and communicate. I believe this progress is partly to do with the way he has settled, the happy atmosphere and communication-rich environment; but it's our regular Attention Autism sessions that have taught him that lessons are a worthwhile activity and have built the attention skills he so needed.

. . . .

Attention Autism aims to engage a child's attention and improve joint attention. It teaches children that adult-led sessions can be interesting and helps them to learn to join a group. The set structure and rules are so effective and encourage spontaneous communication through commenting (both verbally and by using communication books, switches or PECS®). The children repeatedly see others model ways to comment, and each time they see this they are a step closer to doing it themselves. These sessions are predictable in structure but exciting in content. Most importantly, they are a lot of fun. They are highly visual and are a brilliant way to build a child's communication skills.

Attention Autism is so effective at building attention and communication that it is a part of the daily structure in the Early Years Department at Portesbery School. Gina Davies is an inspirational and wonderful trainer, so if there is a chance of attending her training for professionals or parents, I would recommend it.[7]

We find that the Attention Autism sessions are a great way to introduce children to seeing other communication strategies modelled, such as using our class communication book, the 'more' switch or symbol and PECS® (if they are at a stage when they are motivated to comment).

Play

We see a group of children playing with the sand. Maybe there are diggers and the sand is being collected from one area and dumped in another, or there is a dinosaur being buried while a T-Rex is stomping over making big, satisfying footprints and getting ready to attack another dinosaur. Then there is a child who is taking handful after handful of sand and scattering it on the floor or a child who just won't touch the sand at all. We want the children to play in the way we imagine play should look, but the autistic child may see things differently. They may need more time, more obvious modelling (us showing them by playing ourselves and talking through the steps in simple language); or if they are intent on casting the sand, they may need a compromise (a big tub to cast the sand into) or to learn to put the sand into a sand-wheel tower. They may also prefer to play when there are fewer children at the table or no children at all.

We all learn different things at different rates. It is important to meet the autistic child where they are at and allow the progression to be gradual and supported.

Play is such a vital building block towards communication and we

---

7　https://ginadavies.co.uk/training

must invest lots of time and patience into helping the autistic child to learn to develop their play.

Interests, comfort objects and stims
Special interests

A child may have a special interest such as insects, leaves, trains or animals. Having a special interest is a joyful thing. If we trace back to childhood, many careers and hobbies start with a childhood interest and then continue to interest us as adults and bring us fulfilment. It's important to allow children to learn everything about something if that is what they love. It can be a great way to develop play, interaction and communication. Interests can also be a great motivator. If a child has a special interest, this may seem quirky, but the best thing to do is embrace it.

Comfort objects

A child may have a comfort object. Maybe it's a typical teddy or a pillow. Or it could be a toy car or animal or something random like a flip-flop. If they do have something like this, try to get at least one duplicate item. This comfort item can be helpful if a child is tired or anxious or starting something new, like school. Make sure they have it with them on that first day and let the teacher know how important it is to them.

Observe how your child behaves when they have their object. It may be soothing to them, but it may also be something they focus on and use as a stim to block out other things. It may be that if they are holding their CD case, they are completely absorbed in it and they will miss out on everything going on around them. It may be that they will need to learn to manage without their comfort items when they are comfortable in a space or they will not notice what is going on around them. Think about how some people can get absorbed by an app on their phone and will play a game again and again. As adults, we know that this is wasting our time and not doing anything for our wellbeing; we know that if we are on a train with nothing else to do, then playing a game or looking at Facebook is okay, but we would not get our phone out and play a game if we were at a friend's house for dinner or during a meeting (even if we felt like it). So, think of that game on the phone as a stim. We control when we do it. A child does not know about this control. If something soothes them or makes them happy, they will do it again and again and again. A child may love spinning the wheels of a car repeatedly and it's fine for them to do this, but at some point it is important that we direct them to something new to develop their play, such as sending that little car down a ramp. It is important to get the timing of this right. We must not be forceful, but give them the new idea by modelling the skill. Have your own little car and send it down the ramp. I would repeat this many times to plant the new idea without making any demands. If the child shows an interest, offer them the car. Keep language to a minimum.

If your child is not communicating what they want by speaking, they will probably have found some other way. What if they want something that is up in the cupboard? How do they communicate this? Children have different methods. Maybe they will cry and expect you to know what they want (we get to know our children quickly). They cry and we just know that they want a certain snack or drink. Maybe they will take your hand and lead you to the cupboard and push your hand up towards the cupboard. There is no mistaking what they want. They are communicating 'Open the cupboard' and you will then get them what they want (or not). But what if they were at school and they led the teacher to the snack cupboard and there were lots of different things in there. The teacher doesn't want to give them free access, but they really really want something specific. The teacher has no idea what it is. Maybe it isn't even in the cupboard. How will your child feel? They might be frustrated, angry, hungry, thirsty or in pain. How will they communicate these feelings – crying, throwing, banging, biting, or maybe they won't try to communicate at all. They will just feel anxious and exhausted. At home our children can tell us what they want. We know them so well and they know us too. But our children need to be able to communicate what they want in other situations.

Choices

Our children make clear choices and we learn their preferences quickly. As time goes on we almost don't need to ask. We know their favourite drinks and sweets, and we know the things that they would never tolerate. We learn what their favourite toys and activities are. Think about the choices your child has made. Maybe make a list. They can make a choice, but what we want them to learn how to do is to communicate that choice functionally with someone who does not know them so well.

We can begin by offering two things – toys or food are good solid objects. Your child reaches for one and you label it 'car' and hand it to them, then say, 'Bobby chose car' and smile. Once you have a known motivator and your child can make a clear choice, it can be a good time to introduce AAC (augmentative and alternative communication).

AAC (Augmentative and alternative communication)

This refers to communication methods used to supplement or replace speech or writing. They are useful strategies to be aware of for those with difficulties in the production or comprehension of language. As communication difficulties are often a part of autism, we will signpost some of these strategies. If you wish to learn more about any of them, there are websites, books and YouTube videos to explore. Please look, and if you feel they will suit the child, explore options for training and schools that will support them.

PECS® (Picture Exchange Communication System)

If your child is limited by the language they are using functionally and needing to develop a way to communicate, PECS can be so effective. Ideally, it will be introduced with the support and guidance of a speech therapist; but if you are not yet accessing speech therapy, then have a look at the website.[8]

There are six phases. At Phase 1 we teach the child to exchange a picture for a motivating item. As children will have learnt ways to get what they want at home (most often taking an adult by the hand and leading them to open the cupboard or box where the item is stored), it can be trickier to introduce at home than at school. It does take time so don't be disheartened. The more times the child uses the pictures the more opportunities they will have to learn. When introducing Phase 1 we need two adults. One adult will have the motivating item and the other will sit behind the child and physically prompt them to lift the picture and hand it over. As the child puts the picture in the adult's

8   https://pecs-unitedkingdom.com/pecs

hand, they are prompted to tap it, and the adult with the item says, for example, 'Spin toy' and immediately operates the motivating toy or hands over the item. Over time this prompt will fade as the child learns to lift the picture and make the exchange. The thing offered must be a highly desired item. Snack time can be a good time to introduce this (if a child is motivated by snacks). Offer small portions in order to increase the opportunities for exchanges.

Talking tiles and recordable voice switches

Some children are incredibly quick to pick up on strategies such as PECS® that involve using pictures to communicate; but if your child does not show interest in lifting a picture and handing it over to make an exchange, and you have tried this again and again, then it is worth seeing if they will take to using a switch. When using switches, it makes sense to follow stages similar to those used in PECS to help us monitor a child's progress.

Getting set up with switches

A recordable switch is a bit like a recordable button and is simple to set up. To set up, just add batteries and follow the instructions to record a message.[9] Keep it simple – 'more' and 'help' are good ones to start with. The child presses the button and the switch plays back a pre-recorded message. A child who does not have the inclination or motivation to lift a symbol may learn to press one of these buttons or talking tiles to get what they want.

The recordable switches we currently use are called Big Point switches. There is a plastic cover, which lifts off allowing you to put a photograph or symbol underneath. I'd recommend starting with 'more' (maybe they want more snack items or more tickles) or 'help' (to open a packet or to get something that is out of reach). Let your child see these symbolled switches used in context as often as possible.[10] Copies of the colour-coded symbols for your own switches can be downloaded from www.library.jkp.com/redeem using the voucher code KFMSQRC. You could put the 'toilet' switch outside the toilet door and press it

---

9 https://www.tts-group.co.uk/big-point-recordable-button/1003985.html
10 http://www.senassist.com/resources.html

each time you go in and press the 'finished' switch when it is time for an activity to finish. The other two switches can be used to create more opportunities for your child. You could use 'help' by the back door so they can request 'help' to open the door if they like to play outside; or maybe keep a 'help' switch by the remote control so they press 'help' when they want the television on. As your child starts to discriminate between these four symbols, you could start to add other symbols or photographs such as 'outside' or 'water play'.

Below are some tips on how to introduce a single 'more' or 'help' switch in Stage 1.

- *'More' switch:* We are not expecting your child to discriminate and we want to keep it simple. If there is something they like, you could start with a 'more' switch, with the word 'more' recorded on it and a 'more' symbol. To introduce this you will ideally have someone else to help (someone your child likes and trusts). This person can support your child to learn to press the switch by gently directing their hand towards it and helping them to press it. They can also model using the 'more' switch by pressing it and then getting something that they want. This may be 'more' snacks (give them a little at a time), but it could also be 'more tickles', 'more sand' or 'more silly noises'.
- *'Help' switch:* A 'help' switch can be strategically placed on a fridge with a fridge lock, on the wall below the high shelf where a favourite object is kept or on the kitchen table. If there is anything your child might ask for 'help' with, then they can use it to get 'help'.
- *Instigating:* Once your child has learnt that pressing the switch gets them what they want and they no longer need hand-over-hand help to press it, the 'more' or 'help' switch can be placed near them and they will start to press it spontaneously. You could use it on the snack table, for example, if food is a motivator, and the child learns to press it to get 'more' snacks or 'help' opening a packet. Use whatever motivates them – water being poured, flour sprinkled into a tray...
- *Discriminating switches:* Once your child is consistently able to use one switch successfully, it is time to introduce another to see if they are able to discriminate between two switches.

CASE STUDY
Starting out with switches: Adele Devine

We had been trying for some time to get J to exchange a symbol for something he wanted. J might want something, but not enough to go to the trouble of getting a symbol and handing it to us. No matter how many times we tried and J's parents tried, we were not progressing with PECS®. J wouldn't lift the symbol and always needed hand-over-hand help. Often this stage does take a really long time, but despite our persistent efforts over a long period we knew we needed to try something else.

J loved tickles. We had tried to get him to use a 'more' symbol to ask for 'more' tickles. He would do this with hand-over-hand assistance, but we could not get him to make the leap to an independent exchange. J was happy to press a switch to say 'Good morning' at circle time so we decided to try using a 'more' switch. J quickly picked this up and was able to ask again and again. He would press the 'more' switch and we would say 'more tickles' and he would get tickles for about 30 seconds before he would need to request this again. J was very good at using the switch and learnt to use it in other situations. We would have the switch on the table at snack time and J would press it for 'more'.

J was in a class of children with severe learning difficulties and most of these children were using PECS at snack time, so he would see lots of other children exchanging symbols. Seeing other children and staff constantly model using PECS was so helpful. We kept the switch there and also made a 'more' symbol available to him, but continued to encourage the PECS exchanges with support. After about a month, J made his first independent PECS exchange. After this, J started to make excellent progress by using PECS. He was soon discriminating between a range of symbols, turning the pages of his PECS book and making multiple spontaneous PECS exchanges. He learnt to gain our attention and create the sentence 'I want tickles', finding the right symbols in his PECS book. He also learnt to use a communication book to comment on colours and animals during structured sessions and play, and to make song choices. It was amazing to see how he progressed once he realised that it was possible and worth his while to communicate with us.

Note: All the time we use switches, we continue working on Phase 1 of PECS because a child can still learn to use PECS at any time (as was the case with J).

• • • • • • • • • •

Communication books

A communication book contains pages of symbols for words and phrases we use every day when speaking. These symbols are organised by category. Each page has a number of symbols, which will depend on the size and number the child works best with. In the early years class at Portesbery School we find that having 12 symbols on each page works as a resource for the whole class. You could have more or less depending on what works best for your child.

Categories in a book might include:

- I like (favourite things or activities).
- Colours, numbers and shapes.
- Feelings.
- Parts of the body.
- Favourite song choices.
- Farm animals.
- Transport.
- Anything else of high interest – dinosaurs, jungle animals, etc.

The book provides a way for us to communicate and model speech consistently.

When people are speaking, an autistic child might not be able to process the language. They may hear a jumble of sounds, and when they try to get a clue from facial expressions, things become even more confused.

Without being able to decode what's being said, how can a child learn the language skills they need to speak? Frustration may set in. They can't tell us, so we start to see challenging behaviour, or maybe they become isolated. They cannot find a way to join in, so they self-soothe and withdraw.

Even if a child is not ready to point and comment, they will be watching and learning when they see us using the communication book.

One of the lovely things is that access to the symbols provides pre-verbal children with opportunities to make extra comments and requests. They could choose the emotion for 'If You're Happy and You Know It' or the animal in 'Old MacDonald Had a Farm'. We have found that children often love to use the communication book at home and at school.

Some children will use the book as a way of creating calm and controlling adult language. A favourite page is often the transport page. I have found that a child might take your finger and get you to point and name the different transports. They will be hearing 'car', 'helicopter', 'motorbike', 'bus', 'train' again and again, and this activity is calming. While they are controlling, they are also learning the words and the associated symbols, and listening and interacting on their own terms.

The feelings page can be used to label how you think a child is feeling; or if a child is hurt, you could point to the 'pain' feeling and turn the page and point to the area where the pain is. For example, 'pain', 'knee' if they have grazed their knee. Showing the child how to do this might mean that one day when they have an invisible pain such as a toothache, they will have a way of communicating this.

Children often enjoy using the 'feelings' page to make choices with an adapted version of 'If You're Happy and You Know It'. Favourites are: 'If you're sad and you know it, have a cry', followed by pretend crying; 'If you're tired and you know it go to sleep', followed by a dramatic yawn and falling asleep. Funnily enough, they also love an 'angry' verse, and the more cartoonish, dramatic 'angry' you do it, the happier they will be. This control over your emotions is great fun, but it is also a great way of learning to recognise, regulate and communicate emotions.

The book can also provide less assertive children the chance to get a turn at choosing a song or commenting on a colour. All the time we use the book the children are seeing an alternative way to communicate modelled. The communication book seems like such a simple strategy to develop communication but is so brilliant.

PODD

The initials stand for:

- *Pragmatic:* ways that we use language, both socially and with purpose.
- *Organisation:* a systematic way to order words and symbols.
- *Dynamic Display:* changing pages for a wide vocabulary and a wider range of statements.

PODD was developed by Gayle Porter, a speech pathologist with the Cerebral Palsy Education Centre in Victoria, Australia. It was initially developed and used with learners with cerebral palsy, many of whom have severe communication difficulties but are very able cognitively. The PODD system was a huge book of vocabulary organised in such a way to allow the user to develop their ability to communicate.

One of the things that hits home and is highlighted during the PODD training is the number of times we model speech for a child before they learn to use it, and how when children start speaking they choose words they have heard modelled every day. It makes sense that we should model using AAC communication systems in the same way. This system needs to be modelled multiple times with the autistic child, in a way that puts no pressure on them, before they may choose to interact with it.

The communication books we use at Portesbery School were first developed by our speech therapy team as a way of simplifying the more complex and weighty PODD book we had in the classroom. To make the book quicker to navigate, we added tabs or markers at the bottom of the page. Our autistic learners do not always have the same levels of patience to wait for a teacher to find the right page, so we had to make it fast, motivating and fun. Using visuals can seem a bit over-whelming and unnatural at first, so a good way to start is by creating a visual showing different colours. Point to the colour as you say the colour word. Or, if a child has a special interest such as dinosaurs, then link the communication board with this (use whatever will motivate your child). As you model using these visuals, you will be building foundations for your child to use them too. They may not seem to be interested, but they will be observing and potentially listening and learning each time you point to a symbol and say the word.[11]

Signing

Signing can help build communication skills. Imagine trying to have a conversation with someone through a thick glass window and you can't hear what is being said. You need to tell the person inside to

---

11 For more information, visit https://novitatech.com.au/equipment/podd-comm-unication-books

open the door and let you in because you have forgotten your key. How would you communicate this? There would be a lot of pointing and signing. Signing is a natural strategy when we are not able to communicate using speech.

Signing can help us to gain the child's attention and helps illustrate what we are trying to communicate. The autistic child may have perfect hearing, but they may not be able to process or decode language.

Makaton is a language that uses signs along with symbols and speech. Makaton signs are often used by staff in special needs schools. Makaton run training courses and there is a lot more information available on their website.[12]

Search YouTube for episodes of *Something Special* (the BBC's award-winning children's programme) which features Mr Tumble, played by Justin Fletcher, who uses Makaton symbols and signs to support speech throughout each programme.

Good signs to learn to start with are 'more', 'finished', 'help', 'toilet', 'yes', 'no', 'please', colours and the farm animals. It would also be good to learn to sign the initial letter of a child's first name, siblings' names and 'Mummy', 'Daddy' or any other people who are important to the child. There are images and videos of most signs available on the Internet.

Communication through typing

It's amazing how much we now all rely on typing to communicate with each other, whether it be texts, emails, apps such as Discord, or other mediums. Our children are often very tech savvy and this is an area where the autistic child may really excel. If the child is not motivated to learn to type but they are motivated to use the technology, then you can teach a child to type their name by making it a password to access the computer. Typing could become a way for them to communicate in future (especially if they are not speaking). They can type to chat to friends on Discord or by text. Typing to communicate is a skill for life. Think how often people communicate at work through emails and chats. Even Teams and Zoom have a function where typing a message is totally acceptable. We live in an age where technology enables those with the ability to type to communicate effectively in many ways.

12 www.makaton.org

Jamie Knight is a web developer and accessibility speaker with Asperger's. Jamie lets the audience know when he speaks publicly that he might communicate by typing as sometimes he finds speaking difficult. In an interview with BBC iPlayer Jamie explained:

> I started building sites when I was nine, so about 15 years ago. I first built websites about my hobbies (mountain biking, Lego) then started building sites for others such as my school. I have Asperger's, which is a form of autism, so I got somewhat obsessed with the world of the web and as I grew older the obsession grew.[13]

Working in web development, Jamie is able to communicate effectively by typing, so on days when anxiety stops him from speaking he can still communicate effectively. If you get a chance to see Jamie Knight (also known as 'Jamie & Lion') speaking about his experiences with autism and communication, we'd recommend it.

Speaking

Speaking is at the top of the language pyramid. Verbal children may still need help with how they communicate. The autistic child may be speaking non-stop and not listening. Turn-taking activities can help with this. They may be echoing language they have heard on favourite television programmes rather than having conversations. Lots of role play could help build up their use of everyday language. They may need to work on the volume of speech. They may speak in a whisper or be far too loud (almost shouting) and not know this. A visual volume control might help. Speech can also get louder when a child is anxious, so that's something to be aware of too.

There are so many foundations required before a child speaks fluently; and even when they are speaking, they will still be learning communication skills. It's important not to be disheartened and keep on working at whatever stage a child is at. It can be saddening and frustrating for parents when a child doesn't meet communication milestones, but it is very important that parents recognise the stage their child is at and use strategies to meet them where they are. It's tempting

---

13   www.creativebloq.com/netmag/jamie-knight-21410667

to want to rush things, but communication skills will not improve if a child is put under pressure. The words need to be allowed to slip out spontaneously. Interaction and play are the keys to progress.

So go now and sit quietly near the child, observe what they are doing, smile brightly and learn to love what they love.

CHAPTER 15

Eating, Drinking and Nutrition

'I separate foods as much as possible and always give him a choice so he feels more in control. At the beginning this was just showing two choices hurriedly drawn on a white board. As his understanding has developed, I can verbally give him the choice or show him the food to help him decide.'

(Parent reflection)

A child refusing food will trigger all sorts of anxieties. We know that they need to eat in order to survive and thrive. If your child is not eating or drinking or has an extremely limited diet, it's important to start by recognising all the feelings you might be having.

Anxieties you could be passing on to your child

- *Anxiety and worry:* If my child doesn't get the food and drink they require, they will not be healthy. They will not thrive. They may not survive.
- *Frustration and anger:* Why won't they just eat or drink like other children do? Why is it such a battle? Aghhhh!!
- *Hopelessness and sadness:* I'm a bad parent because I can't even get them the nutrition they need.
- *Embarrassment and social anxiety:* People must think I'm a bad parent, that it's all my fault. Is it all my fault?
- *Fear:* What will the future hold for my child? Will they need to be fed through a tube to get the nutrients they need? If they don't eat or drink, they won't thrive. This is serious. You need to eat and drink to stay alive.

If your child isn't eating or drinking, you will relate to some of these feelings. It would be impossible not to. But now think about a time when you or someone you know has been so upset or anxious you either couldn't eat or overate. It can go both ways. As adults, we can often pin these feelings down and look at triggers and rationalise. But your child will not be able to do this. They will be carrying their own anxieties, and they will also be feeling yours. Imagine that every one of your feelings was transferring to your child, that they are feeling all these emotions and they don't know what they are. Every time food or drink are a part of the social conversation, the anxiety bubbles and this leaves them with fight or flight responses. The adrenalin may kick in and all they then feel is fear. What do we do when we feel like this? We probably wouldn't feel much like eating. We certainly wouldn't feel like being daring and trying something new. So, the first step towards getting your child eating is to try your best to remove all of these extra anxieties.

Forming a positive relationship with food

Imagine this scenario. Your child has just got a new pet (let's say a hamster). Your intention is that this pet will bring them comfort and joy. They reach into the cage and the hamster bites their finger and won't let go. When it eventually does, your child's finger is bleeding. You scream and slam the cage shut and comfort your child. You feel angry, panicky and anxious (all natural feelings) and your child picks up on all these feelings, which naturally intensify the situation. It will take a lot of work for your child to ever want to touch any hamster again. They won't just have learnt not to trust that hamster, but all hamsters.

Well food is just like that. Maybe they once took a bite of something and just went 'Yuck' and that yuck moment created a memory meaning they would never take the risk again. It will take a lot of work and time to learn that not all foods are going to be 'Yuck'. In the meantime let them have access to the foods they do trust and introduce the others through sensory play, cooking and modelling by eating a range of foods yourself, enjoying them and being okay.

Your child may be linking food with all sorts of negative feelings, so the first thing to do is to go back to the roots of their relationship with food and start again. Introduce food as something fun without any pressure at all to eat. Make a mess and get your child interested. Let them see you, and ideally another child, having fun – sprinkling and touching and smelling through sensory play. Don't be forceful. They will need time to form this new relationship and understand that you are not expecting them to eat the food (yet)!

Recognise that it's not just your child who needs to rebuild a relationship with food.

Yuck foods

Maybe you are the sort of person who will eat anything, but is there any one thing you absolutely hate? There will be some foods your child may never take to. Bananas and tomatoes are typical ones. Just be aware of this. As you introduce new foods, try to choose ones which are related or have similarities. For example, if they will eat Cheerios, try introducing other cereals of a similar colour or texture. Be subtle in your approach and don't put them under pressure or add demands. Have the new food available and out, or give it to another child first. Use lots of positive reinforcement. Say 'Yum' and smile when you eat some. They might get curious and want to try it.

Routines

Having set routines can help reduce anxieties and enable the child to feel more in control of a situation. If possible, set times for breakfast, snacks and mealtimes.

Don't make mealtimes last forever, but when they are finished put the food away as this will reduce the likelihood of a child learning to graze.

If your child really resists being in the area where food is served and you feel it's the right time to have this battle, then I would suggest using a five-minute egg timer. This will limit the time and provide them with a visual to focus on. You are requesting that they stay in the area for five minutes and then they can leave. By doing that, they are learning that nothing bad happens during those five minutes.

The more anxious people are, the more that routines can help. The more things are the same the more children will be able to make that leap to try new things. Routines will make your child feel safe, in control and likely to have a go.

Daniel Tammet, author of *Born on a Blue Day*,[1] explains the importance of routines to him: 'I get anxious if I can't drink my cups of tea at the same time each day. Whenever I become too stressed and I can't breathe properly, I close my eyes and count. Thinking of numbers helps me to become calm again.'

Counting, countdowns and visual timers can all help calm the anxious child. Keep language simple, predictable and calm. Use visuals where possible. These strategies are tried and tested and they will help.

Drinking

We know the importance of drinking and can probably regulate it, but there are products out there to help us drink water to optimise health. Have you seen those water bottles with markers to indicate quantities of water you should be drinking throughout the day? Without these products we will still drink water. We will get thirsty and get a drink. Your child may not be able to recognise or link the feeling of thirst with going to get a drink. They will need to be reminded by you handing them a water bottle. In time they may make this link.

---

1   Published in 2006 by Hodder & Stoughton.

From bottle to cup

Your child may have learnt to drink from a baby bottle and refuse to transition to a cup. You will see other children transition onto sippy cups or other drinks bottles. They may refuse to drink anything but the milk they are used to from their bottle. As they are starting preschool, you will naturally want them to be like all the other children. If so, take advice from a teacher. Please stop worrying. A good preschool will want your child to start happy and comfortable. They will work with you to support your child in learning to vary their drinks and drink from cups. This will happen, but as with everything else your child may just need a bit more time.

If you want to add more water and reduce the milk, very gradually add water to the milk. Do this in the smallest steps and don't let your child know about it. They will be watching and listening, so you will need to be in stealth mode for this to work.

Overeating

Overeating is a less common issue, but if your child does seem to be overeating and it looks as though they are gaining weight, it would be a good idea to monitor this and not allow them to get into bad habits.

- Keep a food and drink diary and make a note of current weight and height (this is the first thing your GP will suggest you do), so it's better to do it as soon as you are concerned. Ask others to provide this information too (anyone who might give your child food).
- You could consider restricting access if your child is helping themselves to food. You could have a fridge lock and cupboard lock or keep any snacks somewhere they can't access.
- Reduce portion sizes at meals.
- Keep snacks in small pots or bags so your child knows when they are finished. They may not know to stop eating without some structure.
- Think about replacing high-sugar unhealthy snacks with alternative healthy snacks.
- Consider your own eating habits and those of others in the

family. Do the children have good role models? Reflect on your own relationship with food. Do you reach for food when you are worried, overloaded or anxious, or does anyone else close to your child?

- Do not talk about these concerns in front of your child as you don't want to feed their anxiety or make them think there is any issue.
- Seek professional support and advice.

Over-drinking

Some children need to be encouraged to have a sip of water and then there are others who drink a lot more than seems usual.

If a child is drinking a lot and they are still in nappies, they will be really wet and heavy each time you change them.

Monitor the amount the child is drinking and keep a diary. Your GP will ask for this if you approach them with any concerns.

The amount of fluid a child needs will depend a bit on the weather and their level of activity. It will also depend on the type of foods they eat.

Assuming 70–80% of fluid in the diet comes from drinks (20–30% from food) the EFSA (European Food Safety Association) recommendations from drinks only are equivalent to 1.1–1.3 litres per day for 4–8-year-olds, 1.3–1.5 litres per day for 9–13-year-old girls and 1.5–1.7 litres per day 9–13-year-old boys.[2]

Medication

What about when your child needs to take some medication because of illness? A lot of children are persuaded by the sugary taste of children's medications, but a child with a restricted diet will be trickier. A social story or Comic Strip Conversation[3] may help explain the 'why?'. Having a doll or teddy who needs medication to use as a model before your

---

2   British Nutrition Foundation, www.nutrition.org.uk/healthyliving/hydration/hydration-for-children.html#:~:text=Assuming%2070%2D80%25%20of%20fluid,9%2D13%20year%20old%20boys

3   https://carolgraysocialstories.com

child has it can also be helpful. Build this 'feeling poorly' into role play when you can, so when your child needs medicine it all seems more normal. The syringe that comes with the medication may work better than the spoon as it will not have the same food association. Some parents find they can put medication in the child's milk. If that works, then great, but do keep a close eye that only they can access the milk, and think about timings and dosage. It really depends how sensitive your child is to the taste of the milk. For some children this will not work at all and could even put them off drinking the milk.

Some things to avoid

- Don't talk about your child's eating issues to other adults (your child will be listening).
- Avoid always buying exactly the same brand of things they will eat.
- Avoid things like gravy or sauces touching foods they will tolerate (maybe use a plate with dividers).
- Don't cut or break food (if they like things whole).
- Avoid using a tablet or phone as a distraction if you have not started this (it will not always be possible).
- Avoid letting them graze if possible (eating a bit, wandering off, returning or walking around with food).
- Avoid introducing new foods or challenges when your child is tired or anxious.
- Avoid letting your child learn to fill themselves up with milk or high-calorie protein drinks.
- Avoid getting stuck with what they will eat and giving this to everyone else.

Ideas for food play

- Cornflour and water on a tray with some food colouring makes an irresistible and fascinating goop.
- Add wild animal or dinosaur toys to make footprints in dough.

- Add toys, tubs, colanders, spoons and forks to mash, squish and smell jelly.
- Cooked spaghetti or other pasta shapes. Don't be afraid to make a mess. Model by getting your hands in and show you are having fun. Make it funny!
- Feeding the dolls, dinosaurs, mini beasts or trains (whenever they like). The more the child experiences the idea without it being imposed on them, the better.

Cooking

If food is an anxiety, then involve your child in cooking. This can be an extension of the food play. Again, no pressure to eat, but make it fun and don't be afraid of mess. Use the sieve and shake the flour or icing sugar from above. Some children just can't resist the sight of sprinkling or pouring, so go for height to maximise the drawing. It's not about the end result so much as the getting there. The longer your child stays engaged, the more they will build tolerance and develop positive associations with food.

When asked for advice about helping children who are picky eaters, Dr Temple Grandin's advice was 'Food preparation – just get them involved with that. They get to play with it and they might want to taste it.'[4]

Food fears

Never belittle your child's fear of food. When I was a child, I remember how it felt to be terrified of trying certain foods. It wasn't just being fussy. The idea of certain foods was simply revolting. I had foods I would eat and foods I wouldn't. It's important to show you understand these feelings and also respect them. Don't be forceful because a child needs to know they can trust you. Give them lots of time, but never give up, and celebrate the little wins. When they do make a step forward, celebrate quietly so that they don't think it is a big thing. Recently at school, when a child picked up a sausage, I wanted to jump for joy; but

---

4   Autism Live (April 2020) 'Dr Temple Grandin on Getting Kids to Eat Food', www.youtube.com/watch?v=JzeTdFugteQ

if I had, that same child would have put the sausage down in shock at my reaction. A non-reaction meant that they ate the sausage. You might want to shout 'Hooray' and phone your partner, but don't. Your child needs things to be normal, because normal feels safe.

Little wins and celebrations

- Tolerating being around cooking.
- Picking up a new food.
- Tolerating a new food on the plate.
- Touching foods.
- Sitting at the table when others eat.

Make sure the child is around other children eating and can always access the food to have a try (on their terms).

Naoki Higashida, who is non-verbal and disgnosed autistic, wrote an insightful book, *The Reason I Jump*, by typing out words using facilitated communication and rapid prompting when he was just 13 years old. Higashida observes, 'You could say, "because their sense of taste is all messed up" and have done with it. But couldn't you also say that they just need more time than the average person to come to appreciate unknown food?'[5]

CASE STUDY
From cheerios to sushi: Adele Devine

L had a very, very restricted diet and would only eat about five foods which had to be the same brand. He had learnt that these things were okay and 'safe' and there was no convincing him to try other things.

At school L would only eat the things from his packed lunch and never try anything new. If anyone tried to encourage him, he would make a high-pitched noise and do anything to resist. It was a very big and very real issue.

At snack times L had his set routine: Cheerios in his pot from home and nothing else.

We started cooking sessions where the children would each make their

5   Higashida, N. (2007) *The Reason I Jump*. London: Sceptre, p.90.

own food from scratch using their own set of equipment. The first term we made bread. L started to sneak little tastes of the ingredients. We didn't react but turned a bit of a blind eye (secretly thrilled). We started by making bread and were amazed when L decided to eat the bread roll after it was baked. It did smell good! We started to add variety, and each time he ate his creation. He was even eating pepperoni pizza. L's mum started to recreate the cooking sessions at home and gradually L, who had been so anxious around food and so restricted in what he would try, was trying all of his creations. He wasn't just eating bread-based foods, but crab fish cakes and even sushi. L is in his teens now and eats a wide variety of foods. You would never really know that food was an issue.

L's story is just one of many, many children who seemed too anxious ever to move forwards with food. Please know that your child can make this progress too. One day you will take them to a restaurant and see them eat a whole plate of food and a dessert after. Believe in the one day. If you relax and keep up with the sensory play and the cooking, that one day will happen.

Fast forward ten years. Here's an update from L's mum:

> These days he is rather curious about foods/dishes he hasn't tried before and will often ask, 'What does it taste like?' He is usually happy trying them… He doesn't like everything he tries, but I can't remember the last time he gagged when he disliked something. So very different than the little boy who lived on chicken nuggets and cornflakes…

> 'Moving to solids was incredibly slow and was the first time I felt a bit of concern. We try to make mealtimes as social as we can, eating all together where possible to lead by example.'

(Parent of S)

CHAPTER 16

Starting School

'We had the most amazing teacher and staff team at our son's first school place. Not only did they give our son the very best start in life but they supported our family through some of our hardest times.'

(Parent reflection)

Suddenly finding the right school for your child can seem so much more complicated. Maybe you had a plan in place before they were even born, such as the local preschool, which is within walking distance of your house, then on to the local primary school and secondary school. You may have even chosen the location of your home because of the schools in the area. But suddenly that plan doesn't quite fit your child's needs as well as you had expected. Maybe they are already at the local preschool and don't seem happy or settled.

Early intervention

Reading about autism, you will no doubt find mentions of the importance of 'early intervention', and if your child is at home or in a setting that does not seem to be meeting their needs, you may start to feel a sense of panic. We will do anything to assure our children have their needs met, but this can suddenly seem overwhelmingly difficult. Well, the first thing we would advise parents is to stay calm and not to panic. You will be wanting everything in place immediately, which is only natural. But one of the most vital 'interventions' to enable the autistic child to learn is to be in a calm, quiet space with smiling faces, predictable adults and routines. All of these are things a child can access at home. Each child is individual, so there is no set of interventions to suit all, but *every* child benefits from the care of a calm adult providing them with unconditional love, positivity and praise. There are many ideas for ways you can work with your child in this book. You can create an early intervention toolkit tailored to your child. If you are concerned about behaviour, go to Chapter 13. If you are concerned about communication, see Chapter 14 or the online chapter at https:// library.jkp.com/redeem for ideas.

Asking for help

One of the first things a child needs to learn is how to ask for help, but it is something we adults sometimes forget we can do. Don't worry about asking the wrong professional, because it is very likely they will be able to signpost you to the right one. Even taking this step will make you feel you are taking action.

Set some targets

When planning for learning, your child's teacher will have all sorts of outcomes and targets and ways of assessing progress. When a child requires extra support, they will also have targets which are specifically tailored to their individual needs. In the early years (under five) in the UK these targets are evaluated and reset every six months and annually after that. They can be ambitious but they must also be achievable in that time frame.

There is no reason why you can't start thinking about setting targets and tracking progress. In time you should have a group of professionals setting these targets with you as part of the EHC plan in the UK.

Targets can be linked to four areas:

1. Communication and interaction.
2. Cognition and learning.
3. Sensory and physical.
4. Social, emotional and mental health.

Communication and interaction

Think about where your child is in terms of communication. Think of any challenges they have and what the next steps might be. If they have no speech at all, then perhaps begin with a target based on Intensive Interaction (see Chapter 14). Or maybe they need help sounding some words out or putting two or more words together or commenting or waiting for another person to speak.

Every child is an individual, which is the reason we set individual targets; but to provide an idea and a starting point, some communication targets we may set in the early years could be:

- To increase engagement during Intensive Interaction with an adult for three minutes or more.
- To communicate 'more' by using a switch, Makaton sign or symbol – for example, asking for 'more' bounces on the therapy ball.
- To communicate 'help' by using a switch, Makaton sign or symbol – for example, getting 'help' to open a packet of crisps.
- To learn to take turns in conversation through scripted conversation and role play.

Cognition and learning

So much of learning happens through play, but sometimes the autistic child can seem to get a little bit 'stuck' in the same activity. They might be self-occupying and seem engaged in what they are doing – down time is important to us all, but are they learning? This area is vast, with some children needing to learn to look at what others are doing, and others who know the name of and a great number of facts about every dinosaur, and those who can read before they have even been taught to. For the child who needs to work on attention, see the section in Chapter 14 on Attention Autism. For the child who knows all those dinosaur names, you may think they need to learn about something else or learn to follow a teacher's agenda, or it could be working on reading or another area they have less interest in.

Again, to provide an idea and a starting point, some 'cognition and learning' targets the child may be set in the early years could be:

- To sustain attention for five minutes or more during Phase 1 of Attention Autism.
- To sustain attention for three phases of Attention Autism and take part in turn-taking activities.
- To learn to recognise and order the letters of my name through matching activities.
- To complete a set of four structured tasks that I have learnt to do independently without any verbal or physical prompts.

Sensory and physical

Another huge area is sensory and physical development. You may wish to focus on an aspect of personal care (e.g. toileting, dressing, brushing teeth), touching new foods, using cutlery or staying at the table. This area also includes getting dressed, wearing shoes, art and messy play, transitions between activities or locations and things like learning to ride a bike.

To provide an idea and a starting point some sensory and physical targets we may set in the early years could be:

- To gradually build my tolerance of messy play and start to accept messy hands during art activities and sensory play.
- To lift prefilled spoonfuls of preferred food to my mouth independently.
- To learn to recognise and respond to the symbol for 'toilet' and transition to the toilet with an adult when I have had time to process the request.
- To learn to write my name independently when I complete a worksheet or art activity.

Social, emotional and mental health

This is another huge area and such an important area of focus for all children, but particularly the autistic child. The area and range of targets is again huge. You may want your child to be able to communicate to you when they are happy, sad or in pain, to learn to separate from you, to sleep in their own bed (or just sleep!). Or perhaps they need to work on social skills and friendships.

Some social, emotional and mental health targets we may set in the early years could be:

- To build my tolerance of being around other children by joining small groups in the sensory room or soft play area.
- To become familiar with symbols linked to routines using a 'Now and Next' board and placing symbols on transition boards independently.
- To learn to recognise and comment on emotion by using symbols for 'happy', 'sad', 'tired', 'cross' and pain', using the communication book.
- To learn to use Comic Strip Conversations[1] to develop a way to support me talk to adults and reflect calmly on things that have happened.

So, it's time to take that step and find a school to support your child. Don't worry. There is amazing provision out there and there are also plans for new schools to support the growing number of children requiring specialist support. Training and awareness are improving all the time. Most teachers will have some practical experience of supporting an autistic child in their class. You may be absolutely set on your child staying in mainstream school and that is natural, but if you believe they might have a difficult journey, do have a look at other provisions You want your child to be in an environment where they feel comfortable and happy. There is no harm in looking.

---

1   https://carolgraysocialstories.com

Break things down

A lot of tasks can seem impossible and overwhelming unless they are broken down into manageable chunks. Think of driving a car. We don't just get in and drive. We go through lessons – some more than others! We know that there are stages and steps to learning. The autistic child may not accept or understand there are stages to learning. They expect to be able to pick up a pen and draw amazing artwork. Not being able to is frustrating and stops them wanting to lift a pen. It's important that new tasks are set up in a way that allows them to succeed – for example, placing the final piece in an inset puzzle rather than completing the whole thing. Make the tasks visually clear and achievable. It's worth reading up on TEACCH® structure for more ideas about breaking tasks down into achievable steps.

CASE STUDY
Making the overwhelming achievable: Adele Devine

F's primary school requested that all children wear Velcro shoes as teachers did not have time to tie lots of laces. In the final term of school, F came home upset. The teacher had set homework for them to learn to tie their laces. He felt this was impossible. F's mum knew about breaking things down and making things achievable. She set him three targets with visuals.

1. Find a shoe with laces.
2. Put one lace in each hand.
3. Tie a knot.

The first two were easy but the third was a bit of a challenge. However, F kept trying. F's mum sent the 'work' into the teacher. She was really proud of him for staying calm and trying so hard. F was able to tie his laces by the time he got to secondary school.

· · · · · · · · · ·

Things to look out for when trying to find the right preschool setting for your child

1. You should feel incredibly welcome. Staff should give you time, listen and answer your questions, but also ask questions about

your individual child. They should want to know about likes and dislikes, communication, sensory needs and discuss how they could meet these needs.

2. Communication should be excellent from the very start. There should be enthusiasm about sharing information between home and school as this will help your child to settle in, have their social and emotional needs met and make consistent progress.

3. Ideally there should be a 'no set rules to settling in' approach. Can you drop off a little later? Can you stay with your child if they need you? Can they bring their special blanket? The answers to all of these questions should be 'Yes'.

4. There should be a happy, calm, cooperative atmosphere with smiling, friendly staff making you feel at ease. Staff should be instinctive in how they approach your child, getting down to their level and knowing how to speak (or not speak) and how to make them feel more comfortable.

5. There should be clear structure to each day and a space with zones for activities. There should be a quiet area for children who need time and space. Ideally this will be set up with calming lights and blankets and cushions.

6. There should be access to sensory integration equipment and sufficient space for climbing, bouncing, running, etc. There should be an understanding of different sensory needs, and experience supporting children with toilet training, sensory needs and anxieties to progress at their own pace.

7. There should be evidence of the use of visual supports and strategies to encourage communication. Staff should have experience of catering for children with special educational needs, and knowledge and confidence using a range of strategies to support them.

8. There should be a visual timetable and also perhaps individual timetables and sand timers. There should not be too much language or discussion between staff in front of the children, but a feeling of a teaching team working in absolute harmony.

9. There should be an open approach to working alongside and seeking support from other professionals such as speech therapists, occupational therapists or the autism advisory service.

Can you send in a private speech therapist? The answer should be 'Yes'!

10. Finally, and most importantly, follow your instinct. You know your child best. Your instinct should be telling you that this setting is the right place for your child, where they will be loved and encouraged. If you feel happy and confident about a place, your child will pick up on this.

Settling your child into preschool

You may feel that you will never be able to happily leave your child at preschool. This is a natural feeling for any parent but it can be intensified by autism.

When a child has communication difficulties combined with anxiety, they will find a way to ensure that they are in control and in their comfort zone. At home they will have learnt where everything is and how to get what they want and they will be able to read you so well.

Preschool will bring many challenges. It is not a known place, there are new people your child does not know, and they in turn don't know your child. You understand and can predict your child and possibly know that they will be upset. You may fear that they will be traumatised. How can this possibly work out?

The answer is to research and prepare and smooth the transition in every possible way so that when that big first day arrives you feel happy and secure in your own choices.

First email or phone the setting and speak to the teacher about your child. There must be a sense of trust between parent and teacher and they must be willing to listen and adapt what they do to help your child settle. Ask about their settling-in process. Will you be able to stay with your child? What are the rules? The best answer will be that they will be guided by the child (a 'no rules' settling-in policy).

Why 'no rules'? Well, no two children are the same. What is right for one child and parent could be so wrong for another. It may be that you feel you will need to stay with your child until they settle and that is okay, but always keep asking yourself if staying close is what they need or more what you need. Some teachers may tell you to leave your child at the door and no matter how much they cry they will manage to settle them. This may indeed be true, but it is not the case for every parent and child.

CASE STUDY
A quick 'Goodbye'

T, age 3, was very attached to his mum and had learnt lots of ways to maintain his control. He liked to be cuddled, but not just in any way. T liked to be held and cuddled, but he was getting a bit big for this. When Mum came in to settle T, I saw that she had been standing and holding him and that he must be getting quite heavy. I offered her a seat, but she said that T would not let her sit and cuddle him. She did try and he then became upset and would not sit on her to be cuddled. He kept pushing her and pushing her, trying to get her to lift him. I could see Mum was exhausted and I could also see that T was so fixated on regaining his control and getting his lift and cuddle that he was not going to notice anything else. My instinct was that even though T would protest we would not be able to settle him this way. Mum agreed and said a quick 'Goodbye' and we left T with his key worker. He was protesting loudly, but there were no tears. Although it will have felt awful, Mum had done the right thing. Within ten minutes T was being rocked on his key worker's knee. I went to phone Mum and by the time I returned he was asleep.

When T woke, he was again determined to be lifted and cuddled, but not having Mum there he had transferred this demand to his key worker. In order to break this cycle, I suggested she go to lunch. She left the room and there was again a loud protest. I went and got T's lunch box and sat near him. After a short while he moved my hand to open it, then got me to open his packed lunch and he was eating and happy. I gradually moved the lunchbox further into class and T followed. After lunch he started to explore the room a bit. He had a play outside in the water and the mud kitchen. We had some smiles. He went into the sensory room and as he got more comfortable we got giggles.

When T's key worker returned, she sat on the floor with another child. T did go over but he didn't try to get her to lift and cuddle him. It was so lovely to be able to email Mum and tell her that T was completely settled. It had been hard, but Mum had done completely the right thing.

* * * * * * * * * *

CASE STUDY
Time and space to settle in

S, age 4, was very attached to his mum. At his home visit she made it clear that she would stay with him until he was settled and that she would be amazed if he let her leave the room for five minutes. S was used to being with his mum at all times. They had a wonderful bond, and he was very specific about how he liked things to be said and done. To S, Mum did everything perfectly and knew how he liked things just so. Therefore Mum was the best person to be with.

Mum stayed with S the first day and all was good. He was happy in the space and explored the different activities set out. After a few days Mum managed to leave S for nearly an hour (she was amazed). The following day we agreed that Mum would leave S shortly after drop-off and return three hours later. When I called Mum at lunchtime to tell her he was perfectly happy, we agreed to stretch this to another half an hour.

This gradual settling-in worked perfectly for S and his mum. They just needed a little bit more time to acclimatise to being separated during the school day and to learn that they both would be okay. S now walks happily into school and turns to wave at Mum as she leaves.

* * * * * * * * * *

CASE STUDY
A parent reflection about settling in: Portesbery School parent

From my first visit to Portesbery I knew it was the school I wanted my son to attend. I loved everything about the school and after visiting many nursery and school settings trying to find the most suitable setting for his needs, I walked away from my first visit knowing it was perfect for him. Having had a difficult experience with mainstream nursery and having an extremely anxious child who is non-verbal, finding the perfect setting was an extremely difficult choice. Because of his experience at mainstream, I myself felt extremely anxious and worried about finding the right setting for him but after my first visit to Portesbery I felt so comfortable. The one-to-one time they gave us on our visit before they showed us around to find out about him and to tell us all about the school made me feel at ease straightaway. I took him in his buggy and remember going into Caterpillar Class and everyone just being so friendly and kind. They asked what he liked and brought over Peppa Pig toys to show him but gave him space and just said hello. There was no pressure on him or me and it was very relaxed.

After the visit, Adele rang and we had a chat. She answered all my questions and asked lots about my son to check Portesbery would be suitable for him. As he is an extremely anxious child who is easily overwhelmed by new places and new people, we arranged a visit at a time when the rest of the class were not in the classroom so he could go into an empty class. They had lots of his favourite toys out, including lots of Peppa toys and bubbles. I went to the visit armed with two big bags of toys, snacks and his PECS® book, yet he ran straight into the class and started exploring all the Peppa toys and books. They had set the classroom up for him to succeed and have a positive visit, which made a huge difference. There was no pressure on timing — we were offered to stay as long as we liked and for him to stay for lunch if he wanted to. He loved exploring the class and coped so well when the other children and adults came back in. We left shortly after they came back as we really wanted it to end on a positive note, and I was blown away with how well he coped. Having the space and time to explore an empty classroom gave him the time to feel safe and comfortable. There was no pressure and it made the visit such a positive experience.

They also did a home visit and I was so impressed with how well they got to know him before he started. He had a few settling-in sessions and they always said we could stay as long or as short as we wanted. Everyone made us feel so welcome from day one and I met his key worker before he started and had plenty of opportunities to ask all my questions.

He started with half days and then progressed to full days, but there was never any pressure and everything was done on his terms. He settled extremely well within a few days and very quickly school became his safe and happy place. I know that this was down to how well they got to know him before he started, for the amazing settling-in sessions completely tailored to him and for the fantastic communication between everyone setting him up to succeed from day one. The support at the start and the support now is exceptional. He thrives on routine and consistency and everyone supported him well with familiarising him with his school routine and transitions during the day. When he started he was a very shy and anxious child and everyone has worked so hard to ensure he always feels safe and happy.

To have your child run into school laughing, happy and eager to get down to class is all I ever wanted. He has come on so much at Portesbery. He is happy, his confidence is growing daily and his anxiety has reduced so much. Even on the rare days he is upset due to being overtired at drop-offs, I go to work knowing he is safe and that I can 100 per cent trust that he will be okay and that everyone knows him well enough to know when he needs a cuddle and when he needs some space. Having an autistic child who is also non-verbal means you can't just ask them how their day is or how they feel, and I am so grateful that he has a place at such an amazing school and that he is so happy and settled at school. The way he gets so excited when we get to school and how he runs in happily show me how much he loves it. The support for him and me has been outstanding. He is so lucky to be so well supported every day and I know he will continue to come on in leaps and bounds and continue to make progress.

• • • • • • • • • •

What if they don't settle?

If your child does not like lots of talking, ensure that you have had conversations with the school about likes and dislikes, fears and feelings, and potential triggers on the phone or by email prior to their first day.

If you are worrying about how your child will settle or separate from you, then it's important to discuss this with the class teacher and work out a plan. Try not to voice any anxieties around your child as they will pick up on this and it will make them anxious too. On their first day, breathe and smile and exude confidence. They must not see that you are wobbling or worried, because they will mirror your emotions. Don't worry. They will be okay.

If time passes and your child is constantly by the door at collection with a tear-stained face, if you are regularly being called to rescue them and collect early, then these are warning signs. If they are in the right place, they should start to relax and explore and be able to manage most days well.

Signs that your child may not be settling

- Spending most of their time waiting by the door.
- Crying for a very long time after you leave them every day.
- Regular calls from the preschool to come and collect them.
- Resistance to putting on the uniform (when other clothes don't bother them).
- Not eating, drinking, going to the toilet or doing things they usually would when comfortable.

Why might they not settle?

Your child may find the preschool too noisy, too confusing, too cluttered, too different, too bright, too hot, too cold, too smelly or too uncomfortable. Maybe it is personal too. Maybe they don't like the teacher's voice or the smell of their perfume? Any number of things could make it difficult for your child to settle, and you may or may not pick up on what it is. As time goes on, you will be feeling more anxious and your child will also pick up on this and carry your anxiety with them through the door.

If settling is not happening, try to unpick what the reason might be. Phone or email the teacher and discuss ways to make the morning separation work better. Are they offering ideas and support, and listening and discussing with you? Are they easing your anxiety or adding to it? Be calm in the knowledge that there are other preschools and if it doesn't work out at one, it might be time to do your research and find another. And next time you will be armed with more knowledge and you will be able to ensure that you work with the new preschool to get those all-important first impressions right.

Should I consider a specialist setting?

If you are asking yourself this question, the short answer is 'Yes'. There is no harm in considering this option. If an autism diagnosis seems likely and you believe that your child might need some accommodations through their education, it is worth looking into what specialist provision is available and within reach of where you live. Don't be afraid to contact these settings. Email or phone and ask if you can speak with someone about your child. This contact could be a great help, offering you ideas, advice and signposting, even if the setting is not appropriate for your child. If a specialist setting will be beneficial, don't hesitate, because class sizes are smaller and the spaces will be limited. It is harder to get a space in specialist provision later on as spaces fill and only become available again if children move on. There are a lot more spaces in mainstream schools and as spaces in specialist settings are limited and more costly to local authorities, they will only be given if considered appropriate to a child's needs. There is absolutely no harm in looking at specialist settings. To provide a window into the

Early Years Department at Portesbery School we created a video. This could be a good way to see inside one such setting.[2]

An autism-specific school

This is a school set up specifically for young people with a diagnosis of autism, needing more accommodation to learn than most mainstream settings can offer. Staff will be trained in autism-specific strategies and should have a good understanding of autism. Classes will be smaller with less general clutter and the style of teaching will often be geared towards more visual learning styles. The grounds and classrooms will have more safety features in place to keep students with climbing expertise, or little awareness of their own safety, secure. There will be sensory spaces, less visual clutter and sessions will be quieter, calmer, more structured and repetitive.

Not all autism-specific schools have the same ethos, so read their websites and do some research. Does the school website state that it uses ABA or CABAS (Comprehensive Application of Behaviour Analysis to Schooling) approaches, for example? If they use a specific approach, read up about it, visit and make sure you are happy that it will be a good fit for you and your child.

Spaces at autism-specific schools do fill quickly and there is always a lot of demand, so if you think this might be more appropriate to your child then arrange a visit, speak to the head teacher and get things moving quickly.

A unit attached to a mainstream school

Some mainstream schools have a specialist unit that caters for children and young people who might be able to cope with some aspects of mainstream education but also require specialist accommodation. The unit will be led by a teacher with autism-specific training. A unit could work well if your child is able to cope academically but you know they will need a bit more time, space and support and if there are times they can manage better and times when they need space. Have a look at a unit if there is one within easy distance of your home.

---

2   www.portesbery.surrey.sch.uk/Early-Years-Department

A school for students with additional needs or moderate learning difficulties

If you feel that your child will not cope well in a mainstream setting or unit and that they will benefit from a school that aims to meet a range of special educational needs to progress, see if there is a school in your area that caters for additional needs or moderate learning difficulties. There are limited places in such schools, so it is best to do your research as soon as possible to secure a place early on. Call or email the school to arrange a visit.

A school for students with severe learning difficulties

Schools for students with severe learning difficulties might be the right fit for your child if you feel that they are going to take a lot longer and require high levels of support and expertise to make progress.

It is very difficult to assess whether your child has a severe learning difficulty, but pointers to a child benefiting from a specialist setting for severe learning difficulties might be:

- Little or no functional speech.
- Severe sensory issues (these could include refusal to wear clothes or shoes, or to eat or drink).
- Anxiety around transitions.
- Little or no interaction with other children.
- Extreme sensory seeking (this could be climbing, mouthing, chewing or trashing).

Will my child be held back by going to a special needs school?

The idea of a specialist setting may seem daunting and also disheartening. Before our children are born we have high hopes and aspirations, and the suggestion of 'a school for severe learning difficulties' might feel like writing your child off or setting low expectations for what they might achieve. It's so important to be open-minded and consider all options. A while ago a parent in my class commented that a friend had sympathised with her when she told them that her daughter went to a special needs school. She said how funny she had found this as she felt that her daughter was so lucky and happy at school. She felt as though she was sending her to Disney World each day.

Your child will still be stretched and will be able to access higher levels of support with specialist trained staff and a much better child–staff ratio. Visit the setting and try to get an idea of the peer group they would have. The ideal scenario is to feel they would have peers who are modelling things you would like them to learn. If your child is communicating (even if this is not clear speech) and is mainly needing to develop their social interactions and play, they will need other children modelling appropriate language and play skills. Children learn from each other, so when assessing if a setting is appropriate, keep this in mind.

Attending a special needs school should not hold your child back, and if they would thrive and learn in another setting, the teachers will support and encourage a move.

'Not every child will need to attend a special needs school with an ASD diagnosis; but if you are ever faced with this choice, don't feel guilty. Having your child surrounded by people who understand them, are experienced with their behaviours and know how to support them is an incredible gift to give your child.'

(Parent of S)

Contact or visit a range of schools. You may have a gut reaction or instinct that one of the schools is the right fit for you and your child. The decision may seem huge and overwhelming, and you will get conflicting opinions, but your instinct for where your child will be most happy at this point in time is often the best thing to follow.

In the following case study Beth Heinemann reflects on her experiences finding the right setting for her son Freddie, who has been diagnosed with autism.

CASE STUDY
A tale of two settings
Freddie's first preschool (age 3)

Before Freddie turned 3, I'd learnt so much about autism. We'd started to use Makaton signs and PECs for communication, and worked hard to teach him social skills. Before he started at the preschool, I asked for a meeting.

The teacher gave me a standard ten minutes, during which I filled in a standard 'About me' form. She admitted to knowing nothing about autism.

The teacher mentally grouped Freddie with two other boys on the spectrum – one diagnosed and one not. There was no extra support, and she referred to this 'situation' four times in front of me, saying, 'I have been stuck with three autistic kids in my setting with no extra help.'

Freddie was coping, though – not getting the best, but coping.

Next thing, they decided to physically group Freddie with the two other boys, who were not coping so well. They were all to arrive and leave through a different door to the other children and spend the first and last 20 minutes together in a room with the teacher, doing 'IEP[3] work'. Freddie started to regress. When I bathed him, I noticed bruising caused by another child. I asked [the school] to include him back with his peers and explained why, but they replied with, 'He can't do this. He can't do that...' I tried, in vain, to explain that he never would if they weren't willing to give him the opportunity to learn.

I felt I had no choice but to take Freddie out.

A lady from early years came and listened to me after that. She observed Freddie at preschool and got it... From then on, Freddie was back with the main group. I felt at least he was getting play and social skills, if not much else. It's heartbreaking to look back on that time and write this down; I would never settle for that now.

Freddie's second preschool (age 4)

Before Freddie started, we had an amazing two-hour meeting where we discussed autism and Freddie... And the teacher got it! Hooray! I could have cried. I think I did... She came to see Freddie in his home environment. She observed him for about 20 minutes, then started 'working with' him,

---

3   An IEP is an individual education plan.

getting him doing stuff I knew he could do but nobody else (outside the home) had achieved.

We had visits to nursery before Freddie started at his pace. They provided a booklet for Freddie with pictures of the staff and the different areas of the nursery, so I could visually prep him over the summer. While still waiting for Freddie's statement,[4] the school funded a full-time one-to-one for him, so he could have the best start possible. Lots of meetings were held. I was always involved in the decision making and got to meet all the staff who would be working with Freddie.

Freddie's one-to-one had a basic knowledge of Makaton, and the teacher provided extra visuals for her to use with Freddie. They all used a lot of visuals anyway, which helped with inclusion.

Freddie was extremely happy and successful from day one. Each day was clearly structured, and this helped greatly with his expectations and understanding. He conformed from the very start, doing everything that all the children were doing with no issues at all.

I got verbal feedback daily as Freddie still struggles with this type of communication. He also had a visual strip that he filled in, showing what he had done throughout the day, so he could share this with me. They supported us through toilet training, drinking from an open cup, drinking water, extending speech, play, social skills, etc., etc. – everything really. Thank you!

Then I saw the Christmas play and they had taught all the children the Makaton signs to go along with the songs. What a fantastic sight that was!

· · · · · · · · · ·

Teachers

Finding the right school is the first thing to consider. Next, and less in our control, are the annual changes to teacher and teaching assistants. It is a wonderful thing when you feel that your child is in a class with a teacher who understands, enjoys and can nurture their unique personality and learning style. On the flip side is the anxiety and concern when we feel our children do not have this teacher support.

---

4   A statement of special educational needs detailed a child's educational needs and support required. In England this has been replaced by the education, health and care plan (EHCP).

CASE STUDY
A tale of two settings: Adele Devine
Not settling into preschool

R was eyeing the entrance with trepidation amidst the bustle of children getting their coats and bags on pegs. A little girl was crying and protesting about going through the door, and her mum was trying to comfort and cajole her. Teacher 1 took the girl's hand and said in a matter-of-fact way, 'Those are crocodile tears. She will stop as soon as you leave.' She waved to an assistant, who led the now sobbing girl away. The mum left but was visibly concerned. R could see through a window that the girl was still crying. R took his coat back off the peg. 'I'm not going in,' he said with absolute conviction.

R's mum paused. She knew she was in for a battle and didn't want a big scene in front of the other parents. R was soon the only child in the cloakroom. He had put his coat on and his dinosaur rucksack was on his back. His arms were folded tightly and his hands were clenched in strong fist grips preventing Mum's efforts to get things back on the peg. Teacher 1 could see she had another little protester. 'Come on in. It's time to say goodbye to Mummy now,' she said. 'No.' R was defiant. 'I don't like you. I'm going home.' Mum saw the flicker of annoyance in the teacher's eyes. This was not a great start. 'Mum is going home,' Teacher 1 said firmly. 'R is staying at preschool.' She opened the outside door and ushered Mum out.

R's eyes filled with tears. From then on, every morning there was a battle. R did not want to go to preschool. He said that the teacher was stupid and she told lies. In fact, R was so unhappy that Mum eventually found him a placement in a different nursery.

Finding an alternative preschool

Teacher 2 knew a lot about R before he arrived because she'd met with his parents and they'd had a long chat. She knew he loved dinosaurs and books. She was aware that the sandpit might be an issue and that sharing toys could require some supervision. She was also aware that saying good-bye to Mum at the door had been a big problem in the past.

Teacher 2 had suggested R arrive on his first day half an hour later than the other children. That way, she explained, he wouldn't have to deal with the hustle and bustle. She suggested that Mum come in with him, stay for as long as she wanted and leave when she knew he was comfortable. R and Mum arrived at the preschool. They found his peg. R was chuffed to see the dinosaur next to his name. 'Look, Mummy. There's a T-Rex,' he said with a smile. Mum felt instant relief! Teacher 2 came out to greet them with a big, warm smile.

She knelt down and introduced herself to R at his level. 'I've got more dinosaurs in there and I've been trying to find out the different names from this book. I want to make sure I don't put the herbivores with the carnivores.' R smiled right back at her and was totally enthused. 'I can help you,' he offered. 'I know all about dinosaurs.' Mum followed, but actually felt like she could have left there and then. She watched for a while as R became engaged in his dinosaur heaven, naming them all and happily lining them up, leaning in for a closer look and flapping his hands in delight. After a while, Teacher 2 introduced another child to play alongside R with a set of plastic animals.

Mum had already prepped R that she would stay for a bit. Once he was busy having fun she might go home and then collect him before lunch. R saw that his mum was making an exit but was far too absorbed in his dinosaurs to be bothered. Mum blew him a quick kiss and left. She could have hugged Teacher 2.

As Mum left, her eyes filled with tears. What a relief to know that her complex little man was in good hands!

. . . .

Communication with teacher (parents)

Excellent communication between teacher and parents is essential to a child's success. Establish this early on by getting the teacher's email address and use it to set your child up to succeed. If your child hasn't slept, tell the teacher so that they can reduce demands. If they are sitting on a table with a child who taps their pencil or gets in their space, then let the teacher know. They may not instantly move your child but at least they will know what is unsettling them. Don't let anything that is causing your child anxiety bubble and bubble away. If they have told you and your child agrees to it then communicate this to the teacher.

Communication with teachers (the autistic child)

The honesty of the autistic child must be understood. It is one of the many things we love.

'If I'm teaching a group session and one of the children gets up and walks off, I will not take offence but see this as feedback. My lesson was clearly not ticking the boxes and engaging them enough. I will need to up my game. I value this feedback and will improve upon my offer next time.'

(Adele Devine)

A teacher can learn a lot from the feedback they get when they have an autistic child in their class. You will know if you have a teacher who is the right fit for your child from speaking to them. I've included a few examples to show the teacher–child relationship. We hope that the child you have in mind when reading this book will get the intuitive teachers they so deserve. Teachers are accessing more training and support and they are also getting a lot more experience of including and supporting autistic children. We will also, I hope, be seeing more autism-specific schools and units helping to accommodate these children in future. Things are improving.

'Just over a decade ago I was teaching in an autism-specific school. It was raining at playtime. One of the children was standing by the door looking in and doing that tell-tale "I need the toilet dance". I asked if she wanted me to take her in and the answer was "No". The dance continued and I was sure she wanted to go in. "You look like you need to go in." I'll never forget her response. "I do, but I'm waiting for one of the sensible teachers to take me." "Who are the sensible teachers?" I asked. She looked at me as though I was completely daft. "The ones who don't stand outside when it's raining." How could I argue with that? I am so grateful to the verbal children I have worked with. They have taught me so much.'

(Adele Devine)

'M's behaviour started to escalate in class as he was struggling to play and share nicely with his peers. M was given a choice – to say sorry to the friend he had upset or to have a sensory break outside. M refused to apologise so went outside with me for a sensory break. M was visibly upset having to come outside and I gave him some space. When he had calmed down and started to play with some toys, I approached and talked to him about how he was feeling. M ignored my initial question, so I grabbed the emotions (Zones of Regulation™) board from the classroom. I then pointed at the different symbolled feelings and said what they were. M started to take an interest at this point and began to point at some different emotions. I told him each of the emotions (various emotions – "tired", "in pain", "happy", "anxious", "excited", "silly", "annoyed").

I asked M how he thought his peer who he had upset was feeling. M replied, "Happy" and pointed to the appropriate symbol. I said I think he might be feeling a little bit sad as he was crying, and M pointed to the sad symbol and said, "Yes." I then said, "I am feeling tired as I was up very early today. How do you feel, M?". He took his time looking over the symbols and then pointed at "annoyed". I then asked M, "What has made you annoyed?" He replied, "You." I apologised to M for making him feel annoyed and asked if he wanted a different staff member outside instead of me. M replied, "No, not yet." I stepped back from M's play and watched from the distance before a five-minute timer was used to let him know it was time to go back inside.'

(Emma Newman, Reception class teacher at Portesbery School)

Supply teachers

It is inevitable that at some point a child's teacher or key worker may not be in school. Teachers do plan for this and they will leave instructions, and there should still be familiar staff. It is important to have good communication between parents and the school.

CASE STUDY
Comic Strip Conversation to the rescue: Adele Devine

When Mum collected P (age 6), he was distraught. Usually he kept it together well at school, but something had happened that had really upset him. He was very angry and upset by something that the supply teacher had done.

Mum had found that using Comic Strip Conversations[5] could be a good way to unpick events with P at times like this. She drew a stick figure

---

5   https://carolgraysocialstories.com

standing up to represent the teacher. Next, she drew a stick figure to represent P. P drew a board and pointed to it, sobbing. 'She wrote my name on the board because I was talking. I wasn't talking.' Mum knew, and P's regular teacher knew, that P had a habit of talking when working and he was not aware of it. He could also have quite a loud voice. The teacher had told him to stop talking and he had been a bit annoyed, but then when she told him off the next time and wrote his name on the board, he was mortified. The combination of injustice, fear and frustration were too much to take. P responded angrily to the teacher and was then really upset.

Mum was able to email P's regular teacher, who was luckily in the next day. The teacher agreed that P's name should not have been written on the board and made sure that P was okay.

Friends (and allies)

'Our son (age 6) is extremely close to his siblings, but other children haven't been on his radar until recently. Now he actively tries to engage with other children with mixed results, but it's a huge step in the right direction.'

(Parent of S)

CHAPTER 17

Getting Set Up

'Visuals to explain where we were going next, and time to process the visuals, have helped enormously, and have been needed less and less frequently as he has developed a better understanding of things.'

(Parent reflection)

With all the advice and suggestions being offered, you may be looking around and thinking, 'Where do I start?' Well, to begin with, it is important to create order in your child's home learning space. If your home is already ordered, that is amazing and you can skip this part and go straight onto 'Routines' below. If it is not as ordered as you would like, it may be time to declutter and have set places for the things your child needs. It is so easy for things to become disordered with the constant demands of family life. There is never enough time in the day to do it all... But think about how you feel when you are surrounded by mess and chaos and how when everything is tidy and ordered your head begins to feel so much better. Think about all the mess you have when there's a family celebration. It's great, but there is also a sense of relief when order is restored. So, yes, I am suggesting that the starting point is a big tidy-up and declutter because that will make everyone feel so much better. When we feel overwhelmed, sometimes we just stop and freeze, but sometimes worrying can make us tidy up too. Have you ever gone into tidying mode when you should be doing something else? That is partly because our brains are craving order and our bodies need something productive to do.

Routines

We all have our routines. Until we stop and think, we may not even realise how many. Think back to a morning when one of your routines couldn't happen. Was it a broken boiler meaning no hot water, an alarm not going off, a cancelled appointment or even something like running out of teabags? How might any of these things make you feel? When one of our routines – maybe things we enjoy, things that make us feel good or things which keep us on track – is removed, it throws us. This is natural. Hold onto that feeling. Now imagine increasing this thrown-out feeling and intensifying it as if you were turning a bath tap from tepid (slightly annoying) to scalding hot (impossible to manage). That scalding-hot pain may be akin to what the autistic child feels when a routine is removed or changed without warning.

If we remove a routine without warning, we could be setting the child up to fail. But just as we have our own individual routine pathway that gets us from home to work or out and about, so do our children. We don't know how detailed this is for our children, and the reactions can seem extreme and challenging.

Trying to stick to a routine on days when your child is facing a challenge can really help them as it makes things feel predictable and safe. Think of a big wobbly jelly on a plate. We can wobble the plate a bit and the jelly will stay in place; a bit more and it's still okay; but too much wobbling will cause the jelly to fall off the plate. If your child is going to be facing a new challenge, sticking to the same routine reduces demands and will help them stay on track.

Sometimes we only find out how important a routine is when it is suddenly changed – when, for example, traffic lights are broken, a road is closed, the packaging on a favourite food changes (why do they do that?).

So, there is nothing wrong with having a routine and sticking to it if it helps your child.

Take care with routines

We know that daily routines help us. We learn to do things at certain times in certain places, but our children can learn that our routines are like 'laws' and they may decide that if you do something once it will happen every time. Take care which routines you teach them to expect.

Eating

Consider this example: we eat our evening meal around the same time each evening in the same place. We might all have a seat at the table we usually use. This is all okay. Then we have a guest who sits in our usual seat. We adapt to this. The autistic child might not adapt so well. If someone is sitting in their space or Mummy's space, they might make this known.

We need to take care to get the balance right. The routine makes things work well, but always keep in mind that your child needs to learn to be able to adapt to some changes.

Whereas one child may be able to have lunch in front of the television one day because you can see they are engrossed in watching something and you need to make a phone call, another child may think that because lunch was in front of the television once, it will always be in front of the television. Next time you eat at the table, they may protest because they preferred eating in front of the television. Be aware of the future battles you may create by changing things.

All children can be picky eaters and the autistic child can take this to another level. Control reduces their anxiety and makes them feel safe. We all want our children to eat, but do take care of the routines you start in order to get them to eat. Some parents may use the television or tablet, but be prepared for future battles and having to undo routines you establish.

Treats

It can be lovely to be able to treat children – an ice cream on a sunny day, a toy when they have been good on a shopping trip. But be aware that when you buy that ice cream in the park on a sunny day your child may decide that ice cream in the park will happen every time they go to the park. Treats can happen, but make a rule quickly. For example, ice cream in the park happens if the ice cream van comes on a Friday. Don't go to the toy shop in your town and buy a little plastic dinosaur and expect it to be a one-off. Don't buy that magazine with the little toy on the front as you leave the supermarket if your child likes routines and control. Even if you are prepared to do this every time, what about when a friend takes them to the shop, they try to get a magazine and the friend says 'No'. It's not that we can't treat a child, but we must just give it a little bit of thought and future proofing.

Out and about

It's easy to get into routines when out and about. For example, the order you walk around the shops, the place you park, the route you drive to school. Our children may not seem to be taking notice, but they are constantly looking and learning, and all of these routines become a part of their expectations. But then one day a road is closed, a parking space is full or a shop is being remodelled. To set our children up to succeed when these things happen, plan to mix these routines up occasionally. Take a different route, walk on the other side of the road, etc.

Schedules

Why might a visual schedule help? We all use forms of schedules to help us through tricky transitions. Imagine that you are going to be giving a talk at an event in an unfamiliar city. You have the nerves associated with the talk, but also nerves about catching trains, trains being on time and finding the location. What would you do? Well, first you would probably have prepared slides so you are confident about what you are going to say, and have a set structure in place. You would have looked up your route and allowed plenty of time. You would probably have referenced your phone several times to check the time. You would have it all worked out in order to reduce that bubbling anxiety.

These high levels of anxiety are so often a part of daily life when demands are being placed on our autistic children.

The visual schedule shows the child that there is a clear plan and steps taking them through the day to a part when they can relax. They can see things happening in order and this will really build their trust and confidence. You might think they don't recognise or show interest in the symbols, but by you providing them and repeating often they will learn to associate the symbol with the activity. Show the symbol as the activity starts. If every time it's time for lunch they see the 'lunch' symbol and hear the word 'lunch', they will constantly be learning to link the visual and the associated language with the activity.

A visual schedule can really help a child learn about routine and alert them when there is a potential change to it. Schedules should be whatever your child is able to recognise best. It may be photographs or symbols. When creating the visual schedule, be aware that your child might pay attention to details which you don't notice. If you are taking photos make sure the background is uncluttered. Look at each individual symbol and think about whether it is communicating what you want it to if you did not have the associated word.

Visuals lanyard

Attaching a set of the most frequently used laminated symbols or photos to a lanyard can be a good way to have quick access to them throughout the day. Frequently used visuals might be 'more', 'finished', 'toilet', 'help', 'eat', 'drink', 'brush teeth', 'walk', 'sit', 'car', 'wait', 'stop', 'home', 'school', 'shoes on', 'socks on', 'shoes off' and 'socks off'.

The more we show the child, the more they will associate the visual with the action. Demands given with a visual can enable a child to process what you are suggesting. Keep language simple and give them lots of time to look.

Give them time

How long is the activity going to last? The autistic child may be struggling with sensory issues and anxiety will intensify these. They will not want to waste their time.

Your child might not follow simply because something is on your plan. They like to know why and they like to know how long.

Provide a visual way to show time elapsing – a time timer,[1] sand timer or adapted clock. Add timer symbols to schedules. Be aware that the child may process differently. They may not respond as quickly.

A child might take two minutes to process the information you are showing them. You will learn how long their response time can be. It's important to allow them this. Imagine if you took two minutes to process when someone told you to go to the car and before you had done this they were already getting frustrated and repeating the demand. This can build a child's anxiety and make it impossible for them to follow the direction. There will come a day when routine is thrown out unexpectedly. Unexpected change is a part of life and no amount of planning and protection can stop this. So how do we prepare children for this? See Chapter 13 for information about 'Now and Next', dry wipe boards and 'whoops!'.

Motivators

What gets commuters on a jam-packed train? They want or need to get from a to b. Think of your child's day as a journey. Always think: What is the incentive? Are we meeting a want or a need in the child? Do they see the point? Is there any way you could adapt so that they feel more accommodated, motivated or in control?

What if the activity was a little quieter, a little less crowded or a little more predictable? What if the journey involved seeing some dinosaurs (if your child loves dinosaurs). Think Pied Piper tactics. How did the Piper get the children to follow him from Hamlin? He played their music.

---

1   https://www.timetimer.com

CASE STUDY
Reward system to the rescue! Adele Devine

P was a busy boy who liked lots of new activities and attention. P had a baby brother who was taking up some of his mum's time and P did not understand this. P's behaviour was becoming increasingly difficult at home. He was hitting out a lot and trashing things and it was getting worse. First we monitored when the hitting was happening by keeping a record. We quickly established that the hitting was always happening late in the morning. We discussed the possible reasons. We thought that it might be that P was getting hungry. We introduced a snack. At the same time we introduced a sticker system and for every hour P was 'good' (didn't hit) he would get a sticker. There was a morning chart and an afternoon chart. If he got all his stickers, he received high praise. Everyone was happy and he got a reward from a special box. Mum had a box that she had filled with little cars wrapped in tin foil from a pound shop (ten cars for a pound for a non-hitting child was well worth it). When Daddy came home, P would run and show him the charts. He was *so* proud of himself. Those charts, stickers and rewards turned things around for P. Over time the charts became unnecessary and the hitting stopped.

. . . .

Bridging transitions

Lack of structure and movement that creates noise can heighten anxiety. Provide a structure to transition times (maybe your child could look at a book or bounce on a mini trampoline).

In time you might be able to teach them to take a symbol from a visual schedule and place it on a transition board. This can help your child with the transition between activities or areas because they see the transition as a matching task. There is a clear point. They match the breakfast symbol to the breakfast transition board and suddenly they are in the right place.

Using visuals reduces verbal clutter. Some children find demands difficult. Following someone else's agenda reduces their control and creates anxiety. These children can transition, but they need us to understand that they don't want to feel that transitioning is a demand. Planning and preparation are also essential to support transitions as they change school or to a new class.

Add structures

Tasks and activities can also be broken down so that the stages are clearly mapped. We enable the child to master new skills through repetition.

An activity that requires skills they have not yet perfected (such as handwriting) might feel impossible or overwhelming. The child may not see the stages in learning and they may fear failing.

Provide achievable tasks with a set structure, and your child will see that they can have a go.

You can learn more about creating structure by looking up information about TEACCH®, which provides visual structures to promote independence and support autistic learners.

As we build trust, your child will begin to stretch themselves, but we must gauge individual pace. Also ensure that the tasks either have a functional purpose or are related to their motivators (ideally both).

Use rewards

We all like rewards. A reward might be a choice from a reward box or additional playtime. We may need to use a reward board or token board. Reward boards are most effective when they show exactly what tokens are for.

Never remove a reward that has been earned, and listen if the child suggests there has been an injustice. We can add to playtime or going outside as a reward, but never threaten to remove it.

Build their trust

Be consistent, be fair and listen. Love what the child loves. Create a calm, uncluttered space where they feel safe. Keep your promises. If you say an activity will finish in five minutes, stick to it.

We must continually build bridges. Be aware of the sensory issues and anxieties that often partner autism. Take the time to observe and listen, and you will start to see and respond in a whole new way.

CHAPTER 18

Personal Care

'Our son despised having his teeth brushed. The thing we found to work the best was flavourless toothpaste, a double-sided toothbrush and lots of distraction (silly songs and even sillier celebratory dances worked a treat).'

(Parent of S)

We are grateful to Clare Walker (Deputy Head Teacher at Portesbery School) for co-writing this chapter.

There are some things we have to do for reasons of hygiene, and the autistic child may not make the connections that we take for granted. They are filled with alarm and 'why' questions, without being able to ask them or process the reasoning behind them. Their response to all of these typical personal care demands will be to resist them, and this can be frustrating and exhausting.

Sleep

When a child doesn't sleep, it impacts on the whole family in so many ways. Sadly, even after every strategy is put in place, sometimes the autistic child won't sleep through the night consistently.

Often when parents seek our support because their child is not sleeping, they have already tried putting in place all of the typical advice.

Some tried and tested sleep strategies include no screen time in the hour or so before bedtime, routines, lavender baths, blackout blinds, reduced noise, bedtime stories and hot milky drinks.

Do seek advice and support as there is no perfect answer. Having supported so many exhausted, sleep-deprived parents, we wish that there was a quick fix for a child not sleeping.

Your GP might suggest using melatonin to help regulate sleep. Melatonin is a hormone that is found in our bodies, but it can also be created in a laboratory. Melatonin is most commonly used for insomnia and can be used for jet lag too. Melatonin may help some children's sleep patterns but is not a magic fix.

One of the strategies that can also be helpful to the autistic child is having a very, very regular routine, which can include the same bedtime story every night. Carol Gray, who created Social Stories™ and Comic Strip Conversations, came up with an idea for a picture book, which can be used as a calming bedtime social story.[1] The title says it all: *The Last Bedtime Story: That We Read Each Night*.[2] This book is written in Carol Gray's reassuring voice and covers things your child could be thinking or having misconceptions about.

Our children are constantly looking to us for reactions and it's vital that, no matter how exhausted you are, you remain calm and in control (otherwise they might play up at bedtime to try to get Mummy or Daddy to have a funny reaction again). Adult reactions are exciting and interesting. Children won't necessarily know the difference between excited and angry, or may get a bigger buzz from 'angry'. It's important not to take this personally.

If you are regularly missing out on sleep, be open about it. Tag team with your partner. I've heard some parents say that they do all the

---

1 https://carolgraysocialstories.com
2 Published in 2014 by Future Horizons, Arlington, TX.

getting up at night because their partner has to go to work and they don't. This seems a bit unfair, especially if your child is not at school yet or you have other children so there is no time to catch up. Breaks are also important. If you are offered any support, take it. By being more alert and fresh, you will be helping your child. So, parents taking care of themselves and seeking support is another strategy.

CASE STUDY
Not sleeping: Adele Devine

It was a Friday morning. I opened Leon's home–school communication book to find that his mum had written a little note asking for help. She said that their night-times were becoming a nightmare and she did not know what to do. I phoned her right away and we had a long chat.

At night Leon had developed routines that involved turning off all the downstairs lights and the TV before going up to bed.

Leon was an anxious child and liked to be in control. Dad would take him upstairs and get him into bed. They would read a story and another story, and then Dad would stay in the room pretending to be asleep until he was able to sneak out.

Leon would sometimes wake in the night and Dad would go in again and stay until he was asleep. Mum said that this, whilst not ideal, was manageable, but things had changed recently.

Leon had started to want both Mum and Dad upstairs when he went to bed. He wanted Mum in their room with the door shut, and then he would not settle with Dad. He would lie in bed, eyes open, fighting sleep; and if Dad tried to leave, he would cry and try to scratch him. Dad had ended up staying in the room all night, sleeping on the floor.

New routines

Inspired by Carol Gray's *The Last Bedtime Story: That We Read Each Night*,[3] I decided to create a social story about bedtime that Leon could read every night.

The story explained the routine and that Mum and Dad would be nearby, but downstairs, and that he would be safe in his bed. I used cuttings from

---

3   https://carolgraysocialstories.com

an old issue of *Something Special* magazine, knowing that Leon responded to Makaton and loved Mr Tumble. I also made a visual schedule for Leon to follow. I asked Mum to arrive early to collect Leon so that we could discuss the new strategy. Mum was totally on board and relieved to have a plan. She looked exhausted.

Successful slumber!

On Monday morning, Mum arrived with a lovely card and a box of chocolates. The plan had worked! The social story had reduced Leon's anxiety and they were all able to sleep in their own beds. Hooray!

- - - - - - - - - -

'Sleep has always been an issue for us. We have tried different coloured lights in the bedroom (I have read that some children find red relaxing... Not sure what our neighbours must have thought when we went through this phase of trialling), a rigid routine at bedtime and limiting screen time, even topping up his melatonin with a prescription from the paediatrician, which helps him to get off to sleep but not stay asleep, sadly. This is a work in progress.'

(Parent of S)

'Sleeping – never been a problem. Ken has always been fairly sluggish and slept well. A long time ago, I was told ASD kids can either be "Eeyores" or "Tiggers". Ken is definitely an Eeyore. He has absence epilepsy which was diagnosed at 3, so is on anti-epileptic meds which contribute to his tiredness.'

(Ken's Mum)

Consider how a child might think about personal care demands

- Why would you use baby wipes on me when they are wet and uncomfortable?
- Why would I brush my teeth or let the toothbrush near my

mouth? It looks painful and the toothpaste smells and tastes horrid.

- Why would I put my body in water or have my hair washed when the shampoo might sting my eyes? The water will hurt my head and get in my eyes and make them sore.
- Why should I have my nails cut when I hate the feeling after they have been cut? The scissors look sharp and scary.
- Why would I wear clothes when I'm more comfortable without them? Clothes hurt. I don't need them.
- Why would I wear shoes when they feel so odd and uncomfortable?
- Why would I let you brush my hair, let alone cut it?

So how should we respond when a child is anxious about personal care? These are things we have to do. We want them to be clean and to learn to take care of themselves. These things are not really a choice.

However, it is important to remember that when children are young, they are trying to make sense of the world around them. For many children, linking what they see, hear and experience comes naturally. For an autistic child, it doesn't. Add sensory experiences on top and we begin to understand. Add another layer of acute anxiety because they have not made the connections, so everything is new and a perceived threat. As a parent it is frustrating as we label and reassure constantly, but an anxious autistic child is not hearing and processing rationally because they are often living in the survival part of the brain.

Before anything else, we must plan – for the short term and the long term. Our short-term plan is: What do I realistically want to achieve today? Will I be happy if I get one nail cut? When is a good time for us to achieve this? How am I going to approach it?

The longer-term plan is to look at the way we think about success. None of these personal care demands are black and white; they are not either 'achieved' or 'not achieved'. They require a child to cope with a huge array of sensory input. They can all be broken down into little steps or rungs on a ladder. Think about how complex each of the personal care demands is. It is not, for example, a case of a child being toilet trained or not. Think about how many different steps there are, from coming into a bathroom (bright lights, changing smells, lotions and potions, taps and flush button, sounds, touches – hard sinks, soft toilet roll that unravels!) to being undressed, then touched with cold wet wipes, listening to a flush of the toilet, clothes being put back on and having hands put under water. And that's without the talking. There is lots to think about, so how are we going to do this?

The first step of the plan is to ensure that we stay very, very calm. No matter how frustrated or tired we feel, losing our cool will only intensify the situation and make it worse. Introduce a clear visual support showing your child what they need to do. Have a written script along with the visual and stick to it so that they hear consistent language. Rather than 'Hey, Johnny, it's time to have a bath and wash your hair so that you'll be all fresh and clean', just show a visual and say, 'Johnny bath time in five minutes'. You could also show them a five-minute egg timer so that they have a visual countdown. Do not add or layer language. Keep it simple, uncluttered and clear. You could also use a 'Now and Next' visual schedule to keep language consistent and minimal.

Try to reduce your demands and create a new, more realistic set of expectations. Think of the main goal – for example, 'brushing teeth independently' – as being at the top of a bigger set of steps. Some people can easily reach the top and just do these things, but for others each little step is an achievement. When you view it like this, it helps you to focus on your child's achievements and be more realistic in setting goals. Celebrate the small wins. We also cannot hope to achieve everything at the same time, so even though all things seem vital, it's important to try to work out what to prioritise and when. Choose your battles.

As with everything, set a predictable routine to personal care demands. The more routine, the more the child will learn when things are going to happen and they can then mentally prepare themselves for this. Remember that these 'normal' things can cause extreme anxiety and seem completely intrusive and uncomfortable. Be patient – in a child's own time, they will make progress.

Nappy changes and toileting

If your child is still in nappies, it is likely they will have come to accept the routine of having their nappy changed. There may be things they don't like, such as wet wipes or change of person or place, but this routine will have been long-established prior to autism being considered a possibility.

Wet wipes can seem cold and uncomfortable, and some children end up having a full bath when soiled rather than having a wet wipe. A bath will not be an option at preschool, so try to get your child used to some sort of wipe routine before preschool. Also try to get them used to having someone else change their nappy at times. Maybe Nanna or another willing mum. Agree the words you are going to use as a family (toilet – is that what you sit on or what you call the room?) so your child knows what you are saying and what to expect from whoever is taking them. Be consistent – always take them to the bathroom to be changed so they know the place the routine is associated with. This will make the transition to toilet much easier.

There is lots of emotion associated with toilet training and having your child in pads when they start nursery. There are also lots of questions around when to start toilet training, which your health visitor/nursery can help you with.

A useful way to monitor progress with toileting and see what the next steps might be was created by Clare Walker (Deputy Head Teacher at Portesbery School). She has kindly allowed us to include it. She created this so that we could show our parents that their children are making progress. It just breaks down the steps towards success. Just add the date each time your child achieves something.

Name:

Toilet ladder	Achievements so far
I am independent with toileting	
I know when I need the toilet and will go	
I can pull my trousers up	
I can take an appropriate amount of toilet paper off the roll	
I can wipe my bottom by myself	
I know that I need toilet paper to wipe my bottom	

cont.

Toilet ladder	Achievements so far
I can sit and do a wee	
I can flush the toilet	
I can put the paper down the toilet	
I can wait on the toilet for up to 20 seconds	
I can wait on the toilet for 3 seconds	
I know to wash my hands	
I can sit on the toilet with help/ encouragement	
I will have pad removed whilst standing	
I can take my trousers down	
I can tolerate my clothes being altered	
I can enter the bathroom	
I can respond and willingly transition to the bathroom door	

Baths

If your child hates bath time and hair washing, just do a quick body wash, then a body wash in the bath, then add water or maybe paddle in the bath if they don't mind puddles or paddling pools. Make bath time quick and build water play in gradually. In time, include wetting the hair as part of play. You could also do this when swimming (assuming they like the pool). To get used to seeing the process, you might wash dolls/teddies (not their favourite ones) in the sink or bath during the day or play with their cars in a shallow tray of water, adding foam for fun. Your child may not join in but they will be watching. This is another way of showing the process and engaging the child but not adding any demands. If the car is okay wet, then maybe they will be okay too. Build up slowly.

Teeth

If your child refuses to brush their teeth, then start with a dry toothbrush. You could show them how to brush the teeth of a doll or a giant model mouth. A very short song may help – they know then that dolly only has to tolerate it the length of the song and it is finished and okay. Introduce toothbrushes in play – leave them around and let your child come to explore them naturally. You can get toothpaste with no taste. It might be worth a try if you think the taste or smell of the toothpaste is off-putting. Don't start with a three-minute expectation when just getting the toothbrush to go near the mouth is a huge demand.

> 'Brushing teeth – he has always allowed this, but I wouldn't trust him to clean his teeth thoroughly, so this is still managed.'
>
> (Noah's Mum)

Clare Walker has broken down these steps into a ladder showing steps and progress. Again, add the date each time your child achieves something.

Name:

Toothbrush ladder	Achievements so far
I can put my toothbrush away	
I am independent in cleaning my teeth	
I can completely clean my teeth for at least 30 seconds to 1 minute.	
I can spit in the sink	

cont.

Toothbrush ladder	Achievements so far
I can brush my teeth, rinse my toothbrush	
I can put my own toothpaste on my toothbrush	
I can stand at the sink and look in the mirror	
I can brush my teeth for a few seconds	
I can put my toothbrush in my mouth	
I can hold onto my toothbrush	
I can have the toothbrush put back in my mouth after it has been rinsed	
I can tolerate my teeth being brushed for 5–10 seconds	
I can tolerate my teeth being brushed for 1–2 seconds	
I can tolerate the toothbrush in my mouth	
I can open my mouth for my toothbrush	
I can smell the toothpaste	
I can watch the toothpaste be put on my brush	
I can play with my toothbrush – wet/dry	
I can travel to the bathroom when I see my toothbrush/ symbol	

Choose and time your battles

If there is something your child will find hard to tolerate, then the timing is everything. Choose a day when they have had enough sleep, have eaten well and are happy. Make sure it's a good time for you too. How patient are you feeling, how calm and assured and capable? Make sure that you are not under pressure or rushed.

It may feel, right now, that there is never that time, but prioritise, take small steps. What is your biggest battle right now? Break it down. Climb the first rung of that ladder; it is only a small step. Celebrate the achievement for both of you.

Managing your child's personal care is an investment – your time now will allow them independence and dignity later on. They will achieve all these things with time, patience, consistency and routines.

If you have another child, set up scenarios in which they can be a role model showing their sibling that something is okay by doing it in front of them again and again. The autistic child will be watching what your other child does. Brush their teeth in front of your child with both toothbrushes available (just in case), but no pressure to use it, then praise them afterwards. 'Wow, Jenny, your teeth are so clean. Your mouth must feel good. Well done!' The watching it being okay is all a part of the learning. If they don't have a sibling, see if you can get a niece or nephew or a friend's child to be a role model. If no child is available, you can become the role model. Repeat this again and again. The more your child sees something is okay for others, the more they might think it's not so bad after all.

Make the bathroom a motivating space. Add pictures of favourite characters, etc., to help motivate your child. Let them choose a toothbrush, or select one you think they will like.

Reduce and break down the demand as much as possible so they can succeed in small steps. Start with them watching toothbrushing, then holding the toothbrush, then putting it in their mouth without any toothpaste on. Praise your child for each step, because they are working really hard to get past each and every thing that other children can do without any anxiety.

Don't feel you have to work this all out yourself. These issues can be really difficult and daunting to deal with alone. Speak to your child's health visitor, paediatrician or teacher for advice and support.

Keeping a diary can help you see patterns and is one of the first things you might be asked to do if you seek professional advice, so be a step ahead. This diary is also a space where you can write down how things are, which can be a good way to feel you are addressing things. It will also show the progress (you may not believe that now).

Look back at it in a couple of years' time and you will see.

Part 5

THE JOURNEY CONTINUES

CHAPTER 19

Family, Support and Self-Care

'Make time for each other, it's so easy to forget to do this when you're sleep deprived and have been dealing with tricky behaviour all day, but remembering you're in this together is so important.'

(Parent reflection)

Having an autistic child is likely to change the dynamics of relationships with your partner, your friends, family and colleagues, and will probably reduce the time you invest in your own wellbeing. You will learn to tune in to how your child is feeling so much that you start to see through their eyes and will probably start to carry some of their anxieties.

Relationships and marriage

Having children changes the dynamic of any relationship. Having a child with learning difficulties, differences or autism is likely to add additional pressures.

When we feel pressured or anxious, we are most likely to reveal this to the people closest to us. Going through the process of autism diagnosis can cause us to react in different ways. Your response and your partner's are very likely to be different and this can seem strange when you are used to seeing things in similar ways and being on the same page when it comes to your child or children. If you and your partner have a good relationship, be grateful for it and protect it. Some relationships become stronger as couples present a united front (even though they will disagree at times) and work through things together.

Having an autistic child or children does not doom relationships. You will read about the chances of a relationship breaking down being higher, but there is research to suggest that this is not the case. Researchers in Baltimore investigated the 80 per cent divorce rate, which was around the same for parents who had a child diagnosed with autism as for those who did not. This was a huge study, using data from almost 78,000 parents. Of these parents, 913 had a child diagnosed with autism.[1]

It is likely that you and your partner will respond at a different pace and possibly in a different way to the idea or reality of autism diagnosis. Grief, anger, fear, frustration and exhaustion are all typical responses. Denial can also be a response. Intensive research can be another. Think of those fight, flight and freeze responses that are a part of how a child responds. Think of how an anxious child may hold it together all day at school, but then explode at home when in their comfort zone with those who love them unconditionally. We adults are the same. We might not agree on responses and strategies. One side of a partnership could have gone into research mode while the other is in denial. These different responses could cause frustration and anger. Even mentioning the word 'autism' could cause an argument or a communication breakdown. It is important to recognise our responses and not allow our own anxieties or those of our children

---

1   Freedman, B.H., Kalb, L.G., Zablotsky, B. and Stuart, E.A. (2012) 'Relationship status among parents of children with autism spectrum disorders: a population-based study.' *Journal of Autism and Developmental Disorders 42*, 4, 539–548. Abstract.

to create conflicts. Give each other space and time to adjust. Try to rationalise and keep communicating too.

Lack of sleep, anxiety, frustration, isolation and exhaustion add huge pressures to our relationships. These things can drive parents apart, but they can also make them stronger. Protect what you have if your relationship has been mostly happy, and look out for each other.

'A strong team is essential! It's a very tough gig at times and can test even the most resilient of people and partnerships. Partners again vary so much – some struggle with acceptance and others get fully stuck in. I lucked out with my husband being incredibly forward thinking and proactive in terms of research and how to make our son well, gut and brainwise, before the teaching could be maximised.'

(Ben's Mum)

Friendships

Be protective of your own friendships. You may lose contact with some friends during this time as all your energies go into supporting family, but remember that as a parent your wellbeing is important too. You are the most important and vital resource your child has, and letting off a little steam with friends can help with your perspective and builds your own resilience. Friends can also be an incredible support when needed. They can help build our confidence and self-esteem, make us smile, help us to relax and reduce feelings of isolation. You may worry about your child making friends, but be mindful and protect your own friendships too. It is easy to lose contact with friends and isolate ourselves when we become parents, and having an autistic child will increase the chances of this happening. Don't make assumptions about what your friends are thinking. You may believe they are being distant, but they may just not know what to do or what to say and believe that you need some space.

As you go through the diagnosis process, you may be feeling fearful, angry or worried, and these things can change how you respond to others. Be open with your friends about what you are going through and don't be ashamed to seek support.

Remember that you are role modelling for your child, so think about what you would want them to do given the same situation.

We know that talking things through is so much better than bottling things up.

Reaching out

You may find it helpful to join a support group. It can be a real source of support and encouragement to speak to other parents of autistic children. But be aware that their journeys are personal to them and your experiences will be different.

If you are feeling overwhelmed or isolated, don't be afraid to ask for help and support. Consider counselling or other supports if they are signposted. Take care of yourself and be mindful of the wellbeing of your whole family.

When a child is not making friends

Seeing your child on their own and not interacting with other children may cause alarm bells to ring. In this case, read up on Intensive Interaction, and sit near your child and provide some interaction on their terms. Similarly, having a child who wants to play but does things like throwing sand in other children's faces can be disheartening. Set things up so they can succeed. Maybe start with two sets of equipment. Supervise, praise and reward as they build a sandcastle, and react when they squash it. A reward chart or Social Story™ might help.

We must provide the practical support our children need to develop the skills necessary to form friendships.

Having a friend might be a lot more important to you than it is to your child, and whilst it is important to encourage social interaction through structured play, we must avoid being forceful. Some children and some adults simply prefer their own company. They just don't enjoy the interaction and chat. Add to this that young children are not always predictable. They can make a lot of noise and cause destruction too.

If your child is not making friends, try to provide some predictable interaction, cooperative play and structured turn-taking to help build the social skills they will need. They may just need to learn these social interactions and conventions in a safer and more structured, predictable way. It takes time to build trust, and once we have the child's trust, they can relax enough to enjoy our company.

The best friend (or only friend)

Your child may have made one best friend and that friendship will be very important to them. Just as a child can choose one thing they will eat or drink or one type of clothing, they might just find that one friend who fits them perfectly. If they are lucky, then that best friend may be a constant support throughout their lifetime.

Old friends

Retaining contact by staying with some of the same peers from nursery to primary to secondary school can be really beneficial. Children who have grown up with your child will not only be more tolerant but also be more likely to stand up for, and advocate for, your child in future.

Too quirky?

You may worry that your child's quirky behaviour will reduce their chances of making friends. Maybe they have difficulties with communication and are pre-verbal, or maybe they have a very loud voice or don't know how to take turns in conversation, or maybe they struggle with play and interaction skills or have other behaviours such as hitting, scratching or touching other children's hair. These things can of course make it more difficult.

CASE STUDY
Flappy and happy: Adele Devine

I recall having this conversation after picking our son up from primary school.

> **N:** Jo asked me why I bounce and flap all the time.
> **Me:** What did you say?

N: I said I just like to bounce and flap and showed him. [Lots of exaggerated bouncing and flapping followed to make the point.]

Me: And Jo was happy with that?

N: Of course! said N with a big smile.

And that was that! I'd watched the bouncing and flapping and loved N for it, but I had wondered how his peers would react as they grew out of doing this and N didn't. I loved that N had the confidence to not apologise for his boundless energy and demonstration of his 'in the moment' happiness. I also loved that Jo was a good enough friend to ask N and then accept N for doing something that made him feel good. As N got older, the bouncing and the flapping naturally reduced. If being happy makes us want to bounce and flap, it is only society that says this is not 'typical'. I love to see this bouncy behaviour in the children I teach as it shows me that they are happy.

Children will ask questions and it is better that they ask directly. The best response to a child's question is an honest one. This might be a 'because they enjoy it' or 'because they are still learning' but could also be an honest 'I don't know.' One thing I have learnt is that children are often very accepting of other quirky children. If your child bounces and flaps when they are happy, don't try to stop this or see it as an 'autistic behaviour', but love them for being unique. It is often the adults who can struggle more with quirky behaviours than other children. We can learn a lot about how to be from observing children.

* * * * * * * * * *

CASE STUDY
Friends and allies: Adele Devine

Our daughter has grown up very aware of autism and seems to be naturally tuned in to children with special educational needs. Some of her best friends through school have been or probably will be diagnosed autistic.

In preschool she once told me about a little boy who kept on hitting her and I explained that he may just need to learn to play. A few days later she proudly announced that she had taught him how to play. The two of them were great friends throughout their time in preschool.

One day, years later, she came home from primary school and said that she was sad because some of the children were being unkind to another child in the class. She said, 'I don't think that those boys are mean, but they just don't understand that L is autistic. They don't understand why she sometimes runs about and makes noises and things.' We agreed that it would be better for the teacher to explain this privately to the boys who were calling L unkind names. I emailed the teacher that night. The teacher spoke to our daughter the next day and was thankful to her for bringing this situation to her attention. The teacher emailed me to say how this had helped. I'm sure our daughter will continue to look out and speak up for other children throughout school. There are many other children quietly doing this too.

You will naturally worry about bullies in school and other children not 'getting' your child and it's important to build their resilience and be on the alert as the reality is that bullying can happen. But also be aware that there will also be some good friends and allies along the way and these friends will look out for your child during their school day in ways you may never know about.

· · · · · · · · · ·

'Be proactive when they find friends – encourage interaction and play – befriend the friend's mum/dad even if you don't have much in common – friends can be like gold dust to help social interaction/ communication but need energy from you to help them develop.'

(Elliot's mum)

School gates interactions

The usual chit-chat you see other parents have at school drop-off times may become increasingly difficult. It's not easy and you may feel that you are under the spotlight with the child who doesn't do as the others do. You may start to avoid social interactions as these can cause your child anxiety. As time goes by, this may create feelings of isolation from other parents. You may feel judged or alone in your own unique experience of parenthood.

It's so important not to allow too much air time to that little voice in your head that suggests people are judging you.

Imagine this scenario:

Polly has two children. Ellen is age 5 and has started primary school.

Alfie has just started preschool. The schools are very close, but Ellen needs to be at school first. Alfie (not yet diagnosed with autism) does not like having to take Ellen to school. Polly tries to get him to go in the buggy, but he doesn't like the buggy. He wants to walk but he will not wear shoes (no matter what the weather). Alfie likes to go at his own pace and does not like people passing him in the other direction. Some mornings he plonks himself on the ground and he then fights off Polly if she tries to lift him. He will make high-pitched noises and hold his ears; and although he is not that heavy, he is able to wriggle and resist if Polly tries to lift him. Every morning Polly feels the tension build as she knows she will have to go out in front of all those other parents with their perfectly behaved children. She feels worn down, deflated and judged. One morning Polly is waiting while Alfie is having a meltdown after someone has passed him by. She sees two mums talking and her instinct tells her that they are talking about her. Polly assumes that they are being judgemental. She will never know that one of the mums has just said to others how much she admires Polly and how well she copes with Alfie. They are wishing they could do something to help but know that speaking to Polly will not help. She is being so calm and amazing, as she is every other morning.

Sometimes we assume the worst. There are people who will judge and offer unhelpful feedback, but there are also those who will just be wishing that they could help. Then there will be the many, many people we assume are judging who are simply getting on with their own lives and thinking about other things.

Think about how your child's cry has a way of getting to you, but other people's babies can cry and not have that same effect. We are all at the centre of our own bubbles. We are not nearly as conspicuous as we might feel.

Grandparents can sometimes find it difficult to understand as it is not a part of their parenting experience. They might offer helpful (sometimes unhelpful) advice to try to help. The best thing to do is to give them some information to read about autism. Try to stay calm and don't let them feed any anxieties.

Friends and support networks

Try to keep in contact with your friends and any other support networks. Be open with them about what is happening. Try not to shut the doors to any potential support.

Social media

Social media can be a way to find other families who have children with a diagnosis of autism . There are many support groups and networks. They can be a wonderful support and make you feel less isolated. They can be a source of advice, but as with all Internet research and contact, be aware that there will be no filter to who you will 'meet' or interact with. Be mindful that not all experiences are the same and not all of the advice will be the best. Try to speak with and if possible meet up with other parents who have autistic children.

'Back when my son was diagnosed, I didn't really know anyone else in the same boat and felt very isolated. Facebook groups and online forums were non-existent. I recommended to my borough to have a connection facility to link local mums in the same boat together, but it never happened. Nowadays there are so many groups on social media [that are] location specific. Also, umbrella support groups, societies and charities.'

(Tom's Mum)

Advice on relationships
Grandparents

'Grandparents vary *so* much! Some really struggle with acknowledgement and acceptance, others don't know how to handle it and are slightly wary, and others are brilliant, hands on and get stuck in! Grandparents can often say the wrong thing without meaning to – they come from a different generation and, depending on age, may have very limited experience of ASD. Try and stay patient with them – it's a big learning journey for them too.'

(Eli's Mum)

Siblings

If your child has siblings it is natural that you will also worry about their needs. They will be affected by the anxieties they might pick up. Their autistic brother or sister may have behaviours or sensory issues which cause destruction, upset and restrictions on what you as a whole family can do. It is important to let them have their own space if at all possible. Try to get some quality time with them (even a walk and talk can make a big difference to their wellbeing).

We often worry and focus on the negatives, but there can be longer-term positives. All the while, they will be developing their empathy, intuition, creativity and problem-solving skills.

It is interesting how many people with siblings or family members with SEN end up working in health, special education or the care sector. We learn from what we see. Right now perhaps your interactions and support of your autistic child are inspiring their brother or sister to provide support or care for others?

'I've watched with pride and guilt as my older two children develop an empathy and understanding for their brother that has extended to other children they meet. We joined Surrey young carers so they could have a safe space to hang out with children in the same boat and talk freely with peers that understood. As a family we also try to spend regular time with our older children, be it family games or movie night once their brother is in bed. It's important to us that they all get a fair share of our attention.'

(Parent of S)

'Always be open and honest. Answer any questions so they feel comfortable and understand how to explain things to their friends when they come back for playdates. Siblings of SEN children are often incredibly intuitive, patient and very kind individuals. They learn a lot fast, often having to play second fiddle, and this can shape them into wonderful little human beings.'

(Jo's mum)

'Since our youngest has been diagnosed, our eldest has also received a diagnosis. The more we learnt about autism, the more things clicked into place. Both our children are completely different, with totally different needs, but they have a fun relationship and our eldest shows his brother the most extraordinary amount of patience.'

(Noah and Ed's mum)

'Ron is a very sociable boy and loves chatting to others. The problems are being fully understood or understanding rules of games, etc. He has quite limited interests, so we are working hard on social communication. He has an amazing younger brother who has really helped him in many ways (and vice versa!).'

(Ron's mum)

CHAPTER 20

Diagnosis Journeys

'Celebrate those little achievements with your child and make the most of every second.'

(Parent reflection)

We are incredibly grateful that some of the parents we have known have agreed to share their very personal diagnosis journeys in order to support other families through autism diagnosis. We have included these individual reflections with the hope that they will make the path ahead seem a little less intimidating.

Henry's diagnosis journey

We didn't want you to diagnose Henry with autism – we wanted you to tell us that he was fine. Or perhaps a tiny, little bit autistic and that he would grow out of it. We were terrified that a diagnosis would put a noose around his neck. We didn't want the reasons for Henry's lack of concentration, eye contact, upset to be recorded on his medical records for him to have access to these when he is 18. We were both brought up by parents who believed that one should keep a 'stiff upper lip' and that our children would fulfil our expectations of them – i.e. we should treat Henry as we would wish him to be and this was our best chance of making that happen.

We had wanted children for so long and had undergone rounds of IVF to conceive. We had seen all our friends have children and developed so many misconceptions/arrogances about how our children would behave better, mistakes we wouldn't make. To have a child who came downstairs after bedtime crying and upset because something was wrong and he couldn't tell us why was devastating. We tried to understand the reasons he gave but he has always struggled with finding the most appropriate word to use. We tried to reassure him – 'Worries are always worse at night. Get some sleep and you will feel better in the morning.' He did always feel better in the morning but we were none the wiser about the underlying causes for his anxiety. I thought that this might be an indication that he would suffer from depression in the future (his grandad suffers from depression). I was terrified of this happening. We knew that he hated parties – so do I. We knew that he wouldn't look Grandad in the eye – maybe he didn't like the brusque way Grandad spoke to Grandma sometimes.

Henry read very well from an early age, which led us astray as to any problems. He was also excellent at art and wrote funny, intelligent stories. When we received school reports saying that he was not paying attention in lessons, we laughed and said that it was because he did not find the lessons stimulating enough.

We were appalled when, in the following year, Henry was bullied at school, other children making him cry, asking him to meet them by the old shed at playtime and then roughing him up. He dropped notes on their desk telling them how upset he was by their behaviour. He came home with nasty bruises and bumps on his head. He told me how another boy had put his foot on his head in the swimming pool to keep him under water. Very little was done about this by the school, but Henry didn't want to move.

We were defensive when, in Y4, Henry's teacher spoke to us to say that our first choices for secondary school were fanciful and that she believed that Henry is autistic. She was right of course, but we were disgusted at the school's inaction over the bullying and had lost confidence in their judgement. We agreed that Henry should be assessed but took this matter into our own hands rather than using their preferred professional. We wanted an independent opinion.

We got an EP referral and also an appointment with you [Dr Mooncey]. I brought my son to see you – without my husband – our family's typical 'no fuss approach'. I was terrified and ashamed when you recognised instantly how unhappy our son was. How could he be so unhappy? How could you just say it so matter of factly? 'It's obvious', you said [I paraphrase] – he speaks in monotone, he's not happy, he has no joy in his voice when he talks about what he likes, he doesn't have any interests or hobbies. I will take those words to my grave: I agreed with you, I knew that you were right but I needed you to say it first for it to be true. You asked about the ventouse delivery? Yes, he was born by ventouse and he had also inhaled meconium – it needed to be pumped out of his system. Was his brain damaged by lack of oxygen. Is there a link? Does it matter? Your assessment of our son was a turning point – a medical diagnosis – which we needed, a plan of action to deal with. Switch off and get on with it. It isn't about us; it's about our son. We needed to love *him*, not our idea of him.

You recommended that we see Helen (Dr Davies) and you persuaded her to take us on even though she was fully booked. We switched off and went through the motions. A therapist. The first time she asked him, 'So how are you feeling?' I was reminded of all my misconceptions about therapists, but seeing a diagram of the brain and how it works and the 'tools' to help with 'thinking errors' was a revelation for both me and Henry. Endless sessions of Henry and Helen playing Dobble to build a rapport, not doing the follow-up exercises at home – e.g. not keeping a diary or practising relaxation techniques but *sometimes* remembering them – and best of all, hearing Henry explain to his sister her 'thinking errors'. One step forward and two steps back.

So therapy really helps. But so does medication. Helen, my son and I reached a point where we agreed that Henry needed help to concentrate in class. Henry agreed and we saw you for an appointment and you agreed too. That was the start of a two-year (approx.) journey of acceptance by Henry that he can't do this alone as he would wish.

He wants to become like everyone else *and* he wants to do this without help. His determination would melt your heart. He lied – where did he learn to 'palm' his medication like a pro? But I was up to all that and I made him take it. He didn't think it helped. Helen discussed keeping a diary – one week on, one week off. We don't do this of course – but we knew we should – and it made Henry think about the difference on and off the medication. He now takes it regularly when he is at school – without being asked. But he still wants to be normal – like everyone else. More than anything he wants some friends. He is such a funny, kind, clever, interesting boy that he should have friends. The initial dose was too low – it's been doubled and may even need to be increased again. We'll see when he starts at his new school next year.

He's starting a new coeducational school next year – in part because of your suggestion that he might do better at a mixed school: he's handsome and some female interaction may give him confidence. The headmistress said, during the interview, that Henry had 'more outward signs of autism than some other students in the school and that this might make it difficult for him to make friends. As a result, Henry will be taking 'social skills' as a core subject, instead of French, with a special needs teacher who specialises in autism. This would have scared us witless a few years ago but now fills us with hope. The headmistress said that this will reduce the outward signs of autism: is it wrong to want Henry to fulfil his ambition of appearing to be the same as everyone else? This is what he wants and so we don't think so.

Lucy's diagnosis journey

The day we met Dr Mooncey will be a day I will never ever forget. How could I? That memory is now engraved into my heart and painfully sits there alongside the day my heart broke once again when I received Lucy's diagnosis.

I was so desperate for answers on that first meeting and so hopeful that Dr Mooncey would reassure me that my fears were unfounded, so we could put this all behind us, and just go back to that place again when all was well, and my worries and concerns were in line with my other mummy friends. Not to this new destination that I found myself at.

But that wasn't to be. When she was 2.5 years old, I had growing concerns about Lucy and her development, and largely these were being ignored by family, friends, health visitors and GPs. In the first year Lucy reached all her milestones on time – sometimes a little too early. She crawled at 6 months and walked unaided at 10 months. Lucy was engaging and smiled and laughed. However, I noticed that as we entered the second year of her life, her speech wasn't in line with that of my friends' children. Whilst she could whiz through puzzles for older children, she couldn't point to toys that she wanted or ask me for a drink. I noticed that she stopped looking up when new people would enter the room, she stopped waving – and she never played peekaboo. To be honest, I can't remember now if she ever did wave.

That day we met Dr Mooncey, Lucy was 2.5 years old. Her speech by this point was only one-word answers and difficult for most people to understand, except me. If Lucy did speak in sentences, it was from phrases that she had heard from Peppa Pig. Lucy could recite songs and loved to sing. In the morning she would sing before I went to greet her. Lucy could read the alphabet and was able to read and write at 2.5 years old – all of this didn't add up to me. There was this growing feeling that something wasn't quite right, and I couldn't ignore it.

Dr Mooncey confirmed my fears as she was also concerned that Lucy showed some signs that could come under the autism spectrum disorder. Dr Mooncey was gentle in her approach, but did advise that it would be in the best interests of our child to consider that some issues may be concerning. This made us think, but it was hard to accept our child was fine! We set out straightaway on a plan of action by appointing an amazing speech and language therapist that worked with Dr Mooncey in her team, along with everything I would change at home to work with Lucy and to encourage her to talk more. We played endless board games and took turns – Lucy was ace at them and everybody got involved. Lucy's grandparents loved this as well. We encouraged Lucy to make choices in what she wanted to wear and the food she ate. When the doorbell went, I would go to collect Lucy and we would answer the door together and encourage her to greet people at the door. Lucy started nursery and absolutely loved playing alongside other children and learning and signing all the little songs. Lucy loved spinning and walking on her tiptoes, so to give this a place where she could do this freely, she started ballet lessons and loved every minute of them.

There was a huge part of me that wanted to ignore Dr Mooncey, as I know you will want to as well.

It would have been too easy to pretend everything was fine and go back to that happy place. But there was this nagging feeling that kept returning – what if she was right? I just couldn't take that risk and I'm so thankful that I did listen. If I hadn't, I know that Lucy wouldn't be the remarkable lady she is today.

So fast forward and Lucy is a very intelligent articulate young lady. Her talents are simply amazing and there have been countless times when she has completely shocked me with them. Her school reports are exceptional, and she is a kind and caring, beautiful child. Lucy has a few close friends and behaves like most young adults her age. Lucy shows empathy – sometimes I have to point out certain situations to her, but she is clever and quickly learns what doesn't come quite as naturally to her. I read somewhere when I had just started out on this journey that autism is like getting on a plane with the expectation that you're going to Spain and halfway through the flight you're being told that you're not going to Spain but instead your flight is now one way and you're going to Italy. You didn't ask to go to Italy, nothing is what you are expecting, you've packed for Spain not Italy. You want to be in Spain with all your friends. However, if you look and see, you'll see all the beauty in Italy, and you'll realise just how lucky you are to have been chosen to go and stay in Italy, and whilst Spain is amazing, so is Italy – if you look closely it isn't just amazing, it's incredible.

I never look back and wish I was in Spain. I did a lot when I first got our diagnosis. Hopefully this analogy will help you to see this and that all is not lost. Autism is awful sometimes and it is hard work. However, there are so many amazing and exceptional gifts that come with autism. If I could give you any advice, that would be to listen to what Dr Mooncey says – she really did change the course of direction that Lucy was on, and I'm forever thankful to her.

Rose's diagnosis journey

Rose was always my baby girl from the beginning, but as she grew I noticed a difference between her and other children. We went to toddler groups and slowly each child that came in developed quicker than she did. She didn't really play or talk and she had such meltdowns that she would head bang hard objects.

Deep down we as parents knew what was coming, as we knew she was behind in development. We had Portage[1] out weekly and myself and my husband taught her a bit of Makaton, to communicate with us. The Makaton helped calm her frustration down, so she felt heard by us. But the day she got diagnosed with autism and global development delay I cried. This was for loads of reasons. It was a relief that we had answers, but also painful as a group of professionals had told me that our daughter was different.

Rose was diagnosed just before she started at Portesbery School. She had already attended the Little Portesberries group, which we found amazing from the beginning. Little Portesberries was a support/toddler group for children with needs and it was an amazing group to support not only the child but the family as well. You got to meet other families in a similar situation to yours, which would make you realise that you're not alone.

We had a home visit from Portesbery before Rose started at the school. Adele and Clare came to visit in our home and Rose immediately felt at ease. She played with them both and they took notes on what she liked and disliked, to make her transition into her class more smooth for her.

Things really changed when Rose started school at Portesbery. They started her on PECS® cards and carried on with Makaton. Rose had a TA [teaching assistant] called Ashleigh and Rose adored her – they just clicked from day one. She loved all the staff in the school, which truly made life better for her. Day by day we noticed changes in Rose. She was giving eye contact and screeching in excitement more. Then she started making sounds that were similar to words. Adele and other staff would do 'What's in the box?' every day with her. Slowly, over a few months, she went from not sitting for the session to sitting and watching what was going on. After a few weeks in class she started exchanging PECS – it was such a *wow* moment. We were so excited and proud as she had another way to communicate with us. The best thing was that the staff at the school were just as proud and excited

---

1   Portage is a home-visiting educational service for preschool children with SEN and their families.

as we were, which really helped make you feel you're not doing this on your own.

After a year, Rose was getting frustrated as she knew what she wanted to say to everyone, but just couldn't find the words to speak or have enough PECS cards to say it. Speech and language worked with Ashleigh and Adele in her class and they built a file up to prove that Rose would benefit from a communication device. This device is a tablet that has all the words she would need to click on to tell us what she wants. After weeks of her teachers working on this, we found out she had been approved to have the device. This was a major lifeline for Rose. It was going to make things less frustrating for her in communication. Rose started using speech more and we found this was more in excitement. Her first word in class was ball (she was in the hydro pool and saw a beach ball). She shouted to her key worker Ashleigh 'ball'. The excitement from the school and us made Rose super excited. Once the device arrived, it was a whole new ball game. She was learning fast how to use it and would use it in class regularly. Daily they would get her to say what she saw and wanted on the device. But they still kept up with PECS cards and Makaton as well.

Rose fell poorly twice and ended up in hospital twice. Both times she regressed in speech and trust whilst in hospital. This meant she wasn't really talking and she was refusing food and drink. She had a tube put in her nose, which then went to her tummy to feed her meds and fluids. We tried everything to get her to cooperate in the hospital, but she just didn't understand and was stressed. Rose's school sent staff into hospital on both occasions to help us get her communicating and taking food and drink. On both occasions their help and support got Rose through it with us. The second time they came to hospital, they brought a doll in and fed it and explained that way that baby needed feeding. The doll even had a food tube put on. They brought foods she liked and PECS cards for her, to persuade her to start eating. It all worked and the next day Rose had her tube removed. Then the day after that she came home. As parents we have found it's so important to accept help and support. It's okay to need help. I used to think I was a failure as a parent if I couldn't fix things or make things better. But you genuinely can't fix everything on your own. Our daughter has thrived since she went to Portesbery and we accepted help. Working together as parents and school has got her where she is today.

When Rose started Portesbery I thought she would never talk, she would never do this or that. Well, today our daughter is at a school for children with all learning needs. It's a school which is for children who are a lot more capable than I ever thought Rose would be. She is talking, writing, drawing and smiling daily. She continues to use her communication device and PECS cards for words she struggles with, but there's a huge difference in her.

If this has taught us anything as a family, it's that autism doesn't define your child, it doesn't mean your child can't or won't. Autism is a condition that you as a family and other support take on together as one. You push your child to their ability, and if they can't do something, you keep trying or find another way of getting what you need. Our biggest regret is that we judged our child on what other children were capable of at the beginning, when we should have been looking at what she could do or what we could do to help her. We are truly grateful for all the support and care which our daughter and we have had over the past few years.

Is there anything you would like to go back in time and say to yourself at the start of your journey?

We asked the parents who have contributed to this book this question. We will leave you with their insightful words and hope.

'I wish I could tell myself that this journey isn't linear; there will be ups and downs, but the highs will soon outweigh the lows, and the feeling you get when milestones are met will blow you away.'

'You know your child best. If you don't think something is right for your child, fight for it. Don't just accept things because someone in authority told you it's the way things are. There is one hell of a rocky road ahead, but you will come out of it a much stronger person.'

'Life will not be as you had imagined; but don't feel guilty about grieving for the child you never had, because once you get past that, you will learn to love your new, different and unexpected life. Your child will teach you to stop and appreciate much smaller things in life, things that previously you would never have noticed. They will make you so proud when they achieve things that you never thought possible.'

'The diagnostic tool is only as good as the "professional" who uses it... trust your instincts as a parent... If local services fail to diagnose, look further for more knowledgeable Professionals with a capital P.'

'Having an autistic child changes "you", not just your day-to-day life.'

'Ignore the judgements... You're doing an awesome job supporting your child.'

'It'll probably take twice as long as you expect it to. It feels huge, but it changes nothing in real terms. That's still the kid you adore and it'll be okay.'

'You were right...and although it took a court order, the diagnosis helped.'

'To accept the child you have and work with them.'

'To focus more on what your child can do and push them to their ability, rather than comparing them to other children. Also remember that if your child is having a meltdown and you don't know why or how to make things better, it doesn't make you a bad parent. No parent can make things perfect. But just being there through those hard times with them, no matter what, makes you a fab parent already.'

'Don't let people's comments and looks when you're out or at occasions get to you. It's not you or your child that's the problem, it's the people that are too obnoxious to see the reality of what you are all achieving.'

'Celebrate those little achievements with your child and make the most of every second.'

'It's not your imagination. Go with your intuition.'

'To accept help. You don't have to do it all, and to make time for you – date nights and stuff.'

'Focus on what your child *can* do – the strengths, not the deficits. Enjoy every bit of progress, however small. Try and keep a sense of humour – and never give up!'

CHAPTER 21

A–Z of Terms Which Can Be Relevant to Autism

Autism

Autism is a complex neurodevelopmental condition which is increasing in prevalence. There has been a significant increase in public awareness of autism in recent years and most people now have some understanding of what autism means. It is described as a spectrum but it is not linear. It can be described as being like a colour wheel with different shades of each colour signifying the severity of the difficulty in a particular skill.

Behaviours

Presentation of unusual behaviours may be a feature of autistic traits. It is important to be able to differentiate children's behaviour which does not conform to developmental norms. This is not easy, especially for first-time parents.

Caregivers

Caregivers or parents, educational staff and others can also suffer from emotional difficulties. This should not be overlooked or ignored. The emotional trauma that parents experience is immense; learning to understand and deal with a child's behaviours and emotions can be daunting. This is made more difficult with a child who does not communicate or engage. On the one hand, there may be a child who will not want to be touched, looked at or spoken to, and will flinch at any physical contact. The other extreme will be the overzealous, boisterous child who does not understand personal space and boundaries and will invade the personal space of others. Some children may not be able to differentiate between friends, family and strangers. Their lack of awareness makes them vulnerable and they may be a target for bullying.

It is important for parents to manage and express their feelings and fears to friends or professionals, without being judged. Some will share their emotions, and others may not be able to do so. It is important to care for personal emotional wellbeing and learn resilience.

Development

Development is the rate at which a child progresses in different skill areas. Many autistic children may develop normally up until the age of two, and parents may not have any idea that there could be any underlying neurodevelopmental difficulties. This may be that the child acquires milestones such as walking, running, feeding themselves and fine motor control. Speech may be the first area where parents notice their child is not communicating and the child is almost 2 years old. Other signs may be that the child is reluctant to give eye contact and is not responsive to their name. Parents may think the child is deaf and a hearing test may be requested. It is also important to see if the child has learnt to point (using their index finger). Do they show enjoyment in joint interaction and clap and smile and respond to carers and other individuals? Does the child raise their arms to be picked up or are they not keen to be held? Does the young child at the preschool stage join in with actions songs, nursery rhymes and show an interest in others at toddler groups? Sometimes parents may say, 'My child is shy and I was also a really shy child and did not like joining with others.'

Although tempting to compare children, remember that each child is unique and develops at their own rate. Be vigilant and if you have concerns, speak to a health professional, even if it is for reassurance.

Emotions

'Emotion' is defined by the Oxford dictionary as a strong feeling such as love, fear or anger, the part of a person's character that consists of feelings.

Emotions are part of human life and development. The intensity of the pain and suffering can be overwhelming and the impact on our lives at such a tragic time cannot be described. Unexpected events can trigger emotions, and the Covid-19 pandemic is a major life event that has an impact on emotional wellbeing.

Alexithymia is a term that describes the inability of a person to realise when those around them are experiencing certain emotions, and they may also struggle with recognising their own emotions. It is derived from the Greek word meaning 'without words for emotions'.

The area of the brain which is responsible for different emotions is in the limbic system. The limbic system is made up of different parts as follows:

- The amygdala is the area which processes emotional stimuli. It is also linked to the fight–flight response.
- The nucleus accumbens has a large concentration of dopamine receptors that result in the experience of pleasure.
- The hypothalamus regulates emotions such as joy, fear, sadness or excitement, and this further affects body functions such as rapid heart rate. Autistic individuals are unable to link the emotional experience with physical manifestations and find it difficult to understand and explain their emotions.
- The hippocampus is involved with memory.

The limbic system was one of the first areas of the brain to develop and it has evolved over time. The initial function was the fight–flight response in primitive people where this reflex response had to be well developed for survival. Over generations this has evolved to become more complex, although fight–flight responses still remain a primitive response to any danger.

Neurochemicals are brain chemicals which influence mood. There are three main neurotransmitters:

- Dopamine, as mentioned earlier, is connected with feelings of pleasure.
- Serotonin is responsible for memory and learning. An imbalance in serotonin levels can result in anxiety, anger and mood changes.

- Cortisol, which is released in response to stress and anxiety, further moderates mood.

Any abnormalities in the production of these chemicals, or any damage to the brain, can influence emotional understanding and lead to mental health problems such as anxiety, depression and other mental health problems.

There are many studies confirming the release of beta endorphins ('feel good' hormones) after a relaxing activity. Skin-to-skin contact with babies, (kangaroo care[1]) has been found to reduce stress hormone levels.

Friendship

Many of us may take friends and friendships for granted. Friendship is a special relationship that involves mutual feelings of trust, respect and affection. It can develop into a lifelong bond with special times and memories that can be shared and cherished.

What is a friend? This is a difficult question to ask an autistic person. They may have a concept of friendship and many do have some 'friends'. Sometimes a bond develops because of a mutual special interest but may lack emotional depth.

Many autistic people can also go on to have meaningful and happy relationships. They will find those special people in their lives or someone will find them! Friendships for most people are a very important part of their life.

Autistic people's inner desire for this emotional feedback through people may be lacking. Their emotional wellbeing might be regulated by an interest in pets, for example, or things such as Minecraft® or Lego®, world wars or soft toys that give them more pleasure than social interaction.

Remember to promote friendships and social skills by:

- Being positive and hopeful.
- Nurturing friendships and understanding in your children.

---

1   Mooncey, S., Giannakoulopoulos, V., Glover, D. and Modi, N. (1997) 'The effect of mother-infant skin-to-skin contact on plasma cortisol and β-endorphin concentrations in preterm newborns.' *Infant Behavior and Development* 20, 4, 553–557.

- Making opportunities for them to learn friendships and enjoy the pleasure we take for granted through social interaction.

Grief

In life we all come across grief, whether it be the loss of a loved one, illness or even the Covid-19 pandemic. Grief is a complex process and no two people grieve in the same way. The fact that your child may have a diagnosis of autism may trigger feelings of grief, and all individuals will deal with it in their own way.

The grieving process was originally proposed by Elizabeth Kübler-Ross in 1969.[2] However, it is generally accepted within the psychological arena that there are five stages of grieving. Each process lasts for different periods of time and they do not necessarily have to be in this order:

- Denial and isolation.
- Anger.
- Bargaining.
- Depression.
- Acceptance.

Denial and isolation

This process of grieving is the first stage that helps us overcome the emotional pain that we are experiencing. It is hoped that over time the acuteness of this feeling will fade.

Anger

We try to find reasons why things have happened. Guilt can overcome us and we may look for answers when in fact there may be nothing to explain why our child is developing the way they are. There is no logical answer, but it is human nature to try to find answers.

We try to cope with our feelings and may experience anger. Anger

---

2　See, for example, Gregory, C. (2021) 'The five stages of grief: an examination of the Kubler-Ross model.' *Psycom*. Accessed on 10/04/21 at www.psycom.net/depression. central.grief.html may be directed towards health professionals or to ourselves in how we could have done something different. What if I had done this differently? What if I had given more attention to my child? What if I had eaten better in pregnancy? What if I wasn't so stressed? What if I had left work early? What if...? These 'if onlys' are attempts to look for reasons and punish ourselves. The wisdom of hindsight is good, but we know that in reality we cannot change the past. Always remember that as long as there is life there is hope and don't be afraid to reach out for help. Allow yourself time to heal psychologically and things will get better.

Bargaining

As mentioned in anger, the 'if onlys' can overtake your life and your mind. Secretly you make bargains with God or with yourself to say 'I will never do this again' or 'I promise to live a better life', 'I will not get angry', 'I will dedicate my time or money to charity if only things can get better'. This is a desperate plea during a period of helplessness and a stage that often comes with the guilt. However, do not feel guilty. Faith is important to many people, and if you are a believer and feel that God can help you and support you through this time, it can be comforting. If you are an athlete and you feel exercise will help you through it, do so. Do not feel guilty about doing something for yourself. Read, watch Netflix, do yoga, sing and dance! You will feel invigorated and ready to take on the day, as these activities help you to relax.

Depression

All of us are prone to develop some symptoms of depression at times in our lives, mainly around major life events. Mostly we are able to overcome these emotions with support from family, friends, exercise or other activities. A child being diagnosed with autism can be life-changing. We may become sad, withdrawn and find it very difficult to deal with everyday situations. We worry: What will happen? How will we deal with it? What does the future hold? Will my child be able to be independent? Will they live a normal life? Will they get a job? Will they have a partner? Will they have a family? All these questions will cross your mind and the human brain may react by producing feelings of low mood, emotional numbness and withdrawal.

One needs to look at the positives. 'What are the positives?' you may think. There are many. Your child is healthy, they do not have a life-limiting illness. They do not require regular medical intervention and they are physically able. The human brain thrives on endorphins, serotonin and all the positive hormones that give you a feeling of well-being. It is important to keep your emotional strength during this time. A simple act like a short spell of yoga may be what your brain needs. Mindfulness and meditation can relax you and reduce your cortisol and stress hormones so that you are in a better frame of mind to take on the challenges of the day, however big or small.

If you think that you are experiencing low mood or maybe feel depressed, seek support from friends and family or contact your GP or primary care doctor for help.

Acceptance

The time when one reaches acceptance varies. Some parents are ready to accept the diagnosis early in the journey and are proactive. Parents are determined that they will do all they can for their child, however long it takes and whatever the costs. At the other end of the spectrum are those families where acceptance is extremely difficult, particularly if they are from a background where mental health problems are considered a stigma in society. Parents wish to be told there is a cure, this will end, things will change and the child will be 'normal' again. Then there are parents who may take time to accept the diagnosis, or a few who may want to seek a second opinion. This does not necessarily mean that they are any less brave or realistic, but coping and resilience vary in different individuals. After all, we are human and learn to adapt to a different way of parenting. It is a matter of learning to read your child and growing with them. At times it will be through trial and error and you won't always get it right, but keep positive. The entire journey of life is a learning process, which in the case of a child who has any neurodevelopmental difficulties makes the journey different and maybe more difficult than you had thought. Nobody said this would be easy, nobody gave you a handbook on parenting, neither do you have to pass a test to become a parent! Most parents slip into parenthood without thinking about it. When you have a child who is autistic, your parenting strategies will be very different from those you use with a child who is developing neurotypically. But this will pass. I have heard this expression used much more in the last few weeks than I (Sophie) ever have. On a personal note, the passing of my mother in the last year, followed by my father two months later has been an emotional challenge and indeed I have also been through this grieving process, as has Adele who lost her father a few months previously. However, these were the words that my uncle said to me when he visited my mother in hospital: 'Sophie, this will pass, and you will get over it. You will feel pain and the loss will remain with you. You will learn to accept life and move on. You will become strong through love and hope. Over time the acuteness will wane, but the void will always remain. It will take on a different form, but you will learn to accept the loss you have to bear.'

Hierarchy

Humans are social animals and social groups form. Inadvertently they may be ranked, whether it is as a result of age, experience or power. Autistic persons have been found to have difficulty recognising social ranking.[3] This may be where problems can arise. An autistic child may not be able to recognise social ranking and respond to a teacher as they would to a peer. This may appear overly familiar or in some instances rude. If those working with children do not appreciate that the child has autism, the behaviour could have consequences which the child may think are unfair.

Inheritance

Modern advances in genetics and research suggest a possible familial tendency for the development of autism. Autism is seen in all cultures, backgrounds and countries. It is thought to be one of the most common neuropsychiatric conditions which is passed on in families. The severity of core symptoms is variable within the same family as is their intellectual ability. Macrocephaly, or a 'large head', can be associated with autism, and is found in 20 per cent of cases. It is not

---

3   Ogawa, S., Iriguchi, M., Lee, Y-A., Yoshikawa, S. and Goto, Y. (2019) 'Atypical social rank recognition in autism spectrum disorder.' *Scientific Reports 9*, 15657. https://doi.org/10.1038/s41598-019-52211-8

possible to correlate the cognitive ability of a child to the size of the head. There are various theories which postulate possible differences in brain function and anatomy in autism,[4] for example, the size of total brain volume or increase in size of corpus callosum or the limbic system. None of the studies so far have found specific anatomical findings related to autism. There are studies to indicate that the environment has an influence on development of the nervous system.

Autistic individuals can find it challenging to consider things from the perspective of others, and this may be misconstrued as being 'egocentric' or 'selfish'. Sometimes their words or actions can appear rude as they lack a 'social filter'. It is important to understand that this perceived egocentricity can get autistic individuals into trouble. They can appear to be defiant, argumentative, contradictory and difficult. This highlights the literal understanding of autistic persons.

Joint attention sharing

Joint attention sharing is the ability to share something: an activity, an object or an emotion with another person. Developmentally, this skill appears around 6–12 months of age, which makes babies very interactive. It has been noted in the literature that children who have symptoms of autism may not develop the ability for joint attention sharing.[5] Joint attention is crucial in the development of social communication, interaction and future language development. Research shows that autistic children have the ability for joint sharing but lack the motivation to do so.[6]

Joint attention sharing can involve triadic or dyadic eye contact. Triadic eye contact involves attention between the infant, another person and the object. The child shifts their gaze from the person to finger pointing and then to the object. Triadic eye contact usually involves the child making a request by looking at the other individual and the

4   Brambilla, P., Hardan, A., Ucelli di Nemi, S., Perez, J., Soares, J.C. and Barale, F. (2003) 'Brain anatomy and development in autism: review of structural MRI studies.' *Brain Research Bulletin 61*, 6, 557–569.

5   Vismara, L.A. and Lyons, G.L. (2007) 'Using perseverative interests to elicit joint attention behaviors in young children with autism: theoretical and clinical implications for understanding motivation.' *Journal of Positive Behavior Intervention 9*, 4, 214–228.

6   Charman, T., Baron-Cohen, S., Swettenham, J., Baird, G., Drew, A. and Cox, A. (2003) 'Predicting language outcome in infants with autism and pervasive development disorder.' *International Journal of Language and Communication Disorders 38*, 3, 265–285.

object. This shows the infant's awareness of the other person. In dyadic eye contact the child looks only at the object, not the other person. Many studies over the last few decades have shown the importance of joint attention sharing for later language and social development.[7] Encouraging joint attention sharing can have a positive impact on future social communication skills.[8]

A good example of a joint attention sharing activity for children is blowing bubbles! The child looks at the adult with anticipation so that they can see the bubbles being blown.

Kith and kin

It is important for children to be able to distinguish between familiar people and strangers. Babies who have developed a secure attachment with their carers will develop a sense of stranger danger at around 7–10 months. Children on the spectrum may find it difficult to differentiate people. Social Stories™ are very helpful in teaching children this concept. There have been interesting studies looking at autistic children's perception of faces. One study by Hobson *et al.* looked at the responses of autistic adolescents and a group of non-autistic adolescents to photographs of individuals with different expressions. Some faces were also shown upside down. The non-autistic young people turned the pictures the right way up almost instantly, whereas some of the children in the autistic group kept looking at the upside faces, trying to decipher them.[9] This indicates that autistic people may find it difficult to process facial recognition.

Love and loneliness

Love is a strong feeling of affection. Some children on the spectrum may find it difficult to reciprocate the love that you share. Affection

7   Mundy, P., Sigman, M. and Kasari, C. (1990) 'A longitudinal study of joint attention and language development in autistic children.' *Journal of Autism and Developmental Disorders 20*, 1, 115–128.

8   Rogers, S. (2006) 'Evidence-Based Interventions for Language Development in Young Children with Autism.' In T. Charman and W. Stone (eds), *Social and Communication Development in Autism Spectrum Disorders: Early Intervention, Diagnosis, and Intervention*. New York, NY: Guilford Press.

9   Hobson, R.P., Ouston, J. and Lee, A. (1988) 'What's in a face? The case of autism.' *British Journal of Psychology 79*, 4, 441–453.

may not come spontaneously for autistic individuals. They may find it very difficult to hug, cuddle, be held or kissed. It may be that some autistic individuals are more comfortable with animals – animals cannot ask you to do things or tell you off! Their interest may have started with dinosaurs, which may be an obsessional interest in some autistic children. Some children relate better to pets and find them comforting. Chris Packham, wildlife expert and television presenter was diagnosed with Asperger's in his adult years and presented a BBC documentary, *Asperger's and Me*, in which he described his social struggles as a child and how he found comfort in nature and animals.

Multidisciplinary assessment

A multidisciplinary assessment is the recommended assessment for children who may have neurodevelopmental difficulties such as autism. The multidisciplinary team includes different professionals who work collaboratively to assess children for autism. There will usually be a medical professional such as a paediatrician with expertise in neurodevelopment, and at least one other professional. Depending on the needs of the child, this may be a SLT, EP, OT or specialist teacher. Early identification and diagnosis help the child and families to overcome any challenges they may face and contribute to improving the long-term prognosis.

Neurotypical

'Neurotypical' and 'neuroatypical' are new words (neologisms) to describe people's behaviour. This terminology is gaining popularity, including in TV shows portraying autism. 'Neurotypical' describes a person who has normal or non-autistic development and behaviours. A neuroatypical person is one who displays diverse or atypical development or behaviour and includes autism. These terms are commonly used by autistic individuals to explain differences.

OCD and autism

OCD (obsessive compulsive disorder) is a condition in which an individual feels compelled to carry out repetitive behaviours or thoughts.

OCD and autism may appear to have some similarities.[10] Researchers have found that 84 per cent of autistic individuals have anxiety and at least 17 per cent may have OCD. Another way of looking at it is that individuals with OCD may have a higher incidence of autism, which may be undiagnosed or is diagnosed later in life. Obsessive behaviours can occur to some degree in people generally. Obsessive compulsive disorders are present in 1.2 per cent of the population to an extent where it affects their mental health. Brain imaging studies have shown that individuals who have these behaviours can have a dysfunction in the caudate nucleus in the striatum, the area of the brain which influences habit formation. The striatum is also closely linked to social interaction.

A condition has been recently identified called 'Pure O'. This is where an individual has intrusive thoughts but does not need to carry out physical acts.

PANDAS/PANS

'PANS' is an umbrella term used for 'paediatric acute onset of neuropsychiatric symptoms', which includes conditions known as 'PANDAS' (paediatric autoimmune neuropsychiatric disorders associated with streptococcal infections), the sudden onset of obsessive compulsive disorders or tics in children. PANS has been mentioned here as some parents may refer to anecdotal reports of improvement in autistic behaviours after treatment for streptococcal infection. PANDAS does *not* occur more frequently in autistic children.

Quirks

A quirk can be described as a habit an individual repeatedly displays, which often becomes associated with them. A commonly heard phrase is that 'We all have tendencies or quirks which could be autistic.' To have a diagnosis of autism there are very specific symptoms and characteristics which must be fulfilled. It is inaccurate to say that all of us

---

10 Postorino, V., Kerns, C.M., Vivanti, G., Bradshaw, J., Siracusano, M. and Mazzone, L. (2017) 'Anxiety disorders and obsessive-compulsive disorder in individuals with autism spectrum disorder.' *Current Psychiatry Reports 19*, 92.

have autistic tendencies – merely having quirks or eccentric ideas does not necessarily mean we are autistic.

RRBs

RRBs (restrictive repetitive behaviours) are a common feature of autism. They are behaviours or activities which are frequently repeated by an individual and can interfere with daily life. Restrictive behaviours which involve play include lining up toys, spinning objects, wheel spinning, flicking light switches on and off and staring at lights. These are the behaviours which can often cause difficulties as they may have an impact on the family's daily routine.

RRBs can be divided into two main groups:

1. Low-order behaviours involving motor mannerisms such as flapping, rocking, grunting and fidgeting.
2. High-order behaviours usually associated with routines, rituals and obsessive interests.

Stimming

Stimming refers to 'self-stimulating' behaviours which are repetitive and can be rhythmic. They may be physical acts such as flapping or spinning; sometimes they are vocal – for example, grunting. Stimming is not always a sign of autism. Many of us sometimes have stimming behaviours, such as hair twiddling, but they do not interfere with daily activities.

The following are types of stimming:

- Auditory stimming is making sounds such as humming, singing and throat noises. It may be repeating words or phrases.
- Tactile stimming involves the sensation of touch. The young person may like to rub the skin or finger flick.
- Visual stimming may include blinking or side glancing (watching from the corners of the eyes).
- Vestibular stimming relates to an individual's balance, such as flapping or spinning.
- Olfactory stimming includes sniffing objects.

- Gustatory stimming may be licking or chewing objects.

There may be triggers for stimming such as:

- Anxiety.
- Excitement.
- Excessive sensory stimuli such as noise or crowds.
- Under-sensitivity to surroundings.

Stimming may serve a purpose for the child such as:

- Pain reduction – stimming can cause the release of endorphins, which can evoke a pleasure response.
- Managing emotions – excitement or frustration can cause stimming.
- Self-regulation – stimming may help to soothe or relax the child.[11]

Many parents ask whether these behaviours are dangerous and how they can be managed. The behaviours are not dangerous unless they involve physical acts, such as excessive head banging, which could cause injury. They should be managed if they interfere with daily life or learning. There is no evidence to support harm from stimming. In fact, one study examining stimming in autistic adults reported that these adults found stimming soothing. They described stimming as an adaptive mechanism to help them cope with difficult situations and they did not want treatment to stop stimming.[12]

Siblings

The sibling relationship is unique and generally the longest-lasting relationship in life. The sibling relationship will be influenced by the birth order of the autistic child, gender and behavioural difficulties. An older sibling may be more tolerant and nurturing, whereas a

11   Sandman, C.A. (1988) 'Beta-endorphin disregulation in autistic and self-injurious behavior: a neurodevelopmental hypothesis.' *Synapse 2*, 3, 193–199.
12   Kapp, S.K., Steward, R. and Crane, L. (2019) '"People should be allowed to do what they like": autistic adults' views and experiences of stimming.' *Autism 23*, 7, 1782–1792.

younger sibling may be a good playmate or be frightened by outbursts of behaviours. These outcomes can affect the psychological wellbeing of siblings and lead to acceptance or resentment towards the autistic sibling. Sibling relationships have been studied and it is generally accepted that the relationship is complex and multiple factors can influence it.[13] Because it is complex, it's difficult to generalise. What is important is that siblings are also supported during the diagnostic process and after the diagnosis. Autistic children who have siblings benefit from their interaction and the siblings possibly serve as role models for the autistic child. This also teaches the siblings acceptance of difference and inclusivity.

Therapy dog

Pet therapy builds on the pre-existing human–animal bond. Interacting with a friendly dog can help many physical and mental health issues. It may reduce blood pressure and improve overall cardiovascular health. This interaction can also release endorphins and help alleviate pain, reduce stress and improve an individual's overall psychological state.

Studies show that children exhibited a more playful mood, were more focused and were more aware of their social environments when in the presence of a therapy dog. These findings indicate that inter-action with dogs may have specific benefits for children and suggest that animal-assisted therapy (AAT) is an appropriate form of therapy.[14] Therapy dogs are interactive and children appear to relate to them as non-judgemental participants who are outside of the complications and expectations of human relationships. This unique interaction may offer children a valuable form of social and emotional support in educational and therapeutic settings.[15] OTs use animals through

13   Kovshoff, H., Cebula, K., Tsai, H-W.J. and Hastings, R.P. (2017) 'Siblings of children with autism: the Siblings Embedded Systems Framework.' *Current Developmental Disorders Reports 4*, 37–45.

14   Martin, F. and Farnum, J. (2002) 'Animal-assisted therapy for children with pervasive developmental disorders.' *Western Journal of Nursing Research 24*, 6, 657–670.

15   Frieson, L. (2010) 'Exploring animal-assisted programs with children in school and therapeutic contexts.' *Early Childhood Education Journal 37*, 261–267.

approaches such as create/promote, establish/restore, maintain, modify and prevent.[16]

Research indicates benefits in terms of greater interaction and a secure therapeutic relationship (therapist–patient–animal).[17]

Pet therapy can be used in many different ways. Defined objectives are an important part of therapy, and progress will be recorded and tracked at structured sessions.

The goals of a pet therapy programme can include:

- Improving motor skills.
- Increasing self-esteem.
- Increasing verbal communication.
- Developing social skills.
- Increasing willingness to join in activities/motivation.
- Improving interactions with others.
- Making a child happier, lessening depression, and improving outlook on life.
- Decreasing loneliness and isolation by providing companionship.
- Reducing anxiety.
- Helping children learn empathic and nurturing skills.
- Improving a child's ability to trust adults and feel safe in the therapy space.
- Developing trust.
- Building empathy.
- Learning to express and connect with emotions.
- Sensory regulation and exploration.

Umbrella

The autism spectrum is an umbrella term to include the neurodiversity of this condition. 'Autism', 'autism spectrum disorder' and 'autism spectrum condition' describe a range of autistic traits. Previously these were classified as pervasive developmental disorders (PDD).

---

16 Youngstrom, M.J., Brayman, S.J., Anthony, P., Brinson, M. *et al.* 'Occupational therapy practice framework: domain and process.' *The American Journal of Occupational Therapy* 57, 1, 115.

17 Solomon, O. (2010) 'What a dog can do: children with autism and therapy dogs in social interaction.' *Ethos 38*, 1, 143–166.

Vaccines

Vaccination can be a controversial topic, but it is important to discuss some of the facts from the medical perspective.

The MMR (measles, mumps and rubella) vaccine does *not* cause autism. Media publicity in 1998 following Dr Andrew Wakefield's paper published in *The Lancet* linking autism to the MMR vaccine[18] caused a wave of panic. Subsequently, many studies have discredited his theory.[19] Andrew Wakefield was struck off the medical register in the UK for his false claim and the paper has been retracted from the journal. Across the world over three million children have been studied,[20] confirming that no link has been found between MMR and autism.

There have been other parental concerns regarding vaccines, such as vaccines containing toxins, primarily thiomersal. Thiomersal is a mercury derivative which was used in some vaccines for more than 50 years. There was speculation that the mercury could cause 'mercury poisoning' resulting in developmental delay in children. The content of mercury in these vaccines was extremely low, almost negligible, and certainly not sufficient to cause poisoning in humans. As a precautionary measure thiomersal/thimerosal (spelt in both forms in the literature) has been removed from vaccines. There is insufficient evidence to corroborate this link. Despite the removal of thiomersal from most vaccines, autism prevalence has not decreased.[21]

Another common belief is that subjecting young babies to an increasing number of vaccinations increases the immunological load on the child and weakens the immune system. This again is not a valid explanation. The newborn's immune system is subjected to multiple attacks, including viral infections. Although vaccines increase the load of foreign particles in the body, they do not overwhelm the child's

---

18 Wakefield, A.J., Murch, S.H., Anthony, A., Linnell, J. *et al.* (1998) 'Ileal-lymphoid-nodular hyperplasia, non-specific colitis, and pervasive developmental disorder in children.' *The Lancet 351*, 9103, 637–641. Retracted article.

19 Farrington, C.P., Miller, E. and Taylor, B. (2001) 'MMR and autism: further evidence against a causal association.' *Vaccine 19*, 27, 3632–3635.

20 Wilson, K., Mills, E., Ross, C., McGowan, J. and Jadad, A. (2003) 'Association of autistic spectrum disorder and the measles, mumps, and rubella vaccine: a systematic review of current epidemiological evidence.' *Archives of Pediatrics and Adolescent Medicine 157*, 7, 628–634.

21 Hurley, A., Tadrous, M. and Miller, S. (2010) 'Thimerosal containing vaccines and autism.' *Journal of Pediatric Pharmacology and Therapeutics 15*, 3, 173–181.

immune system.[22] Modern-day vaccines contain fewer immunological loads than used to be the case, because of advances in preparation and medical research.

Unfortunately, there will always be the 'anti-vaccination/anti-vax' followers who are against the concept of vaccination. There are said to be around five million anti-vax people in the UK. Sadly, this does not improve herd immunity and it increases the risks for the general population.

'Weirdos'

Quite often you hear remarks like 'He looks weird', 'He says strange things', 'He dresses weird', 'He doesn't understand', 'He is obsessed with animals', 'He says unkind things'. These statements are sometimes made about children on the spectrum. On a superficial level, the words or behaviour of autistic children may appear 'weird'. However, these children can be very literal and cannot see how their statements are strange or rude. This is one of the biggest challenges for autistic children. People on the spectrum do not necessarily look different; they look like regular kids but behave differently at times. The unusual behaviours or quirks are much more apparent in boys than in girls. Autistic girls may be more aware of the reaction of others, whereas boys may not be able to see these subtleties.

These differences may result in stigmatisation. Some cultures are very close-minded to the great neurodiversity that is present in the population. Families with an autistic child may find it very difficult to integrate into society. They may feel that they are unable to enjoy social gatherings because of the additional complexities of having an autistic child. If you have an autistic child, it is important to find creative ways to join social functions, even for short periods of time, and to prepare your child for that experience. There may be challenges within the family. Siblings at times may feel resentful of a diagnosis of autism within the family as they could also be bullied or made fun of by others. This may make them want to dissociate from their autistic sibling, causing difficult dynamics within the family. There is no such

---

22   Offit, P.A., Quarles, J., Gerber, M.A., Hackett, C.J. *et al.* (2002) 'Addressing parents' concerns: do multiple vaccines overwhelm or weaken the infant's immune system?' *Pediatrics 109*, 1, 124–129.

thing as an ideal family and no such thing as a perfect child. As a parent you learn to support your children, try to understand them and help them understand how to be positive and live a rich and fulfilled life.

Xperts (Experts)
Health visitors
For children under the age of 5 years, the first person to consult is the health visitor. Health visitors in the UK are involved in universal screening programmes for childhood development. They are responsible for monitoring growth and developmental progress for children under the age of 5 years.

General practitioners (GPs) or primary care physicians
Your family doctor can guide and support you about concerns and support available. They also implement childhood surveillance programmes for developmental assessments. If there are concerns, they will refer the child on to a paediatrician for a detailed neurodevelopmental assessment.

Community paediatricians
These are children's doctors who are specialists in childhood development and have had specific training. They are able to carry out specific developmental assessments and investigations into the difficulties the child may present with. They also work in a multidisciplinary fashion with other professionals.

Audiologists
Audiologists are trained in testing hearing in children. There are various ways in which the audiologist carries out a hearing test. In babies it is carried out by OAE (otoacoustic emissions). Babies are universally screened for hearing loss to exclude hearing loss, which may be congenital.

Glue ear is a common condition in childhood which can cause hearing impairment and affect speech development.

Speech and language therapists/speech pathologists

A SLT's input is helpful to understand whether the child has a specific speech and language difficulty, a generalised speech and language delay or other communication difficulties such as autism. Speech and language therapy input is very helpful as therapists will advise parents on strategies to promote a child's speech and language and communication.

Occupational therapists

These are specialists who are trained in assessing a child's fine motor skills and mobility as well as sensory difficulties. OTs' roles have changed over the years and they can also specialise in sensory integration – that is, assessing and managing children who have sensory difficulties.

Clinical psychologists

Clinical paediatric psychologists are very important in supporting families with difficult childhood behaviours. They are specially trained clinicians who are able to support children and families on various aspects of behaviour and communication. Anxiety, which may be a key manifestation of autism, can be managed by psychologists using a variety of methods.

Physiotherapists

PTs support the physical motor skills of a child – that is, walking, running, jumping, etc. Children with global developmental delay can have difficulty in their mobility as well as other areas of their development such as their speech and language and communication. PTs can recommend exercises and techniques to support a child's mobility.

Early years team/educational professionals

The early years team is a team of specially trained educationalists who are able to support preschool children with their learning and social skills. They are able to advise whether the child would benefit from attending a specialist nursery even if they may not be of nursery age. There are specialist nurseries where children can benefit from the support of an early years teacher who has special skills in supporting children with developmental delay and learning difficulties. All nurseries have SEN coordinators.

Educational psychologists

EPs specialise in cognitive or learning assessments for children They are trained in assessing the learning profile of children, as well as some neurodevelopmental difficulties such as ADHD, autism and other conditions such as dyslexia. Specialist teachers also have a role in assessing and supporting the needs of children in an education setting.

Mental health support

Mental health professionals may be key in helping parents and families with children's behaviour. A child who is not able to communicate or engage will develop behaviour problems and 'meltdowns' or tantrums.

Child and adolescent psychiatrist

In more difficult cases a child and adolescent mental health practitioner or child and adolescent psychiatrist may be required for assessing and managing a child with extreme low mood, depression, anxiety or mental health needs.

Voluntary sector support

Other services that are available are in the voluntary sector – for example, local charities that support families with a variety of diagnoses including developmental delay, autism, ADHD, genetic problems and other rarer conditions if these have been diagnosed.

The NAS (National Autistic Society)[23] in the UK provides support, training and resources for families.

---

23 www.autism.org.uk

Children's social services

Children's social services departments have teams to support families who have children with additional needs. They can help with behaviour support, respite at difficult times and applications for support such as disability living allowance (DLA) if applicable.

Autism outreach teams

Autism outreach teams provide support to schools for autistic children. They also help families, including parents and siblings of autistic children, to manage difficulties that they may experience.

It is important to be able to reach out to professionals so that parents are supported in times of need in order to understand the difficulties and also manage their own emotional wellbeing. For parents it is difficult to accept that your child may have a difficulty or disability. Being guided by a professional is very helpful.

Youth

Who are youth? For statistical purposes, they are defined by the United Nations as individuals between the ages of 15 and 24 years. However, it should also be noted that the United Nations Convention on the Rights of the Child defines children as individuals up to the age of 18 years. After that, they are considered to be adults with new responsibilities, such as the right to vote. There are 1.2 billion young people in the world aged between 15 and 24 years, which equates to 16 per cent of the worldwide population. By 2030, the figure for youth is projected to grow by 7 per cent, that is, to nearly 1.3 billion.[24]

As the number of young persons/children/youth increases, the demands for healthcare and educational support increase. We also know that further advances in medicine and support for young people with rare conditions means that these children can have a longer life expectancy. Consequently, these young people should be in a position to access education and skills so that they are able to contribute

---

24   United Nations Department of Economic and Social Affairs (UNDESA) (2013) 'Definition of Youth.' United Nations. Accessed on 15/07/21 at https://www.un.org/esa/socdev/documents/youth/fact-sheets/youth-definition.pdf

to society. The United Nations goals for youth and sustainable development goals aim to ensure that no one will be left behind. This means that all youth should be able to access opportunities to attain their potential. Education should be accessible, equitable and promote lifelong learning for a young person, regardless of their ability.

An article in Australia's *ABC News*[25] has discussed 'the autism advantage' in a story of a 34-year-old autistic person who had struggled to secure a job from his early 20s because of the way he performed at the interview (e.g. not giving eye contact). He subsequently secured a top-secret job with the government, which has been actively recruiting people on the spectrum. Their philosophy is that 'the autism advantage is having complex brains that can solve complex problems'. This neurodiversity is becoming a competitive advantage in certain fields such as IT and technology. Some companies and institutions are now realising that autistic persons can be fixated on their special interests, with attention to details and a vision to achieve results. They may not be sociable, but they are conscientious, dedicated and get the job done!

Zen

Zen is a phrase which is commonly associated with Buddhism. Some people think it is a religion or philosophy. It is a state of mind, when one feels completely alive.

We hope that this book has been a journey towards Zen for you, to understand the goodness and the joy that these children bring into our lives. We continue to strive to make our children happy individuals. Good luck on your journey!

---

25   Allen, C. (2020) 'The "autism advantage" at work and how it's giving firms a competitive edge.' *ABC News*, 27 December. Accessed on 10/04/21 at www.abc.net.au/news/2020-12-28/autism-advantage-giving-workplaces-competitive-edge/13016254

Further Resources

Attention Autism
For training, ideas and support in building attention, interaction and communication:

https://ginadavies.co.uk/training

Autism Education Trust
A source of support to improve educational outcomes:

www.autismeducationtrust.org.uk

Intensive Interaction
A source of information and training for supporting the fundamentals of communication:

www.intensiveinteraction.org

Makaton
A unique language programme that uses symbols, signs and speech to enable people to communicate:

www.makaton.org

National Autistic Society
A leading charity supporting autistic people and their families:

www.autism.org.uk

PECS®

Training and support for using the Picture Exchange Communication System:

https://pecs-unitedkingdom.com/pecs

PODD™

Information and training for using Pragmatic Organisation Dynamic Display:

https://novitatech.com.au/equipment/podd-communication-books

SEN Assist

Educational software and resources developed by Adele and Quentin Devine:

www.senassist.com

Social Stories™

Information about creating a social learning tool that supports the safe and meaningful exchange of information:

https://carolgraysocialstories.com/social-stories/what-is-it

TEACCH®

The University of North Carolina TEACCH Autism Program:

https://teacch.com

Zones of Regulation™

Providing a common language and compassionate framework to support positive mental health and skill development:

www.zonesofregulation.com

Index